Praise for *Road of 10,000 Pains*

Road of 10,000 Pains has the first and only accurate description of Foxtrot Company, 2nd Battalion, 1st Marines' combat operation on 21 April 1967 that evolved into Operation Union. Otto Lehrack vividly captures the intensity and close combat during the initial fight as well as the determination of individual Marines to continue to fight against vastly superior NVA forces.

—Maj. Gen. (ret.) Gene Deegan, CO, F/2/1

Just when you thought no more could be said about the Marines' Vietnam War, author and oral historian Otto Lehrack, once again, breaks new ground about the high-intensity ground combat in I Corps.

—Charles D. Melson, Chief Historian, U.S. Marine Corps

A first-class contribution to Vietnam literature by someone who appreciates combat from the ground level. Based upon extensive research and personal knowledge, *Road of 10,000 Pains* is combat history at its best, a testimony to the raw courage of U.S. Marines. This is a must-read for everyone interested in small-unit actions in Vietnam.

—Dr. Alexander S. Cochran, Vietnam veteran and historian, former Horner Chair of Military Theory, Marine Corps University

Que Son Valley was a strategic campaign and watershed event of the Vietnam War. Today, however, it's relatively unknown and forgotten. But those Marines who fought its brutal battles remember Que Son. They remember the sacrifices and the scars of war, but so do they remember the camaraderie and friendships. Author Otto Lehrack's account of the Que Son Valley campaign is a testament to those Marines who courageously committed themselves to one another and to "The Valley."

—Maj. Gen. (ret.) John H. Admire, former Commanding General, 1st Marine Division

In *Road of 10,000 Pains*, Otto Lehrack does a superb job of weaving together the oral histories of the officers and enlisted men who did the fighting. I was especially moved, and at times angered, by the hardships they had to overcome. The historic heavy fighting that followed in 1968 would likely have been even more intense and less victorious for the American troops had it not been for those Marines who fought so hard to defeat their enemy in 1967.

—Christy Sauro, Vietnam veteran, former sergeant, United States Marine Corps, author, *The Twins Platoon*

For Vietnam combat veterans, Otto Lehrack's *Road of 10,000 Pains* will evoke memories of the sights, sounds, and smells of the battlefield. By skillfully interweaving personal accounts of heavy combat between Marines of the 1st Marine Division and the 2nd North Vietnamese Division, Lehrack makes this book come alive as few others have. For those readers who have never experienced war, *10,000 Pains* will transport them into the hell of close combat. Lehrack's book is not for the faint of heart . . . it is a gut-level infantry portrayal of brutal fighting in the style of Eugene Sledge's *With the Old Breed*. It is a must-read for those seeking to learn more about the brutal fighting of Vietnam's Northern I Corps in 1967.

—Col. (ret.) Dick Camp, United States Marine Corps, author, *Operation Phantom Fury* and *Last Man Standing*

Books by Otto J. Lehrack:

No Shining Armor:
The Marines at War in Vietnam

The First Battle:
Operation Starlite and the Beginning of the Blood Debt in Vietnam

America's Battalion:
Marines in the First Gulf War

Road of 10,000 Pains

The Destruction of
the 2nd NVA Division
by the U.S. Marines, 1967

Otto J. Lehrack

Foreword by
General Alfred M. Gray, Jr.,
29th Commandant of
the Marine Corps

First published in 2010 by Zenith Press, an imprint of MBI Publishing Company, 400 1st Avenue North, Suite 300, Minneapolis, MN 55401 USA.

Zenith Press titles are also available at discounts in bulk quantity for industrial or sales-promotional use. For details write to Special Sales Manager at MBI Publishing Company, 400 First Avenue North, Suite 300, Minneapolis, MN 55401 USA.

To find out more about our books, join us online at www.zenithpress.com.

Designer: Diana Boger
Cover Design: Andrew J. Brozyna, AJB Design, Inc.
Design Manager: Brenda C. Canales

Editor's note: Some portions of the oral history interviews have been lightly edited for readability.

Front cover image: The "comma" defensive position that Hotel Company, 2nd Battalion, 5th Marines, occupied the night of November 6 and 7, 1967, after a vicious day of fighting. The photo was taken the morning of the 7th. An experienced air observer who flew over the position that morning and saw "bodies of NVA and Marines everywhere" said it was the worst thing he had seen in Vietnam.
Courtesy Gene Bowers

Maps: Patti Isaacs/Parrot Graphics, recreated from USMC source maps

LIBRARY OF CONGRESS CATALOGING-IN-PUBLICATION DATA

Lehrack, Otto J.
Road of 10,000 pains : the destruction of the 2nd NVA Division by the U.S. Marines, 1967 / Otto J. Lehrack.
p. cm.
ISBN-13: 978-0-7603-3801-8
ISBN-10: 0-7603-3801-9
1. Que Son Valley, Battle of, Vietnam, 1967. 2. United States. Marine Corps. Division, 1st.—History. 3. Vietnam (Democratic Republic). Quân dôi. Su doàn 2— History. 4. Vietnam War, 1961-1975—Personal narratives, American. I. Title.
DS557.8.Q4L44 2010
959.704'342--dc22
2009021213

Printed in the United States of America

For

who led me back into the sunlight,

and for my daughter Angie

Sing, goddess, of Achilles' ruinous anger
Which brought ten thousand pains to the Achaeans,
And cast the souls of many stalwart heroes
To Hades, and their bodies to the dogs
And birds of prey.

The Iliad, Homer

Contents

Maps

Foreword

It is my distinct pleasure to prepare the foreword for this exceptional story of Marines in battle. It is also an opportunity to again salute the courageous warriors of the 1st Marine Division and their allies as they fought to keep South Vietnam free. Our author, Marine Lt. Col. Otto Lehrack, is an experienced infantry combat veteran who also has a sound intelligence background. He has given us a superb account of a series of battles that took place in the rugged, often-fought-over Que Son Valley complex from the spring through late fall of 1967.

In April 1964, while in Vietnam on another matter, I accompanied a senior army advisor on a visit and a reconnaissance of Quang Tin Province, to include Que Son Valley, its sister Phuoc Ha Valley, plus the Army of Republic of Vietnam (ARVN) outposts at Hiep Duc and Que Son. The Viet Cong (VC) were already established in the area and used the valley, the surrounding high ground, and the population to their advantage in establishing base camps, weapons caches, and supplies. The very limited ARVN forces in the area did not have the capability to control the region but seemed to be making progress with the people locally. However, they were viewed with suspicion in the countryside, which was, in part, a carryover from the earlier French Indochina war. The geographical relationship between the Que Son Valley's approach to the sea from Route 1 in the east to the North Vietnamese Ho Chi Minh Trail infiltration network to the west made this a vital strategic region. Experienced infantry could cover the wide corridor from a tributary of this network to the sea in a hard overnight march, which, in turn, could threaten the isolation of the five northern provinces of South Vietnam. The Que Son Valley area also produced a twice-yearly rice crop that far exceeded the needs of the population, and it was a conduit for obtaining salt, which was critical. Finally, the valley was home to a large number of military-age males, many of whom had family ties with the north. The Que Son Valley complex was therefore a rich and vital prize.

In December 1965, Marine and ARVN forces conducted a major operation called Harvest Moon to prevent a Viet Cong attack on the Que Son District headquarters and to trap enemy forces in the area. In August 1966, Marines and ARVN forces conducted Operation Colorado to drive the 2nd North Vietnamese Army (NVA) Division from the Que Son Valley area. As a matter of interest, the last major U.S. offensive operation in Vietnam (Operation Imperial Lake) commenced on August 22, 1970, in the Que Son mountainous complex and continued through the remainder of the year.

On April 21, 1967, Foxtrot Company, 2nd Battalion, 1st Marines clashed with a battalion of the 2nd NVA Division in the Que Son Valley; a fight that ignited a seven-month campaign over control of that vital area. This first phase, dubbed Operation Union, would last well into May. Concurrently, a Marine special landing force (Operation Beaver Cage) also ran major sweeps through the area. Then came Operation Union II and Operation Swift, combined with extensive combat reconnaissance, artillery, and air strikes.

On one side was the 2nd NVA Division. Many of its soldiers were veterans of years of hard campaigning. All three regimental commanders and a good number of their officers and senior NCOs had fought in the iconic battle of Dien Bien Phu. Advance elements of this division marched down the Ho Chi Minh Trail in late 1965, turned east at the Que Son parallel, and staked out command post locations and supply dumps in the jungles around the valley. Then their logistic units brought in weapons, ammunition, medical supplies, uniforms, and other material. Once the headquarters units were in place and the supplies safe in their storage areas, heavily laden combat troops made the long trip south. By early 1967, the NVA thought they were strong enough in the Que Son Valley to control the population and the rice crop. The Marines thought otherwise.

On the allied side was the 1st Marine Division, the Old Breed, heir to the most glorious history in the Corps. An earlier generation of this division landed in Guadalcanal in America's first ground offensive of World War II. Then it fought at Peleliu and finally Okinawa, the end game of the Pacific War. In Korea it was this division that spearheaded MacArthur's landing at Inchon and then later fought its way through six Chinese divisions at the Chosin Reservoir. The 1st Marine Division landed in Vietnam in 1965 ready to take on their latest foe, the Vietnamese communists.

Between April and November 1967, over nine hundred Marines and corpsmen and over six thousand of the enemy would perish in the Que Son

Valley campaign, more than on any other piece of real estate in the entire war. More were lost here than at Khe Sanh, Hue, or Con Thien. Five Marines and one navy chaplain were awarded the Medal of Honor, all of them posthumously. Twenty-seven Marines and corpsmen received the Navy Cross, and eighty-four Silver Stars. The 5th Marines ran most of the operation, and in early 1968, Lyndon Johnson placed the streamer for the Presidential Unit Citation on their battle colors, a well-deserved honor.

This campaign essentially gutted the 2nd NVA Division. In their official history, the Communists admit they failed to invest Da Nang during the 1968 Tet Offensive as their brethren had occupied Hue. Retired NVA officers told the author that this was because of the losses they incurred in the Que Son Valley in 1967.

Otto Lehrack has successfully chronicled the events of this campaign in *Road of 10,000 Pains: The Destruction of the 2nd NVA Division by the U.S. Marines, 1967*. Working from official histories, American and Vietnamese, and from interviews with over 150 Marines, corpsmen, and North Vietnamese Army soldiers, he has compiled a riveting account of men at war. This is a story of real warriors and real combat, and it fills an important gap in the history of the Vietnam War.

In closing, permit me to pay tribute to all the warriors from our armed forces, and our allies, who fought so long and so well in the noble cause of trying to keep South Vietnam free. You are a very special breed of people, and you are the reason we lead the free world. Take care of yourselves, take care of each other, God bless, and—as we say in the nation's Corps of Marines—Semper Fidelis.

—Al Gray, Marine
29th Commandant of the Marine Corps

Introduction

IN SEPTEMBER 1999, I FOUND MYSELF in a van in the Que Son Valley in Vietnam. My traveling companions were several retired officers of the North Vietnamese Army, our former enemy, and a few U.S. Marine veterans of America's war in Vietnam. I was in Vietnam for another project, and the daylong voyage through the Que Son Valley was a side trip, a way to fill an idle day before returning to the States. It was a rainy day, darkened by low-hanging clouds that gave the terrain a somber quality. As the van moved slowly along the valley floor, the volume and pitch of voices rose as the aging veterans from both sides pointed out first one terrain feature and then another. I began to listen to their tales, and it soon became apparent that something special and largely unrecorded had happened in the Que Son basin. Over dinner that evening, I questioned both the Marines and the Vietnamese. "Oh, yes," one Viet Cong matter-of-factly declared, "in the Que Son Valley in 1967, we killed more Americans than at any time or place during the war." The Americans verified that the region had indeed been host to a bloody series of battles. How could this be, I wondered; if this is true, then why isn't the name Que Son familiar?

The answer is this: In early 1967 the Communists were already preparing for their General Offensive, General Uprising—the 1968 Tet Offensive.* Part of their strategy was to draw U.S. forces away from the population centers and to the borders of South Vietnam. They began in the spring by massing troops around Khe Sanh and challenging the Marines in what was called the First Battle of Khe Sanh. Then they threatened Song Be, a provincial

* Editor's note: While there were other Tet offensives (lowercase o), the one in early 1968 would become known to the world as *the* Tet Offensive (capital O).

capital near Saigon, fought a major battle against the U.S. Army at Dak To, and threatened to overwhelm Con Thien. At the same time, they placed several of their divisions within a day's march of the DMZ. The specter of a multi-division invasion from the north preoccupied the allies and, especially, the media. It was much easier and more sensational to describe a conventional campaign, especially one that might involve whole divisions, than it was to figure out the significance of a valley so far removed from the country's borders.

Neither the strategic nature of the campaign in the valley nor its intensity was understood or reported on when the Tet Offensive swept over Vietnam, and the psyche of the American public like a firestorm. The threat to the Marine garrison at Khe Sanh by divisions of enemy soldiers, the investment of Hue by the Viet Cong and the North Vietnamese Army, and the breaching of our very embassy grounds in Saigon captured the public and the media in an unshakeable grip. The events of 1967 in the Que Son Valley were overlooked by both the media and by the historians.

In late 1965, advance elements of the 2nd NVA Division began infiltrating the valley. These men returned to a region that welcomed them. The French plundered the Que Son Valley in their time and, after the French departed, absentee landlords with influence in Saigon took over most of the land. The average peasant here cared no more for the ideological message of the north than for that of the south. However, the Communist proselytizers offered not Communist theory but a brand of nationalism that promised land and peace. They tarred the Americans with the same colonial brush with which they had painted the French in the earlier war. Their message was that the Saigon government was a puppet regime, answering the manipulations of its American master. For many in the Que Son Valley this was an easy sell. All the Americans offered them was democracy, whatever that was; there was no evidence that democracy would fill their rice bowls. By early 1967, the NVA forces in the valley were strong enough to contest control of the valley.

Chapter 1

Foxtrot to Destiny

The machine guns sliced through the formation like a scythe, leaving a windrow of dead and wounded Marines; a grotesque formation, the violently dead in postures impossible in life; the wounded, silent, sobbing or screaming, each alone and desperate within his own skin; their lieutenant, James Shelton, down, his head caved in and his thigh blown out.

These Marines, two platoons of them, from Capt. Gene Deegan's[1] Foxtrot Company, 2nd Battalion, 1st Marines (F/2/1)[2] left the hill mass of Nui Loc Son in the dark that April morning in 1967, trying for all the world to maintain noise-discipline as they stole past somnolent villages toward their objective. Strangely, no dogs barked, but from out of the blackness a bell tolled: not a loud bell, but clear, its vibrations drifting across the valley floor. Dawn approached with tropical rapidity as Captain Deegan aligned the Marines of his 2nd Platoon on an east-west axis in a tree line, facing a tree-choked hamlet on the far side of a forty-meter-wide rice paddy.

Deegan's other platoon, under Lt. James Shelton, moved stealthily eastward near the dirt and gravel track that the map optimistically called Route 534 and then made a large loop to get to the north side of the objective area. Between the dawn and the day, Shelton's Marines struck like a hammer, sweeping southward on line, flushing a score of enemy soldiers, driving them toward the anvil—Deegan's men. The enemy

Marines approach the village of Binh Son (1) on April 21, 1967, during Operation Union I. The battle will become much enlarged as the Marines commit assets to deal with a very large enemy force. *USMC*

scattered like quail; some ran parallel to Shelton's platoon, and his Marines shot them down; others perished in the fire from Deegan's position, and a handful of survivors disappeared into the bush. After the smoke cleared and his men did a body count, Captain Deegan radioed the 1st Marines and reported the contact and eighteen enemy killed. He assured them that everything was under control, only one of his men was wounded, and he needed no help.

Lieutenant Shelton's men stayed in place while Captain Deegan had the blocking-force Marines police up the battlefield, and he called for a medevac for his casualty. While waiting for the chopper, the captain moved among his troops and talked to them about what they had seen.

Gunfire shattered the stillness when one of the Marines cut loose with a full magazine of M16 rounds and another fired an M79 grenade launcher across a large paddy to their right. Privates First Class Lonnie Matthews and John Jackson told their lieutenant that they saw a bush move. Looking closer, they saw four heavily camouflaged North Vietnamese Army (NVA) soldiers, fired at them, and saw a couple go down. The lieutenant told these two Marines and another, Pfc. Thomas "Cotton" Holtzclaw, to take a look.

Marines from the 2nd Battalion, 1st Marines, fight their way out of a tree line under enemy fire in an attempt to rescue wounded comrades on April 21, 1967, the first day of Operation Union I. *USMC*

They started out across the paddy but did not get very far before a smattering of enemy fire sent them scampering back to join the main body of troops. They were unscathed except for Holtzclaw, who was knocked to the ground when a bullet struck his boot heel.

Captain Deegan came over to take a look and then ordered an air strike on the tree line while he lined his Marines up to assault across the paddy and finish off the remaining enemy. His two platoons were about three hundred meters apart, and he ordered them to move toward the objective in a flying wedge.

Just as the air strike ended and the Marines began to move, Holtzclaw came up to Matthews and Jackson, shook their hands, and said, "It was nice knowing you. I am not going to make it." Matthews and Jackson looked at each other and then at Holtzclaw. They told him that he would be okay.

The Marines confidently started across the paddy. The enemy let them get about halfway and then punched them hard with small-arms and machine gun fire. When Captain Deegan gave the order to attack, Lt. Mike Hayes,[3] artillery forward observer (FO), was alongside Lieutenant Shelton and the platoon sergeant, Staff Sergeant Gould.

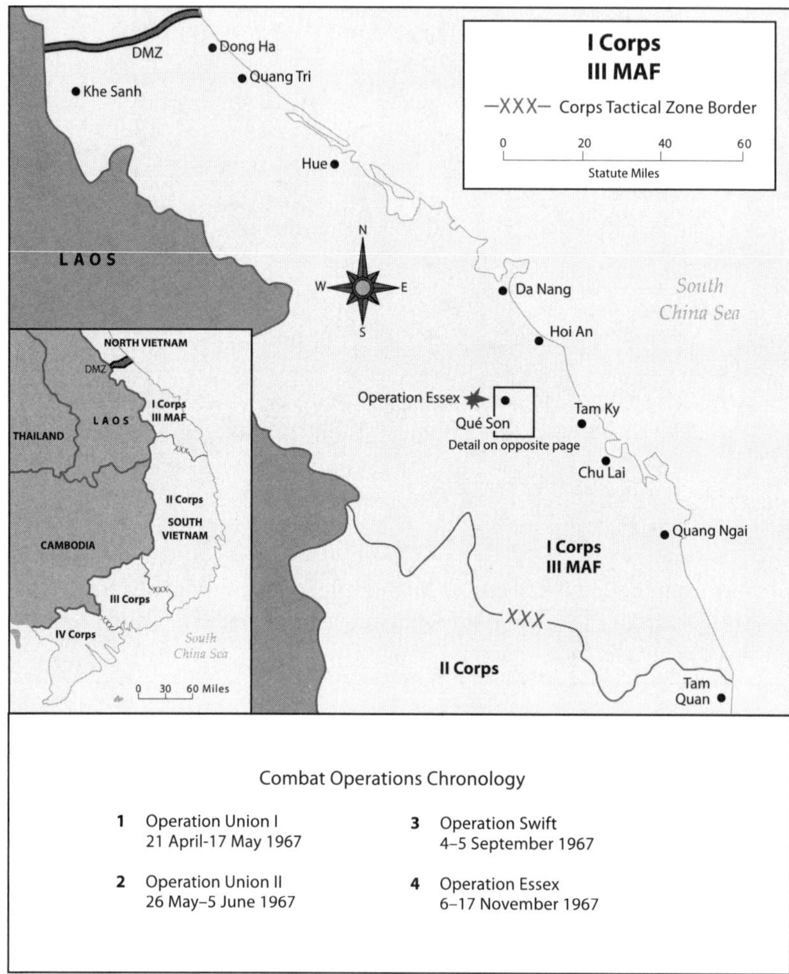

Lt. Mike Hayes: Shelton was hit almost immediately. We had Marines down, and about eight of them made it back to the paddy dike. Of the thirty-one in front of us, there was no way to know how many were killed or wounded.

BULLETS CUT DOWN PFC. HOLTZCLAW at once. Jackson and Matthews picked him up and were carrying him to the cover of a rice paddy dike when he was shot a second time. They lowered him to the ground and called for "Corpsman up." "Doc" Jeffrey Bouton ran over amidst the fire, kneeled down beside Holtzclaw, shook his head, and said, "There is nothing we can do." Then Bouton rose up, and the NVA shot him too.

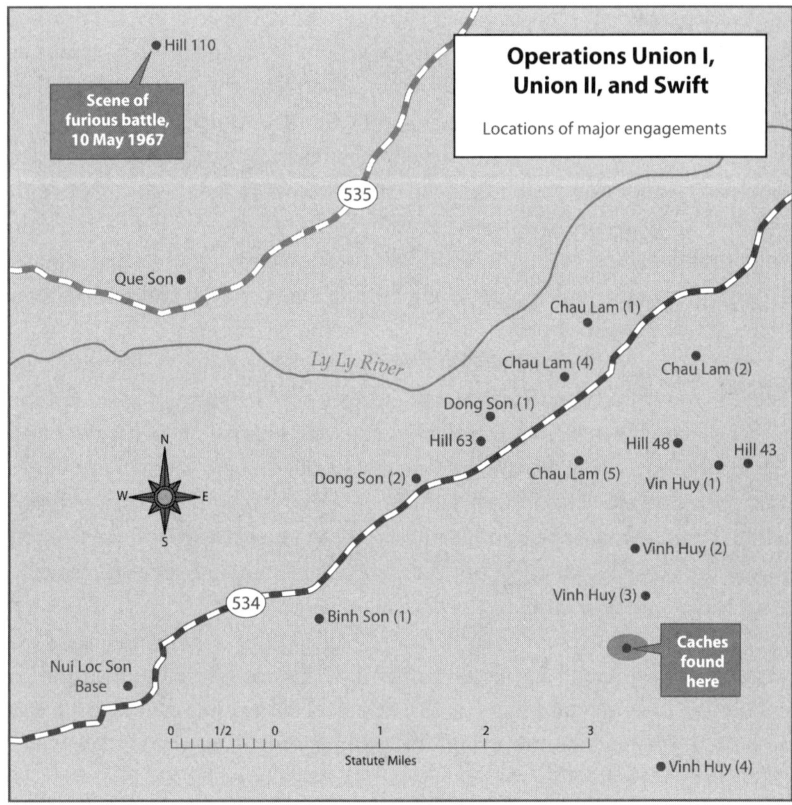

Route 534: "the road of 10,000 pains."

A battalion of Lieutenant Colonel Huyen's 31st North Vietnamese Army Regiment (Red River Regiment) was dug in, and they were ready. They had laid communication wire, strung protective barbed wire in key spots, and positioned mortars inside of houses, the roofs of which were removable and screened the mortars from the air when in place. These mortars barked their presence as they went into action and quickly found the range of the Marines' formation: a round impacted between Holtzclaw and Bouton and finished them both. Simultaneously, enemy small-arms fire hit Lonnie Matthews's left arm and John Jackson's right arm. Everybody around them lay dead or wounded. Captain Deegan motioned for Jackson and Matthews so they ran back to their skipper just as a round slammed into Deegan's chest. Privates First Class Matthews and Jackson, each with one good arm, dragged Deegan behind a hut, where he commenced trying to radio for help.

A corpsman gave morphine to Deegan, which slowed down his thinking a bit, but he got on the radio and told his regiment that he needed all the help he could get, that the enemy had blown his attack formation apart, leaving the exposed paddy awash with dead and wounded Marines.

Just moments after the attack began, Lieutenant Hayes, the FO, was Foxtrot Company's only unwounded officer. He did what he could to organize the Foxtrot Company survivors and summon artillery support. Communications with regiment and with the artillery batteries were complicated because Foxtrot Company had to relay their radio traffic through Deegan's security platoon atop Nui Loc Son.

Deegan's remaining Marines put out as much firepower as they could and held on for reinforcements. The large number of Marines lying in the paddies foreclosed on the option to withdraw. Each Marine lay there in his own small world, compressed to the twenty or thirty yards he could see, a world of heat and noise and smell and hundreds of flying hot steel fragments, any one of which could take away in an instant anything he ever was and anything he would ever be. He was fueled by fear, adrenaline, and a hyper-awareness of what was required of him.

Eighteen-year-old Pfc. Gary Martini rolled over a protective dike and wiggled in a low crawl across the paddy until he was fifteen meters from the enemy. He carefully raised his head to locate a target and one by one lobbed all his hand grenades among the NVA, killing several. He then crawled back through the fire to rejoin the survivors. Martini looked back at the wounded and dead Marines still in the paddy in front of him, turned around, and started out again. Though wounded himself, he ran a zigzag pattern into the killing zone, grabbed another Marine by his collar, and dragged him to safety. A close friend of his, Private First Class Boudreau, called him by name. Boudreau lay wounded less than twenty meters from the enemy. Again, Martini ran into the enemy fire. Hit another time, he shouted at the other Marines in the trench line to stay put and that he could get Boudreau in without help. In the last act of his life, Private First Class Martini pulled Boudreau to safety.

Lt. Mike Hayes: I told everyone to stay down and not attempt to go out. Martini literally broke out of my grasp and went out to aid Boudreau. Martini got hit in the thigh on the way out and in the upper chest just as he got Boudreau back. Now there were about six of us, and Boudreau. We talked to the people on Nui Loc Son who could see the battle and were told that the NVA had us surrounded. The only effective mortar fire support we were getting was from the Howtars on Nui Loc Son.

Pfc. Tom Holloran (with the 106mm recoilless rifles on Nui Loc Son): We could see hundreds of NVA, and we used all our mortar and 106 rounds trying to support our men.

Deegan's survivors grimly faced the battlefield, expecting a counterattack at any time.

Chapter 2

Bald Eagle

Radio operators in combat operations centers (COCs) sat and waited like hotline counselors for fear-laden voices to murmur urgent, static-ridden pleas in their ears.

Sgt. Keith Lamb (artillery forward observer, 3rd Battalion, 1st Marines): We were all sitting around the COC. The day's heat was starting, and the two small electric fans were having a hard time keeping the cigarette smoke down.

"Circumference, this is Chinstrap. Request you monitor frequency Mike 45.9."

One of the radio operators switched frequencies to see what was going on. Someone yelled, "Go get the CO, we are on a Bald Eagle [reaction force]!"

The next thing we heard was Foxtrot Company: "Send help! We have made contact with a large enemy force and are being cut to pieces!"

"Mike Company, saddle up! Let's go! We have five minutes to be in the LZ!"

An officer yelled at me, "Sergeant, where is the lieutenant? We need an arty FO."

"Sir, he went up to Da Nang to division headquarters."

"Okay, you'll do. Get your gear and a radio and head for the LZ."

I ran to my tent and grabbed whatever gear I could fit into my pockets, rounded up John Papcun and another Marine who volunteered as radio men, and headed for the LZ. We busted open cases of C-rations and took out the fruit and whatever else we could stuff in our pockets. Then we milled around, adjusting straps, checking weapons, and waited for the choppers to arrive. We waited for about forty-five minutes.

Lt. Frank Teague (platoon commander, Mike Company, 3rd Battalion, 1st Marines): I was sitting in a hooch reading *Exodus* when I got the word to go see the company commander, Captain Bill Wood. He said, "A company from 2/1 is missing. We lost radio contact with them." We looked at each other, like what do you mean, *missing*? He said that they were over in 2/1's TAOR, "and we don't have any maps of this area, and we are gonna go find them. We'll go in first and then India Company will come in with the battalion CP group. When we get to the LZ, we'll send the three platoons out on compass bearings."

About a week before that, we were issued the M16 rifle. It was a nightmare. Mine jammed all the time. Everybody had been trained on the M14, which was like your right arm, and we got this Tinker Toy that didn't work. I remember thinking that I'm a college grad, and I'm having trouble with this friggin' thing. Some of my men just don't get this shit. This thing doesn't work. So I was off on the Bald Eagle with my M16 in a garbage bag to keep the dirt out. My platoon was going to be first in the LZ, and I was afraid it was gonna be hot.

The helicopters landed and throbbed with impatience as the Marines formed single files, ducked to run under their blades, and boarded. The whirling blades blew dirt, pebbles, and vegetation on the Marines, stinging bare skin where they hit; they blew helmets off and maps out of one's hand. Helicopter crewmen in brightly colored and dark-visored helmets, tethered by the umbilical cords of their radio cables, solemnly stood by their machine guns. All aboard. The pilots raised the ramps, revved up the rpm, lifted a bit off the ground, leaned the birds forward, and took off.

Lance Cpl. Jim Mullen (radio operator for the forward observer): The door gunner began firing, and the guy next to him said, "What do you see, what do you see?" He said, "I see platoon of NVA in the open." I crossed myself and did an act of contrition. Lieutenant Bishop was right across from me, and his eyes got as big as saucers.

Sgt. Keith Lamb: It seemed like a long, long way. Everyone was nervous, and quiet. We knew we were going into a hot LZ. The moment came. No one hesitated. We were lying in rice stubble as the helicopters sped away. Everyone seemed to be firing; bullets were coming from everywhere. More

An emergency reaction force of Marines from India Company, 3rd Battalion, 1st Marines, await their turn to board choppers to reinforce Foxtrot Company, 5th Marines, in April 1967. *Courtesy Howard Olsen*

choppers were coming, so we made our way to a hedge row on the edge of a wooded area that was a village. A few Marines were hit and pulled to cover by their buddies.

My job was to determine where the enemy was and to call in artillery fire. I checked with the forward air controller (FAC) on the coordinates of our

Helicopter door gunner. *Courtesy Lynwood Scott*

position and directed artillery fire on an area to our east, which seemed to be the origin of the enemy fire. Everything was very confusing, and it seemed as if everyone all around me was firing in every direction.

We moved out, and as I ran down the trail through the village, I saw wounded men everywhere. I reached a wall made of earth and logs. There was a low spot between it and the hedge row filled with dead and wounded. One man shot in the crotch was lying there sobbing. I got the radio working and tried to check the location of our troops. Each element of the group I contacted reported heavy casualties. No one knew for sure where they were.

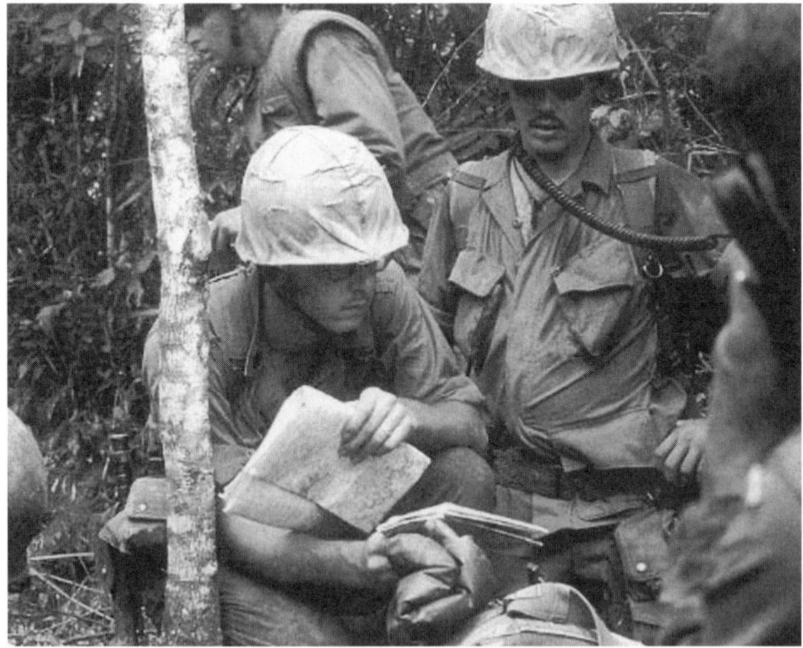

Sergeant Keith Lamb (holding map), an artillery forward observer with 3rd Battalion, 1st Marines, on the first day of Operation Union I, April 21, 1967. *USMC*

Sergeant Samaniego got shot right next to me. I got more information and called in another artillery mission and then had to stop because the rounds were landing too close to our own troops. The first medevac chopper was shot out of the air. Sergeant Samaniego got hit again. I couldn't call in artillery fire with the helicopters in the way, and they couldn't land with all the firing going on. The place smelled like a slaughterhouse. Flies covered the wounded, and the ground everywhere was soaked with blood.

Off to the west I saw another attempt to evacuate the wounded. Four Marines rushed out with a man on a stretcher before they were shot down and became casualties themselves. Explosions start! God, we are being mortared! The helicopter slowly lifted off and, at about twenty feet off the ground, the Marine who was on the stretcher fell out and tumbled into the rice field. A corpsman jumped out of the twenty-foot-high bird and dragged the wounded Marine toward us . . . then he was hit. He staggered toward the lines before he collapsed. Another helicopter tried to land and was driven off. The helicopter left and was the last one we would see for several hours.

THE NVA SCORED SEVERAL HITS ON a Huey helicopter that was providing gunship support to the Bald Eagle insertion. Fragments from NVA mortars crippled the bird, but it was able to get out of the landing zone, attain some altitude, and make an unsteady trip to Nui Loc Son, where it landed safely. The confusion on the ground confounded air support. The pilot of another helicopter later entered in his flight log that medevac birds were unable to get in and get casualties out, because the lack of information about the location of the friendly units prevented them from running fixed-wing strikes to suppress enemy fire.

The position looked like a hospital with dead and wounded Marines all around—a foul perfumery, the steam-bath air laden with cordite, the organic stench of blood, and the reek of the newly dead. The corpsmen doggedly moved from casualty to casualty, ignoring enemy fire, making impossibly difficult triage decisions, decisions that nothing in their lives had prepared them for. The corpsmen's ranks diminished as they too fell victim to enemy bullets or shell fragments, leaving few to tend to the many wounded. As they could, the Marines and corpsmen moved the wounded to one central location and lined up the dead, wrapped in a formation of blood-streaked ponchos.

Sergeant Lamb crouched in the dirt among the heat and stink and enemy fire. He got a fire mission going as he used his map to fan the flies off a dying Marine. Then someone yelled, "Let's go! We're moving out!" Away, they went across an open paddy with all the Marines firing into the treeline at once.

At 1610, lead elements of Lt. Col. Dean Esslinger's 3rd Battalion, 5th Marines, landed far to the east of the battlefield and moved to link up with elements of the 3rd Battalion, 1st Marines. Lieutenant Colonel Van "Ding Dong" Bell's[4] 1st Battalion, 1st Marines, were lifted from Da Nang, landed in the valley, and set out on foot.

There was little artillery support within range of the battlefield. After the fight broke out, four helicopters from Marine Heavy Helicopter Squadron 463 lifted the six 105mm howitzers of Bravo Battery, 11th Marines, to Que Son village. As the heavy choppers moved the guns, airmen from Medium Helicopter Squadrons 262 and 361 (HMM-262 and HMM-361) brought in over forty thousand pounds of artillerymen and ammunition. They shuttled their loads in until well after dark. A platoon of U.S. Army 175mm guns commenced movement by road from Chu Lai to Tam Ky to support the infantry Marines with their heavy guns. In the long hours while the artillery was moving, the Marines had only the Howtars on Nui Loc Son.

In the meantime, the members of M Company, 3rd Battalion, 1st Marines, were on the ground and searching for Deegan's Foxtrot Company.

Capt. Bill Wood: We got a Marine on the radio from Deegan's company who didn't know where he was. He gave a water buffalo as a reference point. He said that their platoons were scattered over rice paddies, and the enemy fixed them in place with 82mm mortars, machine guns, and small-arms fire.

Mortars are fearsome because they do not make much sound in flight, just a hissing noise before they hit, suddenly intruding into one's world with detonations that hurtle hundreds of hot, razor-sharp, life-and-limb-taking fragments. If the battlefield conditions are such that one can hear the rounds leaving the tube, it is just a matter of wait and see after someone yells, "Incoming!" and everyone hits the deck and tries to become as small as possible. A mortar projectile travels in a high arc, and the sound of it leaving the tube outraces it. It seems to hang in the air, giving one's thoughts plenty of opportunity to speed through a wide variety of hopes and fears and "let's make a deal" with one's God. For those who survive a mortar barrage, there is a great sense of relief to hear the last of the rounds impact and know that one has bought another tenuous hold on life.

While the Marines were trying to make sense of what was going on in the paddies, they heard the welcome sound of choppers bringing in India Company. The original landing zone was too hot; small-arms machine gun fire raked the paddy, and mortars bracketed it, so the pilots put India Company down in an alternate LZ. It too was hot.

Pfc. John "Legs" Thompson: We were banking to come in, and I was looking outside the helo, and I could see the green and orange tracers coming up at us. Every now and then the chopper would shudder when it was hit.

The bird came down hard in a muddy paddy. Private First Class Scott Rolston exited the chopper, fell, and jammed the muzzle of this M16 into the dirt. He crawled to cover behind a paddy dike to clear his weapon.

Private First Class Sam Johnson looked up to see F4 Phantoms coming in low and straight. Napalm burst among the enemy like Hell's own fire, instantly vaporizing the lucky ones and covering the less fortunate with large swaths of charred flesh, hideously blistered skin, and painfully blinding them. In the black humor of the battlefield, the Marines called them "crispy critters," but no one was laughing. Some of the aircraft were hit and left the target area trailing black smoke.

The enemy shot Private First Class Hoyt in the shoulder before he could get out of the landing zone. Private First Class Bruce Parmelee, wounded

Posing in front of "Hotel Warsaw," 1st Platoon, India Company, 3rd Battalion, 1st Marines, March 1967. Among those identified, first row, fourth and sixth from left (seated), respectively, Homer Amspaugh, Legs Thompson; third row, third, fourth, fifth, and seventh from left, Glenn Knepp, Doc Wells, Fred Willard, Scott Rolston; last row, second from right, Dick Anderson. The weapons in the front are two M60 machine guns and one 3.5-inch rocket launcher. *USMC*

by mortar fragments and blood-soaked, lay dying. His friend, Private First Class Rolston, wanted to stop and console him but heard the shouted order, "Move out."

Captain Gene Lynch's India Company got itself sorted out and moved to the sound of the guns. Sergeant Tom Darcy, their forward observer, battered the NVA automatic-weapons positions with what artillery he could get from Nui Loc Son. On the heels of this fire, India assaulted the enemy position across a paddy.

Pfc. John "Legs" Thompson: We received heavy fire, and we all had to fight our way to this little tree line, a clump of trees, and then someone was shot; one of the squad leaders went down.

Thompson, Cpl. Ken Kaczka, Lance Cpl. Greg Miller, and another Marine put him on a poncho and dragged him back. The casualty kept one hand on his wound and one hand on the edge of the poncho, repeating, "The Lord is my shepherd, I shall not want."

Pfc. John "Legs" Thompson: We received fire as we ran to put him on a helicopter. We got him on and then ran back to where the tree line was. Lieutenant [Dick] Anderson said we needed to assault the next tree line beyond that.

Lieutenant Dave Livengood's platoon maneuvered over an area lacerated with shallow ditches. As they crossed, the enemy wounded Private First Class Hoyt again, this time in the leg, grounding him. Livengood's platoon found itself in a graveyard, dotted with masonry buildings. A ricochet off a grave marker sent a fragment of concrete into Lance Cpl. Gerry Reidenbach's head.

Back at the first LZ, the commanding officer of 3/1, Lieutenant Colonel DeAtley, had landed, and he stood in the open while Captain Wood briefed him.

Pfc. John "Legs" Thompson: The Marines are tied in* around the LZ but there are about ten meters between holes. If they really want us, they are going to get us.

In a torrent of lightning-bright flashes and ear-popping thunder, a dozen mortar rounds shattered among them, killing or wounding all but two of the twelve Marines in the command group. Fragments hit Captain Wood in the back. A large piece of shrapnel hit Lieutenant Colonel DeAtley in the temple and stuck out of his forehead. Wood thought sure the colonel was dead. The operations officer, Maj. Mike Kelly, looked at his CO and said, "Oh no, they got you too." Incredibly, the colonel got back onto his feet, refused medical attention, and continued to command the battalion.

Captain Wood sent his three platoons in different directions to try to find the survivors of Foxtrot Company. Frank Teague's platoon came upon them first. En route they found a gunnery sergeant.

Lt. Frank Teague: He was in the bush and badly wounded and delirious, calling out, "They are all over, they are all over!" This was beyond anything I

---

* To be set up around the perimeter with no unnecessary holes in the lines, aware of the personnel on each flank and their relative location.

could imagine. My platoon had two corpsmen, Tommy Randolph and Mike Guthrie. They took care of the gunny, and we moved along and came to an old, dried-out rice paddy . . . probably about four hundred meters across. About half way out, there was F/2/1, lined up, dead, wounded, bleeding, screaming. Other than the wounded, it was deadly quiet. About thirty yards out was a small group of maybe three or four guys covered in blood. We started to go get them, and they waved us back.

The next thing I knew, one shot rang out from across the paddy, and it nailed one of my guys. In my experience of four months, the one thing I knew was that the gooks couldn't shoot, especially from four hundred meters. I was thinking someone was shooting at us with a sniper scope. And somebody just wiped out a Marine rifle company. That had to be a big-mother unit over there in those trees. They started shooting, and every shot either hit somebody or was close.

I had everybody get down, and I peeked over the top of this mud berm with binoculars and looked at Foxtrot Company, and they all looked like they are dead or wounded. Most of the survivors were down behind a dike, huddling for cover. I had never seen so many Marines down. I radioed back and said, "I found them; you'd better get up here." Then something came through the trees: a dud mortar round! It was right on us. Now they got mortars.

We managed to get some of the guys right in front of us back. We got this one kid with blood all over him saying, "The shit hit the fan out there." Then some of our battalion officers came up, and they had an arty FO with them and the battalion FAC. They were huddling back there, and meanwhile I got a call on the radio, and I went back, and there was Lt. Bill Koehle and this new operations officer, Major Kelly. Kelly told Koehle and me, "I want you to take your two platoons, go down about three hundred yards, and envelop that tree line." Koehle looked at me and I looked at him. I was thinking we had an FAC here and an FO, and I thought, "What the fuck are you doing? Why don't you evaporate that tree line? You want us to envelop something that just wiped out a rifle company with a couple of platoons?"

But I sidled my platoon down about fifty or a hundred yards, and I was at the base of this tree line and had to cross maybe four hundred yards of open rice paddy. This was going against everything I had ever known. I thought, "I'm not going to take my platoon out into that paddy."

I decided to take a squad out and leave the other guys back as a base of fire. I told them, "If anything happens, open up on the tree line, and if the squad gets across, then we'll bring the other guys across."

So I started moving across with a squad, and we got about twenty or thirty yards out, and everything opened up: tracers coming out of the tree line, machine guns, and mortars; you could hear the pops of the 82mm mortars. Then their fifties opened up. I had never been shot at by a fifty, and the tracers seemed slow. They were like car headlights. It was almost like you could catch them. They hit a couple of my guys. I got everybody back to the tree line, but three or four of my guys were hit. A kid named Stokely was down with a sucking chest wound, and another kid, a radio man, was hit badly.

Doc Tommy Randolph: There were casualties everywhere. As I got to this little strip of land, we put about fifteen casualties in an abandoned old stone house and set up a triage. There were guys crawling in. One Marine looked like someone had skinned him. He had been pinned down behind this rice paddy dike, and a bullet went right up his arm and pulled all the skin off.

Lt. Frank Teague: I looked out, and Emmons, a machine gunner, was still out there about thirty yards away. I saw his face, and he got hit in the jaw. I could see blood and teeth, and he was screaming and out there with the gun and the ammo. It was going to take two of us to go get him. Instead of sending someone else, Tommy Randolph and I went. We got Emmons, and we were crawling with him, the gun, and the ammo and were about ten or fifteen yards from where I wanted to go, and I said, "Let's just pick him up and go." I took about two steps and got really nailed in the right hip. I went down, and Tommy got Emmons back. Then, Randolph and a black kid named Butler came out. Each grabbed a boot, and they dragged me back into the tree line. I was out of it. I got on the radio and called the company commander.

Doc Tommy Randolph: Teague, a guy named Mike Guthrie, Jim English, a machine gunner, and I were up on that point, and all our machine gunners had been wounded, so we moved up on that point toward the tree line where we were getting heavy fire, including mortars. The machine gunner got shot in the face, and the whole right side of his upper cheek was gone, and he was screaming and jumping around. Lieutenant Teague and I held him down and bandaged him up. Guthrie took over the gun. We were trying to move the machine gunner back, and he was flopping all around. As we got up, this NVA opened up on us and hit Frank Teague, and Teague was paralyzed. So, we ended up dragging both of them back. Teague was in a lot of pain, but he wouldn't let us give him any morphine. If Teague hadn't stood up when he did, I would have taken one between the eyes. When we pulled back, Lieutenant Hayes took over from Teague.

Capt. Bill Wood: All three of my platoon commanders were wounded within the first hour. Besides Teague, there was Lt. Bill Koehle and Gunnery Sergeant Ireland. Koehle lost a testicle, and Ireland lost part of his arm. So, I had a couple of sergeants and corporals in charge. We couldn't move. The only thing that kept them off us was air.

Lt. Mike Hayes: Late in the afternoon someone came on the radio and said he was on the way. It was a voice I recognized from Basic School, Lt. David Livengood. He asked me to mark my position, so I did that and that got them oriented.

India Company, 3rd Battalion, 1st Marines, broke out of its own landing zone and was greeted with a large volume of fire from the tree line to their front. Corporal Armenstar Ernest exposed himself to see where the enemy fire came from. They shot him down, a round going through both cheeks of his buttocks.

Pfc. Sam Johnson: We were constantly under fire after we left the LZ—small arms, machine gun fire, and mortars. My fire team found about a dozen wounded and dead Marines. We set up a perimeter around them, and I gave one of the guys my canteen, and this is when we really started getting fire.

Like many other Marines on this operation, Cpl. Ken Kaczka and Lance Cpl. Greg Miller did not take their entrenching tools. Combat in the valley up to that point had been against VC, not regular NVA, troops, and they had not run up against many mortars. The two men tried to dig a hole with their helmets and their KA-BAR knives. Then enemy mortar fire resumed, and they piled into a four-inch-deep hole that they scraped out. Greg Miller landed on the bottom and Ken Kaczka on top of him. A mortar round detonated nearby, slightly wounding Kaczka.

Captain Lynch called, "Mortars up."

Lance Cpl. Greg Miller: "Oh shit!" I exclaimed. Kenny and I jumped up and grabbed the tube.

Howard "Whitey" Olsen fires the 60mm mortar. Note that he is using the base plate but not the bipod. Many times Marines used neither. The 60mm mortar was a company commander's own personal artillery. *Courtesy Howard Olsen*

Cpl. Howard "Whitey" Olsen (60mm mortar squad leader): On operations like this, the mortar men of India Company only carried the mortar tube and ammunition, leaving the base plate and bipod behind. Experience had taught us that most of the firefights in which we could use the mortar were at very close range. We would strip off all the increments, the extra powder bags that increase the weapon's range, and just fire using the base charge. For a base plate we used our helmets. We would fold our soft utility cap so that the thickness of the bill would be under the ball of the mortar tube to keep the ball from punching a hole in the helmet. Rather than use bipods, we would hold the weapon in one hand while dropping rounds down the tube with the other, and eyeball the rounds onto the target.

Lance Cpl. Greg Miller: The muzzle flash for both the NVA's and our mortars was almost straight up. I held the tube and told Kaczka to take all the charges off, and our first round hit really close to the enemy mortar. He yelled, "Fire in the hole," and dropped the second one, and God must have been holding my hand, because the round hit their ammo, and there was a huge secondary explosion, and everybody started cheering. That was the end of those mortars.

There were still NVA in the next tree line before them, so Captain Lynch ordered India Company to get on line and into the assault.

Pfc. Sam Johnson: They were waiting for us.

Pfc. John "Legs" Thompson: We were going across a paddy, and I was carrying the 3.5[-inch] rocket launcher. When we got to the tree line, everyone was moving through it, and the 3.5 got stuck on the vines. This NVA popped up about three yards in front of me out of a spider hole. Luckily, he wasn't looking my way, so I drew my .45 as he turned on me, and I shot him three times, and he came clear up out of the hole.

Six Marines were trapped in some buildings to the front and were catching heavy fire. Lance Corporal Gerry Reidenbach and Private First Class Ramey made two round trips to get them back. Some of them were banged up, and one had lost it emotionally.

Enemy fire stalled the advance. The Marine position resembled half a star, with two or three small points protruding out from the rest of the line. Reidenbach and a machine gunner, Pfc. Rudy Galiana, formed one of these points. Galiana had lost his assistant gunner, so Reidenbach fed the gun.

Four other Marines were stuck out front in a small pocket under the muzzle of an enemy .50-caliber machine gun that fired with a full-throated hammering and sent two-inch-long projectiles over their heads.

Pfc. John "Legs" Thompson: We ran up the hill on the other side of the tree line, and we were instantly pinned down by this fifty. I got down behind this big paddy dike with Cpl. John Paropacic, Pfc. Homer Amspaugh, and Pvt. Glenn Knepp. Knepp had only been in Vietnam a week or two, was very religious, and always carried a Bible. We were trying to lob grenades at this machine gun because it was chewing up the dirt on the other side of us. It was about fifteen yards away. We ran out of grenades, and everybody else was back down over the edge of the hill. I yelled down the hill that we needed some grenades and to throw some up to us.

Gunny Charles Horton saw a Marine go down with a bag of grenades. The gunny got up to go for them, and Captain Lynch yelled, "No!" The gunny went for them anyway and was shot. Captain Lynch yelled, "Shit, they got the gunny. No one else get up." But Cpl. Ken Kaczka got up, grabbed the gunny, and dragged him back to safety. Then he filled his helmet full of grenades.

Pfc. John "Legs" Thompson: Kaczka came running up over the hill with a helmet full of grenades. Kaczka was an FNG.* We watched as the enemy tracers went right over our heads and right past him. He ran up and handed me the helmet full of grenades and then turned around and ran back down the hill again. It totally amazed us. We didn't know if he was extremely brave or if he didn't know what the hell he was doing. We all kind of laughed at it.

Then we realized that we needed to get this machine gun out of there. I was lobbing grenades, but we were not hitting very well, because I didn't want to expose myself too much. "We only have two grenades left." The other guys said, "Okay, we'll jump up and shoot, and you lob them in." On the count of three they jumped up, and they all started firing, and I stood up. The first grenade was wide to the right, but the second one went right in their hole. We fell back down. The new man, Knepp, was instantly killed. The fifty hit John Paropacic in the chest. Homer and I held him while he died. Then I grabbed John's rifle and ran up to the hole, and there were three dead enemy, but I started shooting them to make sure. For some reason, John had loaded up a magazine full of tracers, and they were setting my clothes on fire, so I had to roll out of the hole and put my pants out.

THE MARINES TOOK THE TREE LINE and drove the enemy out. It was an expensive objective, and many Marines went down. Blood trails checkered the objective, and they found a great number of the round-canister magazines that the NVA used on their light machine guns. But the fight wasn't over.

Pfc. John "Legs" Thompson: We consolidated our position on the top of the hill, and we were receiving a lot of mortars and B40s (RPGs). We got all our dead and wounded on the hill and formed a perimeter around them. I was by this old well, and there was a black guy down from 3rd Platoon, and I was trying to patch him up and console him and shoot around the well at the same time. NVA bullets were hitting the well.

Somebody down the line yelled, "Fix bayonets." I yelled out, "Damn, this is just like in the movies." Everybody started laughing. I had three or four

---

* fucking new guy

rifles I'd picked up from casualties, so I fixed bayonets on all of them. All were loaded and were on full auto, and I would shoot one, put it down, and shoot another.

They were so close to us, just on the other side of the trees, and they lobbed grenades, and we lobbed grenades. Sometimes we lobbed their grenades back at them.

PRIVATE FIRST CLASS SCOTT ROLSTON WAS WITH Pfc. D. R. Wells (called "Doc" because of his initials) and Pfc. Homer Amspaugh, a rocket man, and they were told to get into a masonry house. It was dusk. The house was a bad idea because the walls would not stop the rounds, which went right through what Rolston called "socialist cement."

Pfc. Scott Rolston: An RPG zipped by. This house had no roof on it. By this time it was getting dark, so we had illumination up, and out this window I could see large numbers of men moving across my front about forty meters away in a tree line. I was afraid they were Marines, so I got on the horn and broke into a conversation and wanted to know if there were any Marines out there. I didn't find out anything, so I shot a few rounds, and they scattered, and one guy dropped. Homer came up and asked what I was shooting at, and I told him. He was a 3.5[-inch rocket launcher] man and had an M16 in which every third round was a tracer, to spot for the rocket. He fired off a whole magazine from his M16, and of course tracers work both ways, and the enemy knew where we were. They started dropping all this ordnance on us. We were standing next to this door and moved away because we didn't like the angle of the door.

A burst of auto fire came through the wall where Doc Wells and I had been standing. Soon a mortar hit next to the house, and another hit the rim of the wall right over our heads, and it was deafening. None of us were hit, but it caved in part of the wall. I was on my back on the floor and covered with dust, and I said, "Cover the windows," although I have no idea why I said it.

We looked out the windows, and there was a bunch of shadows moving through the thickets outside maybe ten meters away, and we just opened up. It was fairly dark, but we had the light of the flares. We decided that we had to get out of the house, so we ran out and then ran around back to the rear of the house and got down behind the foundation, which was a better idea.

Pfc. John "Legs" Thompson: While I was lying there among all the fire, I looked across and saw the ruins of a masonry house. In one remaining corner of the house was Doc Wells. He was still standing in this corner, and the bullets were going through that corner, and he was trying to hide in about five inches of corner. We yelled, "Doc, get the hell out of that corner," and he dived away, and just then a B40 rocket hit the corner and blew it all away.

Thompson picked up a casualty, threw him over his shoulders, and ran back, staying as low as a six-foot five-inch Marine could while running. A B40 rocket hit on the other side of a bush just as he passed it. The bush absorbed most of the shrapnel, but it wounded both the casualty and Thompson in the back.

Two mortar men, Pfc. Whitey Olsen and Cpl. Art Reader, retrieved dead from the killing field. They found a recently joined Marine, Pfc. Fred Willard, the junior golf champion of California, with most of his head blown off. The two Marines dragged him two hundred meters by his shoulder straps. Olsen still remembers how they wore Willard's boot heels down while dragging him. The two Marines placed his body among the others and then dug a hole together.

Corpsmen were overwhelmed by the many wounded who were intermingled with the dead. Marines cried out in pain, "Corpsman up." Two, mortally wounded, recited the Lord's Prayer in unison amidst the incoming automatic-weapons and mortar fire.

An M60 machine gun stood watch over the wounded and the company command group. Art Reader and Whitey Olsen had bayonets fixed and their grenades out and ready to use. Olsen expected to be overrun, and prepared to fight to the death.

Cpl. Howard "Whitey" Olsen: Somehow, by the grace of God, the artillery fire for effects across our position, helicopter suppressive fire, and the Puff gunship, we survived.

In the fading light, Pfc. Fred Ingham saw an NVA forward observer up in an archway in a pagoda calling in mortar fire on the Marines. Ingham shot the FO and two or three of his replacements out of the pagoda in rapid succession. The enemy finally gave up that position as a bad idea.

Then the NVA sent a ground attack right at the Marines. Private First Class Rudy Galiana stood up to repel them with his M60 machine gun. Four rounds stitched him across the chest. Lance Corporal Reidenbach, his assistant gunner, grabbed the M60 with one hand and Galiana by the collar with the other and turned around. As he ran back, five more rounds hit Galiana.

Pfc. Scott Rolston: A chunk was torn out of my nose by a piece of brick when a round ricocheted off something. Then a mortar round landed, and I picked up a bit of shrapnel in my back. It was not very serious. Another piece went through the end of my trigger finger.

THE FIRE DWINDLED DURING the night, and the Marines counted their ammunition. Rolston had but eleven rounds and one grenade left. They had already stripped their dead for ammo.

Pfc. Scott Rolston: I went out there on the line, and they told us to stay alert, but my mind just unzipped, and I fell asleep.

THE WOUNDED LANCE CORPORAL REIDENBACH returned to his position in front of the India Company lines with Galiana's machine gun and took up the watch. After dark, Corporal Hansen, a weapons squad leader, two other Marines, and a corpsman pulled Reidenbach to where he could be medevaced.

Through the long night, Sgt. Tom Darcy called in twenty-two artillery fire missions, some as close as fifty meters from the Marines, to discourage an enemy counterattack. The two sides exchanged fire until about 0200, when the enemy melted into the night. The Marines found very little the next morning but brass.

Lt. Frank Teague: It was a long time before the medevac choppers could get [to the landing zone]. They pulled me back in a poncho, and a chopper landed close but then had to take off because of enemy fire. Then they got all the wounded guys in one group, and we were there all day. It got dark, and they ran out of morphine. We wounded all had that horrendous thirst, and I thought we were gonna get overrun.

I was sort of half delirious now, and I was thinking that at least I had a grenade if they came and overrun us. Wood was hit, DeAtley was hit, and Kelly was running the op. To this day I don't know why we didn't have artillery support.

SERGEANT FORREST MCKAY AND THE ENTIRE BATTALION were caught on the outermost edge of artillery range.

Sgt. Forrest McKay: We were just far enough out where they couldn't really support us. The 105 battery actually dragged the guns out of their revetments and onto the road so they could try to reach us.

The wounded lay in the landing zone until after midnight, when the medevac birds came in.

Lt. Frank Teague: They finally got choppers in, and they carried me in a poncho and literally threw me into the chopper. I landed right on top of Bill Wood. "What the fuck . . . ?" They took us to NSA in Da Nang, where they were triaging guys. A chaplain came around and gave me last rites, and a surgeon pushed his hands into my stomach.

The executive officer of the 3rd Battalion, 1st Marines, Maj. Art Loughry, got to the field about 2200 and assumed command of the battalion. The insertion of Mike and India Companies and a command group began twenty hours of furious fighting that cost the battalion 79 killed and wounded.

Captain Jim McElroy's men from Mike Company, 3rd Battalion, 5th Marines, marched all night, landing by helicopter after dark and walking for over eight hours. At sunup they fought off exhaustion as they closed the objective. They moved through abandoned enemy fortifications, classrooms, and a hospital. It was deathly quiet, and it was scary. They moved across a dry paddy filled with bright green grass and came upon what was left of Foxtrot Company's assault force. The point man found a machine gun team first. The gun was there, surrounded by the Leathernecks who had manned it until they died. The ground sparkled with dew-covered spent cartridges. Ten yards on were more Marines, strung out on line, in assault formation, halfway across a rice paddy, dead. Some had beer-can-sized holes in them, the effect of fifty-caliber machine gun fire. Their radio operator lay dead among them, his handset clapped to his ear, eyes fixed on the battlefield to his front.

Cpl. Steve Cottrell: Some of them were still sitting up and were still holding rifles. It was like time was frozen.

The 3/5 command group made it to the battlefield in the early morning hours. At sunrise Lt. Col. Dean Esslinger was sitting near his radio operators, Cpl. Norm Bailey and Lance Cpl. Harvey "Newt" Newton. The two Marines saw the colonel stand up, put his helmet on, and salute. They looked and saw a long line of Marines carrying their dead in ponchos. Without a word being said, every Marine within sight stood at attention and saluted as the bodies went by.

Lance Corporal John Lobur found it to be eerie how these Marines kept coming out of the mist.

Lance Cpl. John Lobur: They came four at a time, each guy holding the corner of a plastic poncho, grunting and struggling with the weight of their friends. Dead friends. Heavy dead friends. They scrambled more than walked, in a sort of crab-like shuffle, the corpses face-up, ass dragging, sometimes an arm hanging over the side, looking like pale wax.

THE DATE WAS APRIL 22, 1967; the operation was Union. This was the opening round in the bloodiest series of battles of the Vietnam War. During the next seven months, nearly nine hundred Marines and corpsmen and over six thousand of the enemy would die in these clashes. Five Marines and one navy chaplain were awarded the Medal of Honor, all of them posthumously. Twenty-one Marines and corpsmen received the Navy Cross, and seventy-two Silver Stars. The 5th Marines ran most of the operation and were awarded the Presidential Unit Citation. Between now and the end of 1967, more Marines and navy corpsmen died in the Que Son Valley than on any other piece of real estate in the war. More were lost than at Hue, Khe Sanh, or Con Thien.

Chapter 3

Deadly as a Flytrap

Lush, green and fertile, the Que Son Valley stretches westward from the coastal lowlands near the sea. It comes to a halt against the foothills of what the French called the *Chaine d'Annam* (Chain of Vietnam), the country's jagged spine, a north-south mountain barrier stretching the length of the country. The mountains swing close to the sea here, where they abruptly flatten out into flat paddy land. About 80 percent of the eighty thousand peasants in the valley live and farm three hundred square kilometers of this land. From the air, the valley glows with fairy-tale beauty. In 1967 it was one of the most dangerous places on earth. One Marine said that it was "as beautiful as an orchid and as deadly as a flytrap."

In the early months of the war, the Marines had higher priorities for their limited assets and did not see the need to contest enemy control of the valley. In late 1966 the Communists forced the play when Marine reconnaissance units, the nerve endings of their sensory organs, began reporting large units of the regular North Vietnamese Army moving into the valley from the west. Resources were few, and the Marines could spare but a single company to go take a look. They ordered Capt. Gene Deegan's Foxtrot Company, 2nd Battalion, 1st Marines, to a hill called Nui Loc Son, a limestone outcropping that rises without preamble from the western valley floor and overlooks a choke point through which all but the most determined foot traffic had to pass. The Marines of Foxtrot Company were to monitor enemy traffic, ambush small enemy units, and create a presence in the valley. Their unstated mission was to act as a stake-tethered goat, the sight and smell of which would lure the 2nd North Vietnamese Army Division to do battle. Nothing in the Marines' experience in Vietnam foretold that the enemy would accept the challenge and send large units to contest control of the valley. But the enemy did just that in a bloody campaign that lasted well into the autumn of 1967.

The Marines were young, most in their teens, some but a year out of high school, and a universe removed from anything resembling normal lives. Many had no earthly idea why they were on this battlefield, and few could point to Vietnam on a map. But they were Marines and had been molded in the tradition of their predecessors and schooled in the history of Belleau Wood, Iwo Jima, and the Chosin Reservoir. As they progressed through the downward funnel of command to their units, they found themselves in a spiral of shrinking options. They were in an alien land for which no amount of tradition or training could prepare them. The liquor, prostitutes, and entertainment that characterized the life of some Da Nang and Saigon warriors were not for them. These men were constantly on the move, patrolling off the hill, beasts of burden under the weight of weapons, ammunition, flak jackets, three or more canteens, extra socks, rations, and whatever personal items they had the strength and will to carry without compromising the tools of their survival. They lived in holes they dug themselves, sometimes several of them a day; drank water full of lumps of mysterious origin; ate C-rations, rarely enough for three meals a day; and got by on four to five hours sleep out of any twenty-four. Their only relief from the hell of a thirteen-month tour was a five-day R&R at midpoint that was the reward for those who had avoided death or crippling injury. By mid-tour they had witnessed every form of disfigurement and enough death to last a lifetime. The Marines were obsessed by time—by how much time they had left on their thirteen-month tours, which was the only measurement that truly mattered. They were sunburnt, calloused, and red from the iron-rich soil that they had not the water to remove, their clothing often little more than rags, their boots cracked and broken, and socks scarce. They cut each other's hair with rusty hand clippers.

The Que Son Valley over which they fought was flat paddy bordered by heavily jungled mountain. The paddy land required them to move across large open spaces, and the jungle channeled them into narrow trails. The enemy most often lay in wait in the tree lines that bordered the paddies or set up ambushes on the trails. Both tactics gave the Marines an initial disadvantage, which they paid for in blood. Once battle was joined, the Marines depended heavily on supporting arms, the only American weapons the enemy truly feared, to give them the upper hand while the NVA tenaciously held on until they could disappear in the dark. The enemy developed a "grab them by the belt" tactic, which dictated that they get as close to the Marines as possible, making it almost as hazardous for the Marines as for the NVA when the former called up their artillery and air support. When withdrawing, the NVA commonly hit the Marines with all the firepower they could muster and then quietly retreated, leaving behind a cadre of snipers to slow pursuit.

This was in many ways a squad leader's war; they, the old-salt sergeants and corporals, nineteen, twenty years of age, who trained and led their men, organized assaults, prepared positions, led patrols, called in supporting fire and medevacs, and navigated over mountains and through jungles and across paddy.

The Marines on Nui Loc Son washed as frequently as the water supply would allow. They discarded the hated ham and lima beans from their C-rations but saved the pound cake in hopes of drawing a fruit—peaches were highly prized—so they could make fruit shortcake. When they could, they made tiny stoves of C-ration cans and fueled them with pinches of C4 plastic explosive, which burned at a furious rate, and heated their rations and their powered coffee or cocoa. For entertainment they captured and raced spray-painted rats in the trenches, urging them along with a bayonet on a pole.

Below them lay the valley. In early 1967 it was relatively untouched by the war, a sea of paddies, green, golden, fallow, wet or dry, divided by dikes according to centuries-old pedigrees of ownership. Route 534 lies the length of the valley floor, bisecting it like vertebrae. Here and there are huge, black rocks, scattered around the valley with the randomness of watermelon seeds. Villages rise from the sea of paddies like atolls in a confusion of hooches, coconut trees, and family vegetable plots patrolled by chickens, with small, scabrous, yellow dogs and squadrons of ducks herded from one place to another by a child with a plastic bag on the end of a pole. Bamboo, sixty feet high or more with many stalks four inches thick, girds the little communities and barricades them against sudden entry, channeling foot traffic into narrow passages. There are ancient trails where countless feet have pounded their surfaces a foot or more below the surrounding terrain. Men and women with poles slung across their shoulders, balanced on each end by buckets of slop, baskets of produce, or small, wooden cells confining chickens, ducks, snakes, dogs, and other edible fauna en route to their destiny, move down these trails with the awkward lope of race walkers. Pigs are carried on the backs of bicycles confined by long, woven cages that look like fish traps.

Vietnamese are constantly at work in these fields, planting or harvesting by hand, in rows, their conical hats bobbing like so many piano hammers. Water buffaloes, great, black beasts with sweptback horns, pull primitive plows guided by farmers on foot.

Near every village are graves, planted like special crops on ancestral land, their occupants resting for but a year until the flesh rots, and then the bones are ceremoniously harvested and replanted for eternal rest. Small shrines looking for all the world like dolls' theaters are mounted on posts and festooned with burnt joss sticks, the remnants of food, and other offerings.

It was in this setting that the Marines found themselves in 1967.

Nui Loc Son sits seventeen kilometers southwest of the valley's eastern terminus at the town of Thang Binh. Just west of Nui Loc Son, two 400-meter hills squeeze the paddy land into a 1,500-meter-wide chokepoint. West of there, the valley widens again until it runs up against the triple-canopy-jungled mountains on the far side of the town of Hiep Duc. The allies never ventured beyond this; it was enemy territory, with sanctuary and access to a tributary of the Ho Chi Minh Trail.

In 1961 and 1962, Communists who had fled the south after the partition of Vietnam in 1956 seeped back into the valley and dug up their weapons caches. By 1963, the 1st Viet Cong (VC) Regiment was afoot and ready to fight. No legion of black-pajama-clad farmers, these men were proud regular soldiers, some of whom had been with the Viet Minh for twenty years. Their commander, Quach Huu Hop, commanded a regiment at the iconic battle of Dien Bien Phu in 1954.

They knew how to fight. The 1st Viet Cong Regiment brutalized the 51st ARVN (Army of the Republic of Vietnam) Regiment in two battles in mid-1965. Then, in August, they went up against the U.S. Marines in Operation Starlite on the coastal plain south of Chu Lai. After the battle, the Marines declared the 1st VC Regiment out of action. They knew not that they had fought but two of its four battalions. The allies were yet to learn of the astonishing ability of the enemy to replace slain soldiers from the ranks of the local Viet Cong and infiltrators newly arrived from the north. In December, just four months after Starlite, the 1st VC Regiment popped up again, reconstituted and ready to go, this time in the center of the Que Son Valley, just south of Route 534. The Marines clashed with them in Operation Harvest Moon, the first major foray into the valley by U.S. troops. The fight took place around Hill 43, a location that would twice be fought over again in 1967. Though the VC were soundly thrashed, the allies had not the resources to occupy the valley, and from Harvest Moon until early

1967, the Communists operated there unmolested. Without the presence of an enemy, their force metastasized. Major General Hoang Thao's 2nd North Vietnamese Army (NVA) Division drifted into the valley as silently as smoke in the night in late 1966 and gathered the 1st Viet Cong Regiment into its ranks.

The Que Son Valley was a dependable rice producer and home to a large military-age male population, both critical assets. The valley also formed a broad corridor from the western mountains to the sea, which played on allied fears that the Communists would lop off and isolate I Corps from the rest of the country.

As Marine strength grew along the coastal population corridor of Phu Bai, Da Nang, and Chu Lai, they looked southward to the Que Son Valley. The U.S. Army moved units into southern I Corps in early 1967, relieving the Marines of part of their area of responsibility and freeing up a few assets for action elsewhere.

Reconnaissance teams reported more frequent sightings of enemy soldiers in the western valley. One team leader described enemy units going over steep hills. First, a group of uniformed but unarmed soldiers appeared on the run, carrying ladders. When they reached the base of a steep hill, they linked the ladders together, end to end. Right on their heels, a large infantry unit rushed to the ladders and went, ant-like, up and over the hill. As the last man cleared the ladders, the support troops removed and disassembled them and vanished.

Chapter 4

Foxtrot

In January 1967, Capt. Gene Deegan's heavily reinforced Foxtrot Company, 2nd Battalion, 1st Marines, relieved the ARVN on Nui Loc Son and began operations under direct control of Col. Emil Radics's 1st Marines. It took about a week to shuttle Captain Deegan's company out to the hill by helicopter. The top of Nui Loc Son, corrugated with rock projections, had no helicopter-landing pad. Marines and supplies had to be unloaded under the whirring blades of hovering aircraft. Ammunition, rations, and other supplies were tossed off the choppers. The Marines jumped. The pilots called it "Nui Loc Son International Airport."

Deegan had about three hundred Marines, making Foxtrot Company 50 percent larger than a full-strength rifle company, and the hill bristled with attachments: four 106mm recoilless rifles, four 81mm mortars, a flame-thrower section, a beefed up communications detachment, and a signal intelligence team from the 1st Radio Battalion. Within a month, a battery of 4.2-inch Howtars added real bite to his firepower.

Nui Loc Son was an ideal outpost for observing enemy infiltration into the Que Son Valley. It was easily defensible, and its height made it a good radio relay station for reconnaissance teams sent into the far western reaches of the valley.

Captain Deegan liked his assignment.

Capt. Gene Deegan: The beauty of what we were doing compared with other AORs is that we operated at our own tempo, when and where we wanted to. The other advantage was that there had been only one operation

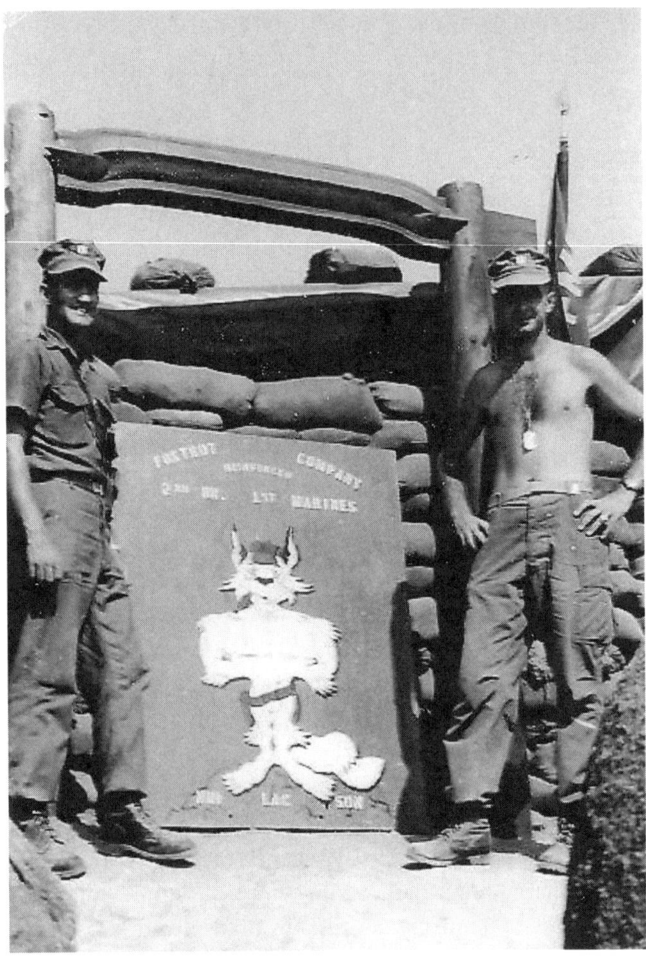

Captain Gene Deegan, on right, with Capt. Warren Walters, the CO of Bravo Battery, 1st Battalion, 11th Marines. The photo was taken atop Nui Loc Son. *Courtesy Gene Deegan*

in the valley, Harvest Moon. There was no history of relationships developed with the villagers and then broken, nor places where firepower had been misused.

THE DISADVANTAGES WERE THAT THERE HAD been no effort in the valley to counter the Communist proselytizers; that Nui Loc Son sat forty kilometers from the nearest other American force at Hoi An, and Deegan had no direct communications with them; and that his outpost was outside the artillery range of all weapons save those on the hill.

The 1st Marines assured Captain Deegan that enemy units in the valley were platoon strength or smaller. Even so, Colonel Radics cautioned Captain Deegan to be very conservative—probe for enemy strength, create a presence in the valley, and establish contacts with the local villagers.

The ARVN had done little to improve the position on Nui Loc Son, so Deegan's priorities were self-generated. The first were to make the position defensible and habitable. The bunkers were inadequate, and the hill was a rat's nest, home to hundreds of these pests who dined and bred without interruption among the residue of modern military affluence.

A Popular Forces (PF) outpost crouched tentatively just off Route 534, just 500 meters south and west of Nui Loc Son in the tiny hamlet of Thon Hai. The Popular Forces were a sort of village militia, poorly trained and equipped, and not noted for their aggressiveness.

The Marines and the civilians had no reason to trust each other, and each regarded the other with suspicion in the early weeks when the Leathernecks began limited-range patrols. As Captain Deegan slowly broadened his operations area, his Marines began killing enemy soldiers on a regular basis, and he also demonstrated to the civilians that he was there to stay and was a force to be reckoned with. As Captain Deegan dilated his operating area, he found only small enemy units, squads, and platoons. But there were a great many of them, so many that on February 18 he reported to the 1st Marines that there was the equivalent of two enemy regiments nearby. The regiment told Deegan not to worry and to keep doing what he was doing. He did.

Other signs of increased enemy activity accumulated. Private First Class Lonnie Matthews remembers that Foxtrot Company captured a fourteen-year-old enemy conscript who told the Marines the NVA snatched him from his village and sent him to a big training camp, just a two-day walk from the western end of the valley. New recruits, whether they volunteered or were abducted, received a minimum of thirty days of training. Nearly 40 percent of the instruction was political. The party cadres heavily indoctrinated the new soldiers on the importance of the party, of the organization, and of their mission in South Vietnam. The cadres rarely used Communist ideology. Instead, they preached the need for peace, land to the tillers, and, above all, the need to rid Vietnam of the "puppet" Saigon regime that was the lackey of the American imperialists.

Once training was complete, each soldier was assigned to a three-man "cell," in many ways the equivalent of a Marine Corps fire team. These

Marines work their way through elephant grass in the Que Son Valley. This was common in many areas and difficult to move through. The grass was thick enough to bring progress to a crawl, and the blades were sharp enough to cut skin. *USMC*

three-man cells ate, slept, and fought together. Vietnam is a very family-oriented society; to a Vietnamese, the family is everything. Each unit had a political officer who was in charge of thoroughly and constantly indoctrinating the soldiers. Using parables, simple poems, and slogans, they worked at supplanting the three-man cells for the soldiers' families. The soldiers were also encouraged to watch their fellow cell members for any sign of weakness of spirit and to report such deviations to higher headquarters.

Infantrymen from the 5th Marines attack across a wet paddy in the Que Son Valley Campaign of 1967. Paddies, divided by dikes and bordered by tree lines, were typical of the ground fought over in this campaign. *USMC*

Much of their tactical training emphasized night combat. The overwhelmingly superior firepower of the allies dictated that the VC/NVA move at night whenever possible. If they moved in the daylight, it was usually because they were driven to do so.

During daylight moves, unless they were under a clear and present danger, they stopped for as long as it took to thoroughly camouflage themselves, and they always tried to move through ravines and along stream beds where the vegetation gave them some concealment. With a compulsion nearly genetic in character, American forces always went for the high ground. The enemy in this war usually went for the low.

Many American commanders thought that the VC owned the night and ceded the hours after dark to them. Deegan, and the other better commanders, thought otherwise and successfully conducted night operations on a regular basis. Deegan nearly always sent his men out under the cover of darkness to find and set-in likely ambush sites that earlier daylight patrols had marked on their maps.

As the Marines demonstrated their success, the villagers became friendlier. One day a village chief came up to the hill and volunteered to lead a patrol. The Marines were skeptical but decided to give it a try. Lieutenant

Marines "battle sight zero": that is, adjust the battle sights on new M16s at the one-thousand-inch range at Hill 69, Chu Lai, early spring 1967. *Courtesy Steve Lovejoy*

George Mallon took the patrol out, and before departing he told Deegan that if the chief led them into an enemy ambush, he would immediately shoot the chief.

Two members of the Popular Forces and the village chief guided the patrol out beyond the PF outpost, where they got into position along a trail an hour before first light. The Vietnamese lay down and went to sleep while the Marines remained on full alert. At dawn, an enemy main-force squad confidently strolled down the trail. The Marines surprised and killed them.

There were about forty rifle companies attached to the 1st Marine Division at this time, and Foxtrot 2/1 was killing more enemy and capturing more weapons than any other ten companies combined. The action around Nui Loc Son attracted the notice of the division commander, Maj. Gen. Herman Nickerson, who soon became a frequent visitor, showing up with some of his other commanders and touting Deegan's methods as an example of how a rifle company could go out and kill the enemy.

Deegan's daily stand-to and stand-down process taught the enemy an early lesson about the Marines' alertness and ability to defend Nui Loc Son. During stand to, everyone was in their bunker before first light, with their flak jackets and helmets on, and all the weapons, including the mortars and recoilless rifles, were loaded, manned, and ready to fire. The Marines would do the same thing in the evening, standing down before dark. One night, at just about last light, they heard the *poof-poof* sound of a mortar firing in the distance and saw the muzzle blast of the weapon in the flat paddy land about two clicks (kilometers) north of the hill. The Marines'106mm recoilless rifle crew blew apart the enemy position while their mortar rounds were still in the air. For good measure the Marines called in an air strike on the mortar position. Their response so intimidated the enemy that they never took another shot at Nui Loc Son.

The Marines kept pushing out the range of their patrols and expanding their influence. One night a platoon slipped out in the darkness and marched farther from Nui Loc Son than any previous patrol. They arrived at their destination before sunrise and carefully prepared an ambush, setting up in a

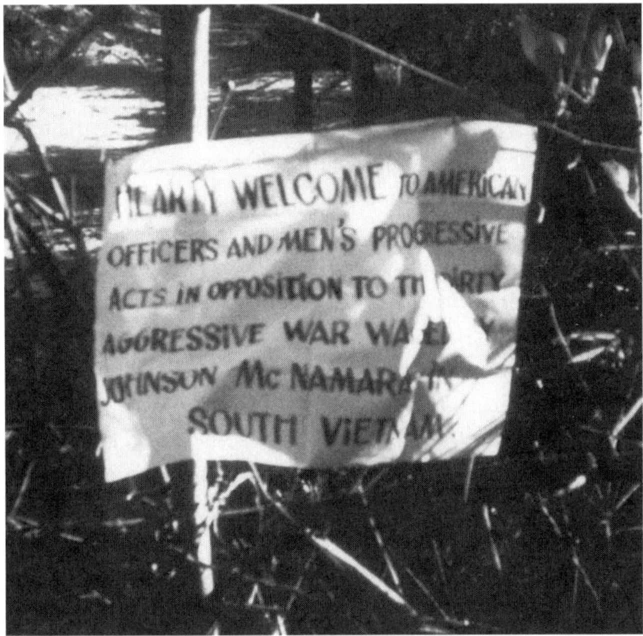

A propaganda welcome by the Vietcong. *Courtesy Harold Wadley*

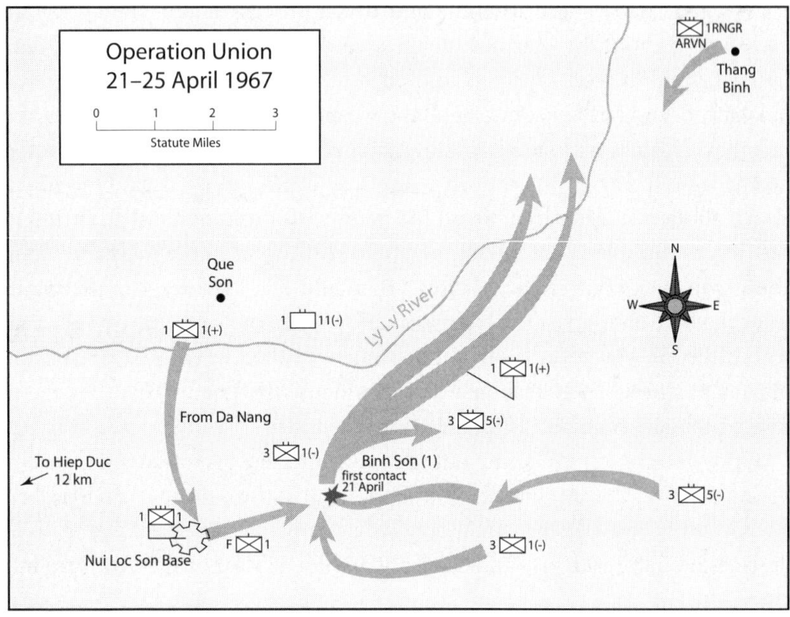

ditch behind a line of bamboo that paralleled a trail. Just as the sun was about to crack the horizon, two women appeared, walking slowly toward the Marine position at an angle of ninety degrees, sweeping the terrain with their eyes. Behind them, one man at a time, a long column of enemy soldiers, about a hundred strong, appeared, cautiously following their scouts.

The women reached the bamboo hedge row, turned right, and led the soldiers down the long axis of the killing zone. They stopped, some of them just a few feet from the hidden Marines, while the enemy leaders scurried about, whispering and passing information from the women up front. The Marines held their breaths, certain that the enemy could hear the pounding of their hearts.

The tension was too much for a sergeant named Tobin. He prematurely sprayed the kill zone with his grease gun and scattered the enemy column. The other Marines opened fire and shot twenty of the NVA dead.

The smoke cleared, the surviving enemy fled, and the Marines took a look at the corpses they had left behind and collected their weapons. The enemy bodies were clad in new uniforms, and they had good weapons, some still with Cosmoline on them, perhaps resupplied during the Tet truce. Lieutenant

Marines from the 1st Marines patrol the paddies of the Que Son Valley, April 19, 1967. Just two days later, the most vicious campaign of the Vietnam War will begin on this ground. *USMC*

General Lewis Walt, the senior Marine commander in Vietnam, flew to Nui Loc Son to congratulate the Marines and look at the captured weapons.

On April 11, Sgt. Tom Manion, the chief scout sniper for the 1st Battalion, 5th Marines, received information from an intelligence source that pinpointed the location of some enemy automatic weapons in the western Que Son Valley. He went out in a helicopter with a fire team and three Kit Carson scouts, former enemy soldiers who had rallied to the allied side, to take a look. Not far from the LZ the enemy opened up on them, crippling the chopper, which came crashing down, staggered forward a bit, and toppled over, blades tearing up the earth. Exiting the crippled aircraft, Manion looked up and saw Vietnamese in uniform and thought they were ARVN.

Up to this point, all the Vietnamese he had seen in uniform were our South Vietnamese allies. He quickly changed his mind when the soldiers began shooting at him. An Alpha Company, 1/5, reaction force under Lt. Rick Zell rode to the rescue, landed, and set up a perimeter. At dark, a flare ship came up and illuminated the area until about 0430. When it left to refuel, the enemy mounted a halfhearted attack that the Marines easily fought off, with only two minor wounded in action. At sunrise, they found two enemy bodies lying outside their position. Sergeant Manion sensed, for the first time, that there was something in the valley that a Marine rifle company could not handle.

By April's end, Deegan's Marines were seriously disrupting enemy activity. For three months the enemy had been leaving an increasing number of bodies on the battlefield. The Marines suffered not a single killed in action. Their world changed on April 21.

The official account of the war says Union I was a planned operation and that on the night of April 18–19, the 1st Marines' staff worked through the night to come up with a plan of attack to take on the units of the enemy division that had invaded the valley. The plan committed elements of the 1st and 3rd Battalions, 1st Marines, as heliborne forces. Another, unidentified, battalion would move from Chu Lai to act as regimental reserve. Deegan says that this was fiction, or, if true, no one told him. He asserts that the fight of April 21 set off the entire operation. Major Art Loughry, the executive officer (XO) of the 3rd Battalion, 1st Marines, agrees that if Union I was a planned operation, it was supposed to begin later. He also agrees that no one told them that the 2nd NVA Division, made up of the 1st VC Regiment and the 3rd and 31st NVA Regiments, was in the valley.

Documents declassified since the war show that even the National Security Council in Washington knew that the 2nd NVA Division was in the Que Son Valley in late 1966, but nobody told the Marines on the ground. Major Loughry talked with Maj. John Murtha, the regimental intelligence officer, about enemy in the valley without Murtha so much as mentioning the 2nd NVA Division.

Lieutenant John Dunn, a mustang and patrol leader with the 1st Reconnaissance Battalion, regularly played hide and seek with the enemy in the western end of the valley. On April 20, the day before Operation Union I began, his handful of Marines set in on a six-hundred-meter-high hill at the west end of the valley and took turns observing the lowlands from atop a tree. All morning the Marines spotted large groups of NVA as they scurried between tree lines, moving eastward. Dunn's men struck them with one artillery barrage after another before the NVA figured out where the Marines were and sent a reinforced platoon toward his hill. It was Lance Cpl. Raymond "Gator" Pheilan's turn in the tree, and he threw a branch down to get Dunn's attention and whispered, "I think there are a bunch of people coming at us. There are about thirty or forty of them." Pheilan came down out of the tree, and Dunn went up. By the time he got up to take a look, the NVA were at the bottom of his hill, on line, and coming at the Marines. Dunn called for an emergency extract and got his team out safely, the choppers raking the enemy with their machine guns as they flew from the area.

Chapter 5

Hot Pursuit

By dawn on April 22, all Marine elements had lost contact as the enemy that had mauled Captain Deegan's company fled to the north. Lieutenant Colonel Bell's 1st Battalion, 1st Marines, and Lieutenant Colonel Esslinger's 3rd Battalion, 5th Marines, moved north and east to pursue them while three battalions of ARVN Rangers moved southwest from Thang Binh to try to cut them off.

Major General Nickerson had both an opportunity and a problem. The opportunity was a chance to do battle with the 2nd NVA Division. The problem was that he did not need all the fingers of one hand to count the assets he could send to the Que Son Valley. He reallocated his forces as best he could, and on April 25, Col. Kenneth Houghton's[5] 5th Marines flew in from Chu Lai to take command of the operation, and the 1st Marines returned to the Da Nang TAOR, except the badly battered Foxtrot Company, which remained at Nui Loc Son.

For two weeks, the Marines fought a series of vicious little running engagements, ambushes, and counter-ambushes, the enemy fighting delaying actions while withdrawing to their sanctuaries in the north and west. The two sides fought over the lower elevations, across rice paddies and through hamlets, many of which were fortified with extensive trench and cave systems that afforded protection from aerial observation, air strikes, and artillery fire; they fought along a ten-kilometer stretch of the river valley south of Hiep Duc which ran eastward into the Que Son Valley proper, the mountains on either side rich with staging areas and hiding places; they

A squad-size patrol from Charlie Company, 1st Battalion, 5th Marines, takes a break in a village. *Courtesy Harold Thrasher*

fought around the village of Hiep Duc itself, where neither the ARVN nor Americans had operated for years.

By late April, Marine radio direction finders had located the headquarters of the 3rd NVA Regiment nine clicks northwest and the headquarters of the 2nd NVA Division about six clicks due south of Nui Loc Son. Both enemy command posts were in rugged mountain terrain. The 1st Marine Aircraft Wing pounded them with bombs but with little effect. The NVA were not unaware of allied intelligence sources, and the radios on which they transmitted were not in their actual command posts but located in remote sites, linked to their headquarters by communications wire and runners.

Lieutenant Colonel Peter "Highpockets" Hilgartner was one of those bright, hard-charging, no-nonsense officers that make the Marine Corps what it is. He was six feet five inches tall, a Naval Academy graduate, and had extensive combat experience as an artillery officer in the Korean War. He took command of a demoralized and ineffective 1st Battalion, 5th Marines, early in 1967 and immediately began cleaning house, transferring the officers and senior enlisted men whom he thought contributed to the battalion's sorry condition. Axing so many people earned him the whispered name of "the Dragon" among the officers, but the enlisted men called him "Highpockets" and liked him. Consciously or not, he followed the model of Gen. Omar Bradley, who once stated that 90 percent of success in battle is knowing one's subordinates. Within a few short months, Hilgartner transformed the battalion into a premier fighting unit. One of his former officers called him a "highly professional hard-ass who turned the battalion around." Rather than hide his rank insignia from snipers and the like, he had the big silver leaf of a lieutenant colonel on the front of his helmet, which, with his height, made him an enticing target. One of the first things he did was to send the bodyguard assigned to the previous battalion commander packing back to his rifle squad, where he was most needed.

On April 30, helicopters inserted Hilgartner's battalion into the mountains thirteen kilometers east of Hiep Duc, where they patrolled west along the Chang River.

Lt. Dave McInturff (commanding officer, Delta Company, 1st Battalion, 5th Marines): We went over to Hiep Duc, and one of my squads ran into an NVA regimental storage area, a big cache of uniforms and medical gear. We pulled about seven thousand pounds of gear out of that place and hundreds of enemy uniforms and a brand-new—still had the wrapper on it—Spring 1967 Sears and Roebuck catalog.

Evidence abounded that there was big game in the area, but it continued to elude them. The first day out, a squad from Bravo Company apprehended a young Viet Cong guerrilla. He told them that a company from a southbound regiment had passed through the area just to the west the night before; they had a .50-caliber machine gun and a 105mm howitzer with them. Over the next week, as Hilgartner's Marines worked their way to the north and slightly east, there was no shortage of minor encounters with black-pajama-clad VC, but they had yet to engage the first team. They soon found them.

Lieutenant Rick Zell, 1st Platoon, Alpha Company, 5th Marines, remembers May 1 as the first time the battalion had contact all day. It was the first time for certain that they knew they were fighting NVA. Large groups of camouflaged soldiers moved against the Marines in the open.

Lt. Rick Zell: We knew something was very, very different. We began to have pitched battles in broad daylight. The first time we had a firefight with a large force, we were trying to set up an LZ for medevacs. As soon as we started clearing the area, we began to come under very intense fire. We couldn't tell where it was coming from.

THE ENEMY SHOT LIEUTENANT ZELL THROUGH THE LEG, but he felt he could still function and chose not to be evacuated, staying in the field until the company commander ordered him out later that day. Lieutenant Joaquin Gracida, of Kilo Company, 3rd Battalion, 5th Marines, was also hit on May 1. In his case a bullet creased his forehead and blew his helmet off. Lieutenant Gracida was in a fury because of the inadequacies of the newly issued M16 rifle. He thought he was going to be relieved because of what he had told the battalion commander he thought of the weapon. He remembers that the attached engineers still had the M14, and some of the grunts, who had seen men needlessly die because of the inadequacies of the M16, were paying the engineers one hundred dollars to swap weapons with them. It gave the infantrymen a more reliable weapon and made the engineers feel like real grunts with M16s.

Chapter 6

Soldiers from the Sea

THE NEXT MARINES TO JOIN THE FIGHT with the NVA came from the sea. On April 28, Lt. Col. Peter Wickwire's 1st Battalion, 3rd Marines, the special landing force (SLF), lifted off from the ships of Task Group 76.4 and alighted in the eastern end of the Que Son basin. They swept to the northeast, working their way toward the mouth of a spur on the northern edge of the valley floor, screened from the valley proper by a seven-kilometer-long, east-west hill mass. The paddy land of the valley resembles, on the map, a Rorschach left hand placed palm down with the fingers pointing west, the spur extending, thumb-like, along the top of the valley.

The Marines from the SLF moved into the base of the thumb and immediately clashed with elements of Lt. Col. Tran Kim Tung's 3rd NVA Regiment, whose soldiers resolutely pestered the Marines with small-arms and mortar fire but refused to stand and fight. The Marines pursued them, constantly moving by helicopter and on foot, daring them to come out and meet in a major engagement.

Captain Jerry Reczek's Charlie Company, 1st Battalion, 3rd Marines, neared its first assigned objective, found no enemy, and set in, passing the night without incident. While waiting for a chopper pickup the next morning, Reczek scanned the valley and saw a large man, who did not appear to be Asian, dressed in black and kneeling out in the middle of a field like someone kneeling along football game sidelines. The man's attention was fixed on the Marines. A gun team loosed a burst at him, and the man dove into a bush. Just then, the helicopters set down, and Charlie Company flew to a new position.

Captain Reczek's Marines patrolled along the valley floor and then, at the end of the day, dug in. After last light the enemy cautiously probed them but did not attack. The next morning, May 3, the operations officer, Maj. Dick Ossenfort, gave the company commanders a frag order (brief or fragmentary order) assigning new zones of action to each and cautioned them that as much as an NVA regiment might be nearby.

Capt. Jerry Reczek: We looked at our zone of action on the maps and took off. We immediately ran into small enemy outposts that took us under fire. After the first contact, we moved through a village, and all the women and children were in one hooch, and yelling and crying and jabbering, a sure sign that the enemy was nearby. Our objective was the village, which we moved through, and we came up on a nice knoll, a good position that already had trenches in it. We got up just about dark and set in after moving all day.

CAPTAIN RECZEK AND CAPT. BILLY WEST, his artillery FO, walked outside the perimeter and were looking at the terrain with a map and compass. Reczek looked up from the map and saw a Vietnamese face peering at them from behind a nearby banana tree. The two Captains hurried back to their lines just as the enemy struck their position with machine gun and 57mm recoilless rifle fire, killing one of Reczek's mortar men and wounding his first sergeant and an admin clerk. Captain Durant, the FAC, hit back at the enemy with close air support just as fast as he could summon the birds, and the Marines got one of their 81mm mortars up and firing and ran through their limited ammunition just as it got dark.

Captain West set up a curtain of steel around the position with box-me-in artillery fire. That night the enemy harassed the Charlie Company Marines, but Puff kept them at bay. Using a flashlight wielded by a Marine on the ground as a reference point, the gunship hosed the enemy down, the line of tracers from the aircraft an unbroken wand of red light fingering the target area, the guns sounding like the tearing of heavy canvas and putting a round into every square inch of an area the size of a football field each minute. Often the enemy .50-caliber machine guns would duel with Puff, the graceful arc of their green tracers trying to swim up the river of red light. When the airship ran low on fuel and ammunition, it went back to base, loaded up, and went back to work. About 0300, Captain Durant suggested that they try to get a medevac in. Captain Reczek decided against it, as he had no critically wounded. Later, when things quieted down, a Huey showed up, and they were going to use it, but when the pilot tried to land, the green tracers erupted again from the ridgeline and punched holes in his aircraft.

On the morning of May 4, Capt. Ed Aldous's Delta Company, 1st Battalion, 3rd Marines, got into a good fight, and Lieutenant Colonel Wickwire sent Captain Reczek's Charlie Company out to assist. After some initial confusion as to where Aldous's platoons were, Reczek spotted them and moved out, closing Delta Company at dusk. After dark and behind a barrier of supporting arms, both companies withdrew and set up on Hill 65 a few hundred meters to their northwest. Captain Aldous had appointed Pfc. Ken Hicks, a machine gunner with Delta, to be one of his radio operators. The skipper sent him off to take a VC suspect back to the battalion CP, and he missed the fight that morning. As soon as Hicks got back and found out about the firefight, he detached himself from radio duty without authority and happily went back to humping ammo for his gun team. They were glad to see him.

That night, against the advice of his experienced NCOs, the Alpha Company commander sent a patrol out to the Ly Ly River to get water. They departed at dusk but returned under a full moon. According to Corporal Jim Murtaugh, the NVA had set up an ambush just outside the American lines.

Cpl. Jim Murtaugh: They knew the returning patrol would be relaxed when they got this close to the company position.

The enemy concealed themselves in haystacks, waited for the returning patrol, and hit it hard. Bits and pieces of the fight lasted well into the night, and when the sun rose, the Marines counted heads and found that the water patrol cost the Marines fourteen dead and eight wounded. Lieutenant Colonel Wickwire relieved the company commander. After the bodies were retrieved, the sergeant major told Corporal Murtaugh to remove dog tags from the dead. The first tag he removed read, "Joseph Rhuben La Rose." Murtaugh carefully wrote the name on a scrap of paper and has carried LaRose's name in his wallet ever since.

The enemy continued to play cat and mouse with Wickwire's Marines.

Capt. Jerry Reczek: We'd move all day, set up at dark, move again after dark; move out at first light, and take more incoming mortars.

The increased activity meant that either they were cornering the enemy or he was waiting for an opportunity to take on the Marines when the odds were in his favor.

On May 5, the command group of the 1st Battalion, 3rd Marines, and most of a rifle company tried to lift off again by helicopter but were hampered by enemy fire. Diligence tempered with luck was on their side. They suppressed the fire and evacuated over two hundred men and three thousand pounds of ammunition without taking any casualties.

Lieutenant Colonel Hilgartner's 1st Battalion, 5th Marines, and Esslinger's 3rd Battalion, 5th Marines, kept pressing the enemy and got into some minor fights. On the night of May 6, an India Company Marine, Lance Cpl. Earl Heister, went to investigate a cave, but at six feet three inches, he was too tall to go in very far. Lieutenant Kenny Moore took Corporal Terrell, one of his squad leaders, and entered the cave and had a running gun battle with some NVA until the Marines expended their ammo. They came out, loaded up, and went back in, shooting and tossing grenades. After the smoke cleared, they threw in tear gas and went in with flashlights and saw the NVA they had shot, six of them. By that time it was dark, and Moore's platoon set up outside the cave. They went in the next morning and pulled the bodies out along with weapons and a collection of records and maps.

Chapter 7

Union I: The Battle for Hill 110

A few days later, Capt. Russell "Jim" Caswell's Charlie Company, 1st Battalion, 5th Marines, set in for the night several clicks south of a hill numbered 110 on the map. Corporal Tom "Kid" Kintner and Lance Cpl. John Rusth dug a chest-deep hole together. After sunset the enemy began chucking rocks at them, trying to get them to fire and give away their locations. Gunny Marcelino Rivera-Cruz ran over and told them to not fire. Then a grenade sailed out of the dark and landed in the machine gunner's hole, but he bailed out before it detonated. The rest of the night was quiet.

The next morning, May 10, Captain Caswell's Marines moved to a small ville two clicks south of Hill 110, picking up a couple of military-age men and one woman. Then, using an existing trail for a guide, they headed up and over a steep two-hundred-meter hill and found themselves on the southwest side of Hill 110's base.

Cpl. Tom "Kid" Kintner: We were walking toward Hill 110. In between there was a small hill covered with these huge rocks, and the gooks opened up on us from this hill. I had to slow down and remove a stone from my boot, but we assaulted up the hill. We had a gunny that carried a .45 and he came face to face with a gook on the trail from about twenty meters. The gunny got hit in the ass, and he killed the gook with his .45. At the top of the hill there was this huge bush. Lance Corporal John Rusth and I were on one side of it, and there was a gook we couldn't see, shooting down at the Marines from the other side. I told Rusth, "Let's sneak around and capture him." All of a sudden, John said, "Duck." The gook had snuck around the bush and was ten yards in back of me. When I ducked, John shot him in the face, and it took his whole jaw off, but he was still alive. He was making this horrible sucking sound and was in shock. We took him down to the bottom of the hill. We started back up again, and no one knew what to do with him, so we gave him to a guy named Corky and said, "Give this guy some permanent medical attention." Corky took him off in the bush, and that was that.

THEN CHARLIE COMPANY MOVED ON to Objective November, Hill 110 itself, which is neither high nor steep and is girded with flat paddy save the southeast side, where it abuts a higher mass.

Captain Jerry Shirley's Bravo Company and Jerry Reczek's Charlie Company, from Lieutenant Colonel Wickwire's 1st Battalion, 3rd Marines, were nearly a click north of Hill 110, near the hamlet of Nghi Ha and astride the Suoi Cho Dun, an east-west stream. They ran into a determined enemy who pounded them with concentrated fire. That morning, Captain Reczek

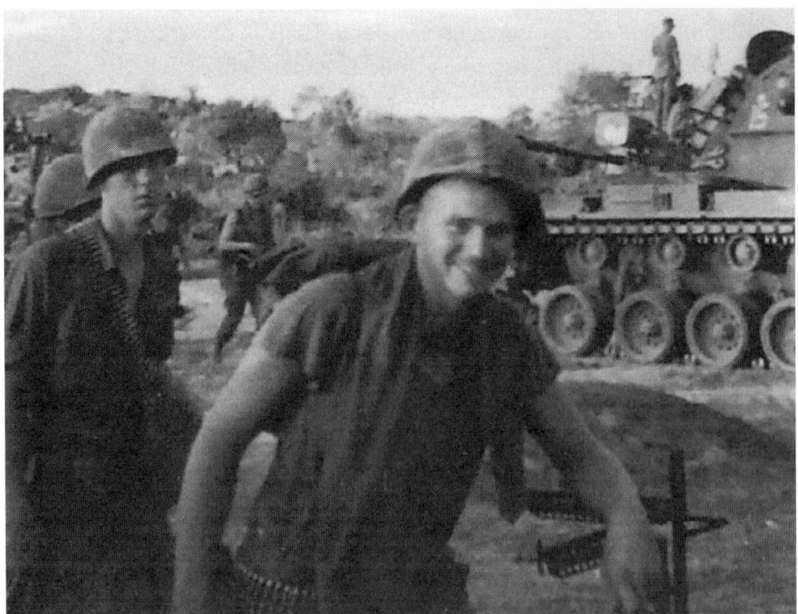

Harvey Cunningham with his M60 machine gun. Note the belt of ammunition around his waist. *Courtesy John Rusth*

Captain Russell "Jim" Caswell, commanding officer, Charlie Company, 1st Battalion, 5th Marines. His commanding officer, Lt. Col. "Highpockets" Hilgartner, said he was "the hero among heroes" of Operation Union. *Courtesy Jim Caswell*

had moved his Charlie Company out at first light, not even taking time for chow. A rattle of small-arms fire sounded across the battlefield from the south, and he could see the puffs of rifle fire on Hill 110. Before he could respond to the struggle on the hill, there was more gunfire to his direct front. Captain Shirley got Reczek on the radio and said, "I've got something going on here."

One of his platoons had run into a superior force. As Reczek was putting out some 60mm mortar fire to support Bravo Company, the volume of small-arms fire picked up and became steady. One of the Charlie Company platoon commanders, Lt. Dick Chapa, could see Captain Shirley's fight and told Reczek that he was afraid Bravo Company would be overrun. Captain Shirley managed to get another platoon across the stream to the right and now had two platoons facing the NVA. Since Lieutenant Chapa had a view of the firefight, Reczek sent him around to the left and enveloped the enemy to take the pressure off Bravo.

The Charlie Company command group was near the stream bed. Reczek saw a heavily camouflaged NVA and pointed him out. No one else could see him, so the skipper grabbed a rifle and shot him.

Capt. Jerry Reczek: We were in real thick scrub in the riverbed, and I could see the concussion of the mortars shaking the leaves of the trees. Captain Billy West, the artillery forward observer, said, "Captain, they've got us bracketed. They have dropped one behind us and one in front." Chapa got on the radio and said he could see the enemy in khaki uniforms and needed help, as he was becoming overrun. I took the CP group and went off to where Chapa was. I could see dead from 3rd Platoon but couldn't see the rest of the platoon. I looked over and there was my XO, who had come up to see if I needed some help. Either a mortar or grenade hit nearby and took off the leg of a Marine at the hip and hit my XO, Lieutenant Ron Sutton, who was knocked unconscious, and I thought he was dead.

Both of the 1st Battalion, 3rd Marines companies were in fights of their own, and neither was able to provide any significant support to Charlie Company, 1st Brigade, 5th Marines, that afternoon.

Capt. Jerry Reczek: A chopper from HMM-263 came in with ammo, and the pilot wanted to know if I wanted casualties to go back. He sat there on the ground while the ammo was off-loaded and some casualties were put on, and he took off and got back to the ship. He had thirty-four bullet holes in the bird when he got back to base.

Captain Shirley sent his 3rd Platoon under Lt. George McGuire off to envelop the enemy from the right. McGuire was immediately shot down and badly wounded, and Shirley couldn't get to him, because he was stuck behind a terrace. The lieutenant lay out there until after dark. Captain Shirley continued to maneuver the platoon by sending orders through Lieutenant McGuire's radio operator.

During the movement to assist Captain Shirley's Bravo Company, two of Captain Reczek's young corporals stepped up and into the legend that forms Marine Corps tradition. One was Cpl. John Reid, a squad leader with the 3rd Platoon. His platoon was going at it hammer and tongs with the enemy when mortar fire wiped out one of the Marine machine gun teams and fire pinned his exposed platoon. Reid ran across open ground to the gun, picked it up, and ran toward the enemy, firing all the way until he found a place that suited him, then set up and laid down heavy fire on the enemy guns, silencing them and enabling six other members of his unit to reach covered positions. When the enemy attempted to overrun him, he stuck to his gun, stacking up enemy bodies until they killed him.

Corporal Thomas Sanders, an African-American machine gun squad leader, attacked the enemy single-handedly with his machine gun after they shot down all the other members of his squad. When the enemy got into a trench and fought their way toward Marines who were also in the trench, Corporal Sanders jumped in, placed himself between the enemy and his comrades, and delivered a hurricane of fire down the long axis of the trench, stopping the enemy attack and blowing the life out of one soldier after another until he went down, wounded.

Capt. Jerry Shirley: The Marines had the high ground on the west side of the stream, which was a good marker. Artillery was out of the question because the 5th Marines were nearby, so Jerry Reczek called in A-4 Skyhawks and controlled strikes in the riverbed to our front and dropped some snake and nape (Snakeye bombs and napalm) very close to us.

Capt. Jerry Reczek: We tied in with Bravo to the right and one platoon from Delta on the left. A company from 5th Marines, led by Capt. Hank Stackpole, was coming up the river bed toward us.

Capt. Jerry Shirley: Battalion decided to send the Sparrow Hawk reaction force out there, and in the meantime Jerry Reczek came up on the left and made contact with my northernmost platoon. The Sparrow Hawk platoon came out in a couple of Hueys and started to set down between my unit and the enemy position, and I saw what he was gonna do and threw a red smoke grenade to try to warn him off. He didn't get the message, and the enemy put twenty-one rounds in the helo and wounded one of the pilots, but the troops made it off the helo. One of the choppers lifted up and slowly moved behind me but had taken so many rounds it couldn't fly.

LIEUTENANT COLONEL WICKWIRE ORDERED Delta Company into the mix, but Delta had to cross the Suoi Cho Dun, a stream only about twenty feet across but armpit deep on the six-foot–three-inch Private First Class Hicks. With help from the tallest of their Marines, Delta Company got across the stream and set up in a tree line within sight of Hill 110. Hicks no sooner reached his platoon CP than his platoon commander ordered him to carry a wounded Marine back across the river and then ford it a third time and bring ammunition to the platoon. The casualty was shot in the face, and his blood ran down Hicks's uniform, soaking it. He started across the stream and saw Marines vigorously waving at him and yelling, but he could not hear what they were shouting. He set down the wounded man down on the far side, and they told him a sniper just killed a Marine crossing in that very spot. He was greeted by the saddest possible sight for a Marine, a row of a dozen dead Marines covered with bloody ponchos. Hicks picked up the ammo and recrossed the river to join his platoon.

Captain Caswell's Charlie Company, 1st Battalion, 5th Marines was closing Hill 110 from the south.

Cpl. Tom "Kid" Kintner: We came up over this rise and could see the valley in front of us. The whole valley was alive with fire: Phantoms and helos and small arms, auto fire and mortars everywhere.

Capt. Jim Caswell: I got to the base of Hill 110, and a platoon from 1/3 had called in an air strike on the hill. The lieutenant had been told by his company commander to take the hill, and they were under fire. I told this platoon commander that we would take the objective and for him to rejoin his unit. He left, but he popped a yellow smoke to show the aircraft our lines, and the NVA used the location of the smoke to mortar our position. This indicated to me that there was a fairly sizeable force in the area. I swept the hill with 60mm mortars.

The extra mortar round that Caswell insisted each of his Marines carry, except for machine gunners and corpsmen, paid off.

The Marines sat on paddy dikes, nonchalantly smoking and waiting for the Phantoms to drop ordnance and for mortar rounds to rake the hill. They did not even take cover from the occasional sniper round, because the shooting was not much and not accurate. They knew they were going to have to take the top of the hill, and they thought that most of the enemy was there.

Capt. Jim Caswell: I had a good man, Sgt. Juan Sanchez, who had weapons platoon. Sanchez was one of those incredibly good NCOs who saved the day for Charlie Company. To offset the M16 problem, Sanchez had all the crew-served weapons inspected and serviced with extra care before leaving on the operation. He also made sure that the Marines carried extra machine gun ammo.

Cpl. Tom "Kid" Kintner: We got to the bottom of Hill 110, and it was covered with chest-high elephant grass. We got on line and assaulted up it. This gook looked up over the grass about twenty feet in front of me. I dumped a whole magazine at him.

Cpl. Bill Pettway (Captain Caswell's radio operator): As we got near the crest of the hill, all hell broke loose. We started receiving intense fire directly in front of us from the fields near the river area. Lance Corporal John Rusth clearly saw a grenade that an NVA lobbed down the hill.

It seemed to fly in slow motion until it bounced off Kid Kintner's pack and went off with a loud explosion. It was a concussion grenade, and the blast knocked Kintner down. He thought that he had been wounded, but he was only shaken.

Cpl. Tom "Kid" Kintner: The NVA took off. I think the guy was down there to lead us up the hill. The left side of the hill was steep and kept the 3rd Platoon Marines from getting up on line as they would have liked, so they reached the top in a staggered column.

Sgt. Hillous York: After we got to the hill, we started up the northwest side. The 3rd Platoon was on the left, 2nd Platoon on the right, and 1st in reserve. We got a little fire from the top of the hill, and then the Phantoms bombed it. On our way up, as we got closer to the top, they used mortars. It is not a very big hill. There were no trees but a lot of chest-high bushes and grass. Then it thinned out, closer to the top. As we get closer, the fire got hotter. As we got over the crest and started down, the firing really picked up from a cane field to the southwest.

Capt. Jim Caswell: As we took the hill, the lead elements of the 3rd Platoon ran past me, and this lance corporal said, "Sir, my rifle malfunctioned. May I have your rifle?" and I said, "Yes," and traded rifles with him. A few days later he gave it back, and I said, "How did it shoot?" and he said, "Not worth a shit, sir." As we came over the top of the hill and down the slope, we came under the most fire I have heard at any time.

The roar was intense, the sound of a single shot could no more be made out than the sound of a single drop of water cascading down a waterfall.

Capt. Jim Caswell: The NVA took me and three companies from 1/3 under fire and didn't seem the least concerned about taking on four companies. We

Sergeant Hillous York, great-nephew of the famous Alvin York of World War I. The photographer snapped this photo just as Sergeant York got the word that his point man was down, and he was rushing to the sound of the guns with a weapon in each hand. He was a Silver Star recipient for his valor on Hill 110. *Courtesy Hillous York*

took this hill, and my troops were still thinking they were chasing VC and didn't realize that we needed to change tactics to regular company tactics against a regular enemy, the NVA. We took up defensive positions as high on the hill as possible, to be on the military crest, but there was very poor cover and concealment. We were in a horseshoe defensive position, which saved our ass, along with our M60 machineguns. I had 3rd, 2nd, and 1st Platoons, going from north to south.

Charlie Company was engulfed in a storm of flying hot steel. Caswell's lieutenants were cut down early, and his sergeants took charge.

Capt. Jim Caswell: I had five sergeants who saved everybody and ran their platoons and ran them in the best manner possible and kept the company together. They were extremely brave. Sanchez was one of them. The 1st Platoon commander was Lt. Robert Kirkpatrick. Sergeant Harris was his platoon sergeant. Lieutenant George Selke commanded 2nd Platoon, and he had Sergeants Lynch and Teague. Third Platoon was [commanded by] a gunny that insisted on taking a platoon back when we received a new staff NCO who couldn't keep up. While we got him into shape, the gunny asked if he could take his platoon back. He was a wonderful man, Gunnery Sgt. Marcelino Rivera-Cruz. Troops called him Gunny Cruz since they couldn't pronounce all that. He was my friend and a very good man. His platoon sergeant was Segt. Hillous York, from Tennessee, a descendent of the famous Sgt. Alvin York, U.S. Army, from World War I, his great uncle.

Cpl. Bill Pettway: We couldn't get artillery, so the FO went down the hill to help out the infantry and was wounded three times. He said, as if surprised by the fact, "They're killing people down there. They're using real damn bullets!"

As the enemy shot Marines down, their comrades would shout their names. "Tague is down." "Washington is down." "Suapaia is down." "Gunny Cruz is down." Corporal Nick Tague had nineteen days to go on his tour. He could have stayed behind and not gone on the operation but chose to do so. Private First Class Clarence Washington was a tall, lanky, much-liked black Marine, always eager to help a struggling comrade. Lance Corporal Suapaia was a popular Marine from Hawaii. All were killed almost immediately. The rocket round that killed the gunny and his radio operator blew their radio all over the landscape, where chunks of it lay smoking.

Cpl. Bill Pettway: I was talking to the 3rd Platoon radio man, Lance Cpl. Fred Tate, Rivera-Cruz's radio man. He and Rivera-Cruz were killed as I was talking to him. The 2nd Platoon radioman, Jacob Lauff, called me and

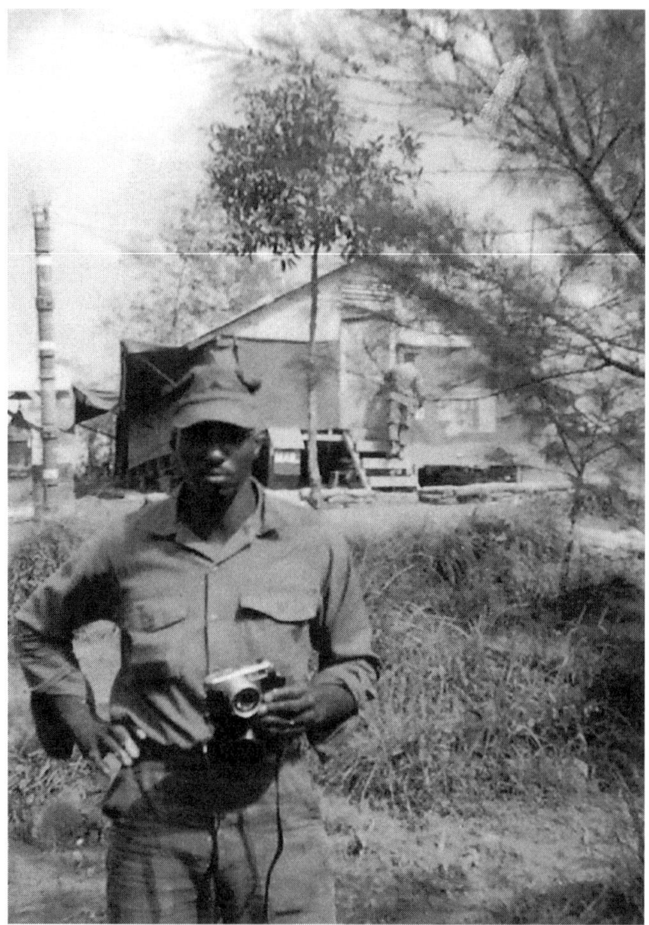

Private First Class Clarence Washington, killed in action on Hill 110, Operation Union I. *Courtesy John Rusth*

said, "I've been hit and need a corpsman down here." I said, "Jake, all the corpsmen have been hit except one." About fifteen minutes later he called me back and said, "Bill, I am bleeding to death. They hit me again." I said, "Jake, how bad is it?" He said, "They broke my arm this time." About thirty minutes later, I tried and failed to contact him, so I thought he had died.

DESPITE HIS WOUNDS, Lauff came up on the radio with Captain Caswell and told him were the enemy positions were located.

Sgt. Hillous York: You could see them, their uniforms with the red stars on their helmets and the red-starred belt buckles. We could see canned goods on the ground where they had been eating. The NVA were trying to get around the end where we were. The fighting was point blank. There was just a little strip of grass between the two forces. After the fight started going good, we were nose to nose across this strip of grass that in places was no more than twelve feet across. They were in this little notch, and they were on the high side of the hill. They couldn't go to the north, because they would have to go across the open and then across the river. The other Marine companies were there.

We couldn't get artillery or air [support], so we just had to lay to it. They were coming across that strip of ground and coming right up in your face. They looked like bees working. They had a lot of firepower and were slinging steel. They had mortar tubes and RPGs and were desperately trying to get through. I didn't hear anything from Rivera-Cruz or his radio operator, Lance Cpl. Fred Tate. After the fire eased off just a little and I was down by the cane with some new Marines, I told them, "Stay here and hold. Just stay here and hold." I started moving to the left to find Rivera-Cruz. Every time you moved, they'd get after you pretty hot. So I'd have to move a little bit and stop. Finally I found Rivera-Cruz and Tate.

Late in the afternoon, we were getting low on ammo, and I was taking ammo from those who didn't need it anymore. I went back up the hill several times, getting our wounded up. Captain Caswell was our anchor.

Cpl. Bill Pettway: Sergeant York took over 3rd Platoon. He called Captain Caswell and said, "I see the end, they are coming."

Sgt. Hillous York: We could see them moving up behind the cane field. That is when I told Caswell I could see the end coming. There just weren't enough of us. We were still holding on.

Rounds were hitting all around Pfc. Harold Thrasher, a rifleman with Lt. George Selke's 2nd Platoon, but he couldn't see where the fire was coming from. A sergeant nearby said he could see the enemy, but his rifle had jammed, and he asked Thrasher for his. Thrasher passed it over to the sergeant, who fired away. As the enemy fire increased, Thrasher remembers politely asking for his rifle back, and the sergeant refused. Thrasher took it stoically, straightened the pins on his hand grenades for easier removal, and waited for the enemy to appear. The NVA never did attack his section of the line, and after a while the sergeant gave him his rifle back.

During the worst of it Corporal Pettway asked Captain Caswell if he could handle the radio himself, and Caswell asked him where he was going. "They are coming up to meet us, and I don't want to wait until then." The captain agreed, so Pettway took a rifle and went down the hill. Pettway found a corpsman with a Marine who had been badly wounded by a machine gun and was hit in his right leg and lower abdomen. Pettway helped them as much as he could and then went around the hill and found another critically wounded Marine. Six Marines put the casualty in a poncho and started up the hill. The fire was very intense. Pettway was on the front of the poncho. The Marine on the back got shot in the leg; he and the Marine in the middle went down, and the weight pulled Pettway down.

Cpl. Bill Pettway: The man in the back said he was okay and that it was just a flesh wound, but the guy in the middle said, "Oh Jesus, they shot my dick off." His crotch was filled with blood. He said, "I am going to pull my trousers down, and you look and tell me if I still have it." He pulled them down and said, "Well?" And we said, "You've still got your skivvies on." So he pulled them down, and a spent bullet fell out and bounced on his boot, and he said, "Oh Jesus, my dick just fell on my boot." We looked, and except for a little skin damage, his genitals were intact.

Capt. Jim Caswell: The platoon commanders and radio operators were all down, and that is when the platoon sergeants and squad leaders took over. These five sergeants, York, Teague, Lynch, Harris, and Sanchez, took over everything. They took over the squads, they took over the platoons, they redistributed ammo, they made sure the lines were tied together, and they evacuated casualties back to my position. We were clearing jams out of M16s with ramrods and sending them back down the hill. With the inferior rifles, we felt like it was 1775.

I called all the company commanders in 1/3 to find out if they were firing on us, because I could not imagine that all that fire was coming from the enemy. They all said they were not firing on us, but they knew where we were. After that first air strike, we had no fire support except from the battalion mortars until they used up the forty to fifty rounds that they carried up the hill.

By midafternoon, the command group and Delta Company of the 1st Battalion, 5th Marines, had driven the enemy off the crest of nearby Nui Nong Ham, Hill 185, and called in mortar fire to support Caswell. This relieved some of the pressure on Hill 110, but it wasn't enough. At 1530, M Company, 3rd Battalion, 5th Marines, landed at the 1st Battalion, 5th Marines' command post. The battalion had a clear view of the battle from the crest of Nui Nong Ham but, except for the mortars, could not support the Marines on Hill 110 by fire.

Capt. Jim Caswell: I did not receive another air strike until about 1400–1500. It was all up to the platoon and squad leaders. I thought I could move arty around the battle area, but we got nearly no arty. Most enemy casualties were caused by our M60s, with help from our rockets and M79s.

Once again, Marine artillery support was in short supply. It was a matter of extremely poor timing. The artillery battery that was lifted into Que Son Village on April 21 was in the process of moving back to their original position on the morning of May 10. Another battery was on its way in but was not yet in place. Just like on April 10, the only artillery support the Marines had for most of the fight was from the howtars on Nui Loc Son. And even then, they were worried about safely clearing the hill mass of Nui Nong Ham, the location of the battalion CP, to strike Hill 110.

Sgt. Hillous York: Two of the three corpsmen, John Tate and William Fowler, were killed. Several Marines were wounded real, real bad, and no one knew what to do for these guys. There were people yelling for corpsmen all around. The casualties were scattered all over the hill, down below, and on top of the hill. It was real rocky and real open. We could see the NVA in their uniforms swarming like an anthill below us, and we kept thinking that we were going to get some help here, arty or air. As we got organized, we realized that the NVA were not on the top but were on the hillsides all around us. Most of the fire was coming from the cane field where they were swarming in and out.

Cpl. Tom "Kid" Kintner: We were on line and decided to assault down the other side of the hill after the gooks. They opened up on us from the bottom of the hill, with mortars and everything. I don't know how many there were. This was the time we fixed bayonets. We got part way down the hill and had to stop. John Rusth was on my right. I couldn't see him, but the gooks could see us plain as day. Everybody around me was dead, and I figured John was, too. I was in the sitting position behind some bushes and decided to put my head down and play dead. If you moved, they would turn their fire on you.

Left to right: Jim Reed, John Rusth, Bill Ryan. Rusth would be awarded the Navy Cross for carrying nine wounded Marines to safety during the fight for Hill 110 on Operation Union I. *Courtesy John Rusth*

The small-arms fire was intense, and the leafless branches were cracking and falling down the back of my neck. I kept thinking, "Prepare to get hit." The firing slowed down, and all of a sudden I heard John off to my right. There was a guy down the hill that I couldn't see who was screaming for help. Somehow, John and I started talking as I was sitting there playing dead. So he said, "I'm gonna go down and get him." I thought he was nuts. He was always getting me into scrapes. He used to get me into more shit, and once I told him, "Being the best friend to you isn't the easiest thing I have ever done." He said, "Cover me." I said, "Don't go down there. We need to get back to the top." At that time, I thought we were the only two live Marines on the side of that hill. But I said, "John, I'll cover you, but I am heading up the hill." He said, "Okay, I'm going," and the fire was all around his ass. I got to the top, and a while later here came Rusth up the hill, shot through the thigh, and he had this guy over his shoulder. He just shot it out with them.

Though painfully wounded himself, the 130-pound John Rusth went back down the hill again and again and carried nine wounded Marines to safety. He was trying to save his tenth casualty when he collapsed from his wounds.

Lance Cpl. John Rusth: I could only hear guys down the hill needed help, and no one was getting to them. A lot of the Marines had pulled pins on grenades and were rolling them at whomever came up the hill. I still had an M14 because I was designated the squad sniper. That helped a lot.

Many of the M16s jammed, and angry, frustrated, and scared Marines threw them as far as they could because they would not shoot. When Rusth was wounded, his M14 was hit in the gas cylinder, so it became a single-shot rifle. Other than that, it still functioned, and he used it well.

One Marine said, "It was beyond being scared. I was sure that I was going to die."

Cpl. Tom "Kid" Kintner: After it quieted down, we moved down the hill a little farther. They called in air strikes, and the Phantoms were coming in so low I could see the colors of the helmets on the pilots. They were lower than us, and when they dropped their bombs, the shrapnel was flying all over us. The whole valley quieted down as it got dark.

The Marines put Lance Cpl. John Rusth on a medevac helicopter at dusk with several other wounded and most of the dead. He looked down from the chopper and thought the Marines still on the ground were never going to make it.

Capt. Jim Caswell: York was amazing. He found the sniper that killed his corpsman and was killing his troops.

Sgt. Hillous York: I had moved around because the 2nd Platoon commander had moved his men a little to the right, leaving a thirty-yard hole between our platoons. When I first moved around to the hole, it was a little rough. It was too hot, and I had to move back. I kept thinking that the NVA were going to come around the left end of us, or they were going to come through that hole, one of the two. I moved from the hole to around the left side and back. Every time you moved, they were on you like a chicken on a June bug. I had just moved over to the edge of that gap. I heard one single shot and "Corpsman up." I could tell the sniper was to the right of us. I knew about where he was, but I couldn't see him. "I know you are there somewhere, but there is no sense wasting my ammo until I get a close bead on you." I kept watching and listening, and he popped again, and I heard somebody yell, "Corpsman up." I then knew about where he was, within twenty feet. Then he shot again real quickly and killed the corpsman, Fowler. When he shot that time, he moved his rifle. It was a long rifle with a scope, and he had one of those soft hats and khakis and a piece of camouflage over his shoulders. When he pulled his rifle back to move it around a limb, I saw the rifle, and I could see his arms and his head. My M16 had jammed two or three times. I had it on automatic. He was probably twenty-five to thirty yards from me. My weapon worked that time, and he dropped his rifle, and it fell and hit a limb. I didn't have to worry about him anymore.

Capt. Jim Caswell: All five of those sergeants were what sergeants were supposed to be. Hillous York went to the top of a little hill and killed six or seven of the enemy by himself. Hillous told Hilgartner that the machine gunners had killed them all. A few years ago, he admitted that he had killed them all himself. The troops were magnificent.

I was talking to Bob Crabtree, Wickwire's operations officer, during the battle, and he kept asking, "Are you going to be overrun?" I said that I thought I was, and he kept saying, "Then why are you so calm?"

Sergeant Sanchez's efforts in making sure the crew-served weapons were in top shape and supplied with plenty of ammunition saved the day for Charlie Company. He kept the M60 machine guns firing all day and the company's 60mm mortar ammo was a blessing. During the battle, the enemy used captured American radios to jam the Marines' frequencies.

At day's end, Marines from Caswell's Charlie Company, 1st Battalion, 5th Marines, brought Pfc. Jacob "Jake" Lauff, the 2nd Platoon radio man, back up Hill 110. He had been hit in his left wrist, his left leg, and his lower abdomen. Corporal Pettway didn't think he would live long enough to make it to the chopper. Pettway asked him what happened down there. Lauff said that when he was moving from one place to another, the enemy didn't hit him. He dove behind a little stick, with the desperation in combat that anything serves for cover. When someone ran from cover to where he was trying to get to, the NVA would shoot at them and hit Lauff. After being hit a couple of times, he pulled his .45 out and thought, "The next SOB that runs across there, I am going to shoot him myself." He remembers no more.

Then the helicopters started coming in, and one was shot down, but the crew got off with minor injuries. A chopper finally landed in one piece,

A CH-34 is setting down. *Courtesy Lynwood Scott*

and they evacuated Lauff and others. When he reached the hospital, the surgeons wanted to amputate his leg, but he wouldn't let them, and he eventually walked a route as a mail carrier.

Lance Cpl. Jack Smith (Charlie Company): When they tried to send part of Alpha Company in, they hit the shit. There were two CH-34s [transport helicopters] coming down, and they collided. The tail was ripped off of one chopper, and the gunner was sucked out and fell about two hundred feet.[6]

Capt. Ron Burton (assistant operations officer, 1st Battalion, 3rd Marines): One of the 34s managed to land. The other one crashed on its side and caught fire and burned, and the 1/3 Marines rushed over to try to get the pilot and copilot out, but they had to watch them burn to death because of the heat of the magnesium burning.

The CH-34, or H-34, though old, was very reliable. But one of its big disadvantages was that the skin of the birds was made of magnesium, which unlike aluminum, burns furiously. One pilot called it a "six hundred thousand–dollar flashbulb."

The remaining two platoons of Capt. Jerry McKay's Alpha Company, 1st Battalion, 5th Marines, two thousand meters to the east, moved toward the 1st Battalion, 3rd Marines, and had just gained initial contact with the NVA when a Huey gunship erroneously marked the Alpha Company command post with rockets. A flight of Marine F-4 Phantoms rolled in, strafing and bombing the Marines, killing five and wounding twenty-four. Lieutenant Rick Zell of Alpha Company, wounded and medevaced earlier, monitored radios in the battalion combat operations center and can never forget the air strike hitting his company. He attributes the mistake to the pilots recently becoming aware of large units of uniformed enemy troops in the valley and mistaking the Marines for the NVA.

Cpl. Tom "Kid" Kintner: The next morning they were gone, and we went to the bottom of the hill, and the gook bodies were just lying on top of each other. I rolled over a gook to get this beautiful starred belt buckle and belt, and his entire back was gone. I threw up and left the belt.

THE TROPICAL SUN AND VERMIN quickly claimed the dead after a battle—bodies rigid, swarming with flies, ants, and maggots that were oblivious to the violence and single-mindedly taking advantage of this bountiful harvest of corpses; bodies so black and swollen that their living allegiance could only be determined by their uniforms and equipment; bodies encased in a poisonous aura of foul air.

Capt. Jim Caswell: My feeling was that this (NVA) colonel was who they saw again on [Operations] Union II and Swift. This guy was really good. No other Marine has ever said that to me, but this guy was good. He was one of the finest tacticians I have ever seen. Unfortunately, he just about blew us away and was trying to make me into a grease spot on the side of that hill. He was a really good soldier and an extremely good tactician. I'd like to shake his hand. Of course, we didn't have any rifles firing, but that is another story. He may have known that the M16s were not functioning well. He also knew that our artillery battery, the one that supported 1/5, was moving. Somehow, an air strike got called in on Alpha Company to the east. I am not convinced the enemy did not have something to do with that. He jammed all my radio frequencies. He put a heavy base of fire on me and enveloped my open flank. I was a good tactical student and had had a company for a while, and I thought, "Wow, this guy read the same book I read." His only disadvantage might have been an ammo shortage, but it wasn't noticeable in the first three hours. I had never heard fire in which you never heard a single shot. It was a roar. We had ten KIA and forty to forty-five WIA. None of us should have survived the day.

Capt. Jerry Reczek: We held our positions that night and sent out night patrols, trying to catch enemy stragglers that were attempting to escape.

Capt. Jerry Shirley: We had some coordination problems with the 5th Marines. I wanted to move but couldn't, because they were firing these huge flares, and about midnight I finally got them stopped. That night the enemy moved up the stream to the north. We captured a Maxim-type machine gun with wheels that weighed about three hundred pounds. Some of the NVA corpses had photos of themselves in a dress white uniform, probably taken up north.

Daybreak shone on 116 enemy bodies around the Marine position. Total Marine losses for this phase of the operation were 33 killed in action and 135 wounded in action.

The battle for Hill 110 and the surrounding terrain was fought with courage and grim determination on both sides. At least eight Marines were awarded the Navy Cross and fourteen the Silver Star.

Capt. Jim Caswell: The next day, Lieutenant General Walt and Colonel Houghton flew in, and Hilgartner, and they wanted to see the bodies. I called the patrol leader, who had just returned, and I told him I had bad news, that he had to take another patrol to the bottom of the hill, and I would be on the patrol with him, but he would be the patrol leader. He said, "Aye aye, sir." He was a lance corporal. I told Walt and Houghton and Hilgartner that there would be no radios on the patrol except mine. "We're not going down with a whole parade of radio masts." I thought they would chew my ass or tell me I was going to be court-martialed, but they, including Lew Walt, said okay. I told them where to stand, and we walked along with the six or seven enlisted Marines.

As we passed through the lines Walt stopped at a little Hispanic Marine and said, "Let me borrow that rifle, son." The Marine would not let go of his rifle. I was horrified, and Walt was nearly picking this tiny Marine off the ground and shaking him like a dog. The kid said, "No, I don't care how many stars you have, you are not getting this rifle." I thought, "I am going to jail." I handed my pistol to the Marine and said, "Look Marine, give the general your rifle. I will be back within an hour." He was very skeptical but said, "Aye aye, sir," and took my pistol.

We went to the bottom of the hill but didn't see too many corpses at that spot, and all of a sudden a Huey landed, and Walt hopped on it and left. He didn't get shot, anyway. I returned the Marine's rifle. I was really proud of him.

Lt. Col. Pete "Highpockets" Hilgartner: Caswell is the hero among heroes in Union I.

Capt. Ron Burton: After we worked back up the valley, we were up in this big, dry, open area, and these guys who had been in this desperate battle . . . the whole battalion sort of simultaneously shed their gear and began sunbathing. Then they got the word that Punjab 6, the division commander, was on his way in, and the word was passed. All those Marines were dressed and in all their gear in seconds. The whole 2nd NVA Division was there within striking distance, and that hadn't been enough to keep the Marines from using a lull to do a little sunbathing. But one Marine two-star, and . . . .

Sergeant Dwight Faylor, who had been in Korea, had access to a fifty mounted on a mechanical mule. We spotted an enemy soldier sitting in the doorway of a hut about 1,200 meters away. Faylor said, "Watch this, this is how we used to snipe from ridgeline to ridgeline in Korea." He had the fifty sandbagged into place on the mule, and he took his time setting up the shot. He pulled up some grass and let it drop and checked the strength of the wind, and he wet his finger, stuck it in the air, and bore-sighted the weapon. I thought this was a joke when Faylor said, "Keep your eye on him, I'm going to take him out." I was practically rolling my eyes, wondering if Faylor thought he was Sergeant York, and was ready to take my binoculars down when Faylor got the shot off. I was watching and watching and was just ready to turn and say it was a miss, when the enemy soldier jumped straight up in the air, his shirt turned red, and he fell spread-eagled back into the hut.

Chapter 8

Dangerous When Cornered

The Leathernecks saw many groups of fifty or so enemy soldiers fleeing toward the safety of their sanctuaries and slaughtered them with artillery and air. Those who remained tried to avoid the Marines. Several captive NVA troops told their interrogators that they were supposed to be fighting the ARVN at the town of Que Son but kept running into the Marines. The fact that the NVA were on the run did nothing to diminish their lethality when cornered.

The Marines found them again two clicks north of Route 534 and six clicks east of Hill 110. As Lieutenant Colonel Esslinger's 3rd Battalion, 5th Marines, marched down a small hill toward the hamlet of Phuoc Duc (4), an enemy battalion hit the lead company, Lt. Dave McInturff's attached Delta Company, 1st Battalion, 5th Marines, hard. The NVA spotted the Marines' route of advance and were waiting in ambush. Using a common ruse, a few enemy soldiers showed themselves and then scattered. Without thinking, a few Marines took off in hot pursuit. Two Marines were killed and a dozen wounded. Private First Class William Myers, an assistant machine gunner, was near the front of the formation when violence erupted—small arms, automatic weapons, and mortars. His gunner tried to move around to the enemy flank, and the enemy shot him dead. Myers picked up the gun and ran straight at the enemy's fire and into a 150-meter-wide paddy. He ignored the fire, set up in the paddy, and put the gun to work. When he used up all his ammunition, he ran back across the open paddy to the dead gunner, retrieved his ammunition, and again went across the paddy after the enemy. He lasted about three more minutes before the enemy killed him.

His covering fire gave the other Marines the break needed to get organized and drive the enemy from its position. Lieutenant Colonel Esslinger's other companies moved into the fight.

Captain Henry Stackpole's India Company, 3rd Battalion, 5th Marines, which had been moving behind Delta, maneuvered around the southern edge of Delta to support them. They immediately ran into heavy enemy small arms, mortar fire, and a counterattack. India Company had Marines down. A large enemy force in entrenched positions to the front threatened the casualties and their rescuers.

Corporal Lawrence Caine, weapons squad leader with India, hit the enemy with machine gun fire to cover the evacuation, killing an estimated twenty North Vietnamese Army soldiers. Then, he saw fire coming from a series of nearby caves, charged into them, his gun spitting death, and killed two more of the enemy. When he returned to his original position, the enemy was at it again. He battered the NVA with machine gun and rocket fire. Under his cover, medevac helicopters landed and took off the dead and wounded. Caine was seriously wounded by mortar fire but refused to quit until all casualties were evacuated.

Then the NVA sent a large force against India Company, forcing the Marines to withdraw two hundred meters behind the shield of supporting arms. Corporal Caine stayed put, pouring automatic-weapon and 3.5-inch rocket fire into the enemy's ranks during the withdrawal, though wounded a second time by a bomb fragment. When he withdrew, Marines counted sixty-two enemy bodies on the field. One of the platoon commanders, Lt. Kenny Moore, stayed on his feet during the counterattack and moved around his lines, personally directing small-arms and crew-served weapons, and repelled the enemy. His actions were crucial in throwing back the enemy advance. Lieutenant Moore's men killed another five NVA as his platoon moved through the battle space.

Lt. Kenny Moore: Delta [Company] was hit in ambush near this ville. I was lead platoon, and I could see them. I told Stackpole we could envelop from the right side. Stackpole told me to get in position. We set up on a line and were set to attack when it got delayed; night fell, and we sat there in that linear position all night long. Regiment wanted to regain contact the next morning with the enemy, and Delta 1/5 sent out a patrol, and they didn't come back. My platoon was sent out at 0830 to try to find them. We found the patrol directly south of us. Of the eleven or thirteen Marines that had been sent out, all but two had been killed. The Vietnamese patched the two

The command group of India Company, 3rd Battalion, 5th Marines, huddles for a conference in the Que Son Valley, mid-1967. *Courtesy Howard Olsen*

survivors up, gave them water, took their weapons, and left them. The others were covered up with a couple of inches of dirt. They had been moving in column, and the enemy was set up in ambush and killed most of them very quickly. One was wounded in the stomach. On the other casualty, the enemy used duct tape on his sucking chest wound. We found that patrol and evacuated them, and they brought Kilo [Company] in, from our battalion.

This is the day, May 11, that Tilley [Lt. Robert "Bob" Tilley, commanding officer of Kilo Company] was wounded. They patrolled down near a village called Phuoc Duc (4), ran up against a prepared enemy position, and took a significant number of casualties in the first fifteen minutes.

Lance Cpl. Frank Jurney: The NVA hit Kilo hard as they moved onto a plateau and across some dikes, trying to get to a knoll. There were about seven or eight dead Marines lying on the dikes. Kilo had an M60 set up, and everybody around it was dead.

Lance Cpl. Harvey Newton: The ground was very hard to dig into, so the machine gunners built a parapet next to ours and put the M60 on it with bipods. When the firing started, the gun was knocked down, and three of us jumped into a hole. I was on top, and my backside was above the parapet, so I rolled out of there and actually went to sleep right in the middle of the firefight. Later, I got up, went to take a leak in a trench, and found a Marine body in there from Delta Company. Delta lost four MIAs. Two of them wandered out of the woods while I was taking a leak and came to our position.

Lance Cpl. Paul Malboeuf: We moved over the top of the ridge and stopped. We covered the back. All the stuff was happening in front of us. Everyone who was on line in front of us was hit and down. We got slammed, and we were not moving. They were walking mortars over us. It looked like the whole company was getting hit, and they were bringing wounded back to our area. The 1st Platoon took care of a lot of the medevacs. Before that, we called in air strikes, and the only reason the NVA broke off was because of napalm. You could feel the heat way over on our side of the knoll. It gave us a window of relief.

Lance Cpl. Larry Mazurkiewicz: It was hot as hell, and the napalm sucked the oxygen right out of my mouth. We were out of water and very low on ammo.

Lance Cpl. Paul Malboeuf: Tilley and Rich Wilson, his radio op, were on top of this hill and near the tree. Gunny Armstrong was in front, maybe twenty feet away, and I remember sitting in a small slit trench where the bad guys had been the night before; it was covered with Ho Chi Minh [rubber sandal] tracks. An NVA company opened up from the tree line and immediately killed Gunny Armstrong, and they hit Doc Buci in the foot. We put fire from the machine gun into the tree line, and they started dropping stuff around us.

Pfc. Patrick Mosey: Tilley got hit; Bill Bresnahan and Jim Keilly were killed. The Indian guy, F. W. Weahkee, was hunkered down and burning out machine gun barrels. [Weahkee was a member of the Pima tribe, and the Marines called him "Fearless Warrior," for his initials. It was a well-deserved moniker.]

I dumped my M16 because it was useless. I was good about cleaning it, and it still didn't work, so I just threw it away. All I had was a .38

revolver. I dragged back up the hill a Marine who was hit in the forearm, and both bones were shattered. He could not move, and I was dragging him up the hill. Another Marine was shot in one leg and then the other, and he was screaming, "They shot me in the other leg." There was a little African-American guy named Moses who was bare to the waist and with no weapons, running around like a jackrabbit. He was bringing up ammo from the Marines with the CP group who didn't need it. He was lightning fast. He'd drape bandoliers around him and run up and drop them off.

Cpl. Norm Bailey (Lieutenant Colonel Esslinger's radio operator): When Mike [Company] was relieving Kilo, one round went off, and a guy next to me was shot by a sniper. The round went all the way through him and went through my canteen. It spun my cartridge belt around, and I thought I had been shot and went down like a sack of shit. Lieutenant Tilley was standing right next to me.

He said to us, "Grab a rifle." I only had a .45, and I grabbed a rifle from a kid who had got hit. Tilley said, "I want to fire three rounds at that tree line, and then I want to go up there and roust that guy out."

I thought, "This guy is crazy." About three or four of us ran across this paddy, and when I got up there, the shit hit the fan. I was near the CO, Colonel Esslinger. I looked over, and in the elephant grass was a guy about fifty meters away, looking at me with a pith helmet on. First one of these I ever saw.

He and I looked at each other. I said, "There is a gook over there, and he is looking right at me." The colonel said, "Better get your head down because the next thing that is going to happen is that he is going to shoot you between the eyes."

Shortly after that, we walked up to the military crest of this hill, and there was a bit of a river down in the valley. We spotted some dinks who were on the other side of the river but were taking cover on our side of a dike, about twenty of them, because there were some choppers that were strafing near them. We really got into the shit with these guys, and it is the first time I remember that we called in 81s. We had advantage over these guys because we were up above them, and we shot the shit out of them. It was late in the afternoon, and a couple of squads went down there to set up an ambush and come up with any bodies, which they did.

At midafternoon, Lieutenant Colonel Esslinger committed Mike Company, and Captain McElroy began to move toward the fight.

Lt. Kenny Moore: My platoon was closest to the action. I was dispatched to pull out the survivors of Kilo, evacuate the wounded, and stack up the dead. I got there in midafternoon, and as we were doing this, Tilley got hit across the back of the neck, right under the back of the helmet, and was bleeding like a stuck pig. Captain Stan Holmes, the FAC, looked like Governor Arnold Schwarzenegger and had been a Naval Academy football star. Holmes got shot through the thigh, but he picked up Tilley and carried him down, and Tilley said, "Put me down, put me down." It turned out that what he wanted was a cigarette. In late afternoon, about 1630, I had about thirty bodies in a pile and another thirty wounded adjacent to them, and there was an enemy sniper that started shooting into the pile of bodies. I put out two fire teams to find the sniper and take him out. About that time, Mike Company was ordered to come over and reinforce my effort and provide a greater degree of security until we got the medevacs out.

ENEMY FIRE KEPT THE MEDEVAC HELICOPTERS at bay, preventing evacuation. Corporal Melicio Ortiz, of the 2nd Platoon, India Company, stood up with a machine gun. Silhouetted against a helicopter landing behind him, he delivered suppressive fire into the enemy position until the enemy shot him down. He saved the chopper and the wounded that were aboard.

Lance Corporal Christopher Mosher, Kilo's forward air controller, moved through the heavy enemy fire that bedeviled his company. He called in air strikes while on the move and finally placed himself in an exposed position from which he called in and adjusted air strikes for five hours. Under his guidance, the aviators hammered the enemy with pinpoint accuracy.

Pfc. Thom Heidtman (Kilo Company): The shooting started, and I never fired a single round that day. The gun team, Cpl. Ernesto Sanchez, gunner, and Paul Malboeuf, assistant gunner, killed many NVA. I spent all day dragging our casualties back up Hill 10. There was a big ditch behind Hill 10 where the helos were landing, and all you could see was their blades; they were bringing ammo and water. Our air was pounding the NVA with bombs and napalm. When the napalm hit, some of them would run out of the tree line on fire, and others just ran for their lives, and Ernesto Sanchez would just hose them down. One time we were dragging up a guy on a poncho, and the guy next to me was shot in the throat. I was mad at him because he got hit, and I had to carry both sides of the poncho. I picked up two more boxes of machine gun ammo, and I ended up in a hole with the FAC. Just as I got in the hole, I heard him say, "We are getting a traffic jam up there. Make one pass and drop all your ordnance." The jets came around and dropped everything, all their ordnance, and went back to the base to reload. A five-hundred-pound bomb would hit a pine tree, and the tree would take off like an ICBM.

I went to the next hole and dropped some more ammo. Some guy came up early in the fight and said the lieutenant got shot and the gunny was dead. I thought Tilley was dead when we threw him on a helicopter, but he survived. They pulled us out at 5:30 or 6:00 and took us back about two hundred meters. I was walking back, and there was a ditch about four feet deep and ten feet wide. As I was climbing up, I saw a Vietnamese standing there with a kid in his hand and a cow with a rope in his nose, and the guy had a crutch, but he looked healthy to me. He was young and the right age group, and I could tell by his shoulders that he had been carrying a pack. I went over and took the rope out of his hand and threw it down and took the kid and gave it to mama-san. I put my rifle in his back and poked him, and he limped along toward Kilo. I pushed him down into the ditch and was pushing him up the other side, and just then a corporal came running up and grabbed this guy's crutch and hit him over the head with it, and the guy took off like a track star. He was headed for this village, and a machine gunner hosed him down with the M60.

Capt. Jim McElroy: I was marching along behind my 1st Platoon, and we had channeled ourselves along a small path so we could get up there in a hurry. Someone from Kilo was waving our troops toward the slope where they had been hit. They were splattered all over the place. We piled in behind them to get their wounded, and some of my lieutenants got banged up.

Lance Cpl. Frank Jurney: They opened up on us, and the mortars started coming in.

Lance Corporal Jurney retrieved a radio from one of the wounded Marines, Gunny Hitchcock spotted for him, and Jurney called in artillery on the enemy. Two NVA machine gun positions were tearing up the Marines, but Jurney and Gunny Hitchcock located them with binoculars and destroyed them with artillery.

When Mike Company relieved Kilo, Lance Cpl. Chris Mosher volunteered to remain at his position to continue directing the air support and relay information on the enemy's location and strength to the air controllers attached to Mike Company. While briefing his Mike Company counterparts, he was severely wounded in the back by mortar fragments and was evacuated. He lived but never walked again.

Lance Cpl. Harvey Newton: I went to get ammo, and a 60[mm mortar round] landed nearby, and I was airborne and thought I must be dead. My T-shirt was speckled, but I was unhurt. I returned with the ammo, and we fired off all the rounds and got behind these big, black rocks. We had two M16s and two .45s. We could see the NVA in the tree line and some of our guys. It looked like they were trying to flank us from the left across an open space. I noticed that the walking wounded going back to the LZ by themselves were making it. Those being carried were drawing fire and getting hit. We pulled out, and I went over the crest to the rear. There were bodies and people down with heat stroke. Staff Sergeant Paul Orlett grabbed a five-gallon jerry can of precious water off a chopper and drenched a naked black Marine with heat stroke, whom they were trying to cool down. He died. We had left our packs back, and I found mine. My towel and New Testament were shredded by mortar fragments, and my food was stolen.

Lt. Kenny Moore: McElroy came over, and we got behind a rock, and I told him what was going on. We were in front of Kilo and were bringing back the casualties. We were on the military crest, like a butte, that fell down about thirty meters. I told McElroy where the enemy was, which was to our south and a bit to our east. I told him to stay down and not go over there. He chose to set up as a shelter for our battalion on my left flank. The battalion was about a thousand yards behind us. I was the forward, south-facing unit, toward the enemy, covering about a four-hundred-yard front. I was out ahead of Kilo, and I had people bringing back the casualties. We had a pretty solid defense between Kilo and the enemy.

McElroy used his map case to carry Red Man chewing tobacco, and cigars when he couldn't get Red Man. He turned around and said, "Kenny, don't worry about me. I can take care of myself. You are doing a good job." He spit some tobacco juice out, turned around, and was shot through the shoulder, right under the left collarbone: a through-and-through shot. He looked at me and pulled out this ugly, stained, dirty, red bandanna from his hip pocket. He said, "Why don't you stick that through that wound and tie knots on either side of it." The wound wasn't big enough to get a wire through, much less a bandanna. I put a piece of duct tape on each side of it. I went and got his gunny, [Dennis] Dinota, and we dug a shallow hole for Dinota and McElroy, and I told Dinota to stay with him. "If you have a problem, call me." He had three platoon commanders, and I didn't know any of them. That was the way we went into nightfall.

The India Company Marines were set in an old trench line facing down a hill. The advantage was they did not have to dig it. The disadvantage was that the enemy knew where it was too, and probably had mortars registered on it.

Lance Corporal Raul "Squez" Vasquez of Mike Company remembers the enemy being around them all night and trying to unnerve them.

Lance Cpl. Raul Vasquez: The NVA were relentless. It was like New Year's Eve: bugles, drums, cowbells, screaming, the whole nine yards.

Just about sundown a recoilless rifle round slammed into the India Company lines and killed Cpl. Peter Boets. About that same time, an India Company 3.5-inch rocket squad leader, Cpl. Jerry Richardson, was shot in the thigh by a sniper in a tree, probably the same sniper that shot Capt. Jim McElroy. Ignoring his wounds, Richardson took out the sniper with his rocket launcher before he allowed himself to be medevaced. He turned the rocket over to Lance Cpl. Roy Bowles, and Lance Cpl. Dennis Delaney became the rocket squad leader.

Night blackened the battlefield. Lance Cpl. Ken Fields's squad leader with Mike Company pointed to a spot twenty feet from the machine gunner and ordered Fields to dig. The ground was rock hard, and Fields had scraped out a depression five inches deep and five feet long when a listening post (LP) fifty meters in front of the lines radioed a whispered report of enemy talking and moving all around them.

LPs are the loneliest of duties, very often just two to four Marines and a radio placed outside the lines in the darkness to act as a trip wire, their mission to warn the Marines on the line if they hear movement. For their survival these Marines could not talk, smoke, or eat, and even when the rain fell, they could not use their ponchos, because the glare of the wet material might give them away. And there they would shiver in a muddy hole, praying for sunrise. They turned down the volume of their radio and, when the enemy was nearby, communicated by pressing the key on their handsets: for example, "If you are okay, key your handset twice; if the enemy is near, key it three times," and so on. If the enemy drew near, the Marines would send up a red star cluster, a military roman candle, to signify their passage back through the lines, and hope they would not be killed by nervous fellow

Marines or by the NVA. This duty most often resulted in nothing more than a miserable, frightening night without contact.

Cpl. Norm Bailey: That night, we had moved, and we could hear music and see camp fires all around us. Somebody called for illumination, and the paddies got lit up, and this was the first time I could see the NVA walking across the rice paddy. They were moving in fire teams. "Holy shit, look at these guys." I probably saw a couple of hundred, and they were not moving toward us but further down the valley.

After Captain McElroy was wounded, he worried about the running of the company. But his Marines responded like Marines.

Capt. Jim McElroy: Everyone knew exactly what to do without being told. I sent Lt. Byron Hill, an artillery FO, down to where a platoon commander had been shot very wickedly in the leg. Hill went down and took the platoon over and did all his artillery work down there too.

To get there he had to crawl because the hill was scrub brush and dirt. I have never seen troops so excited in my life. We had been walking around there for two and a half weeks, and they finally got into something. I was just amazed. I had guys that I thought were dunderheads who were mapping our coordinates and setting in for the night.

Lt. Kenny Moore: About 9:00 in the evening, my defense was a line formation, and McElroy was on my left, and there was nothing on my right side. Bravo 1/5 had come in, in a single-line formation, about 8:30 that night. They were supposed to be on my right flank and extend down to the ridgeline. I went over and met their platoon commander and worked out coordination and all that, and at about 9:30 they set in. At 10:30 I checked the lines, and we are all good, lots of ammo, no casualties and a great defensive position.

About 11:30 I was checking lines again, and I started over toward McElroy's company. I found him and Dinota. and they were in a good defensive position going from the southeast corner of the ridge back to the east and around to the north.

He had a platoon in reserve about one hundred meters back, behind his position, and my position too. As I got down toward my right flank, one of my guys said, "Hey, lieutenant, that company that was on our right moved and took off about thirty minutes ago."

I went out about a hundred yards, and there was no one there. I was on my way back when the first enemy attack took place. They started off with about twelve rounds of 82mm mortar fire into our position, no damage.

Lance Corporal Dennis Delaney thinks the enemy used cover of the mortar barrage to move their automatic weapons into place. After the fight started, Lance Cpl. Bob Kreuder saw that the NVA had placed a machine gun directly in front of him and not far away.

Lt. Kenny Moore: They came up the hill at midnight exactly, and we had our hands full like I had never seen before. The battlefield was illuminated. They fired two illumination rounds from their mortars about a hundred yards apart in the air. We had those little hand-held illuminations that always worked great. You could see extremely well.

Illumination rounds turn night into day, magnesium flares tethered to their parachutes, slowly descending and swaying, trailing white smoke and creating a melee of shadows—lengthening, contracting, crisscrossing and then retreating—stealing color and gray tones and casting the world into the surreal opposites of the ghastly clarity of blinding light or total blackness, a malevolent disco-light at its most extreme. Lance Corporal Delaney remembers the light shining on a row of enemy faces as they came up the hill.

Lance Cpl. Dennis Delaney: They were close, maybe thirty yards away before we knew they were there.

Delaney's 3.5-inch rocket malfunctioned, and he found that the electrical connection was broken. He hastily rigged a field expedient while under fire, using a piece of communications wire, and got it operating again.

Lt. Kenny Moore: I could see four hundred to five hundred of them coming up the hill. About four hundred of them were in front of us, and another seventy-five to one hundred were over in Mike Company's area.

They came in the night, shadows dancing across the landscape to the accompaniment of bugles and drums, confident they knew the Marines' positions and convinced of their own success. They came on until the Marines vaporized their attacking force into nothingness. The survivors ran, crawled, or limped out of the killing zone.

Lance Cpl. Bob Kreuder: I had two rifles, and both of them kept jamming up.

Lt. Kenny Moore: I took a machine gun and had it repositioned directly out to the right, so if they [the enemy] spread out in that direction, there was no one out there. I had no reserve. Fortunately, they didn't come around to the right.

IN THE MIKE COMPANY SECTOR, Gunny Dinota looked at the line after the Marines had set in. He didn't like what he saw and, amidst much bitching and moaning, repositioned his Marines and made them dig new holes. When the attack came, the NVA found that the Marines were not where they expected them to be but had moved and were firing down the long axis of their advance, killing them by the dozen. Lance Corporal Ken Fields's gun team leader called for more ammunition. Reluctant to expose himself, Fields tried to sling a can of ammo to him. The ammo fell short of the gun position, so he was forced to run out, pick it up, get it to the gunner, and make it back. He accomplished all this in what seemed to be a very long time but was only a few seconds. To Fields's right rear, Gunny Dinota stood in his fighting hole with his left leg on the front parapet in what Fields described as "a classic John Wayne movie pose." He waved his .45-caliber pistol in the air and shouted fire directions. The gunnery sergeant was everything a Marine should be, and more. He was very bright, physically very strong, and absolutely fearless. Captain McElroy said of him, "He was the best soldier that I ever knew."

Lance Cpl. John Lobur: They came at us in the dark, marching up from a hedge row and not even bothering to be quiet. We could hear the jabbering, and some of them were even smoking. During the fight, we had to yell over to Hatfield and tell him that his barrel was burned out and his tracers were dropping into the ground. Ron Pizana changed the barrel; he knew how to do it fast and do it right. On two occasions Gordon Seablom ran up from behind us, knelt, and fired his 3.5 rocket launcher right into them.

Lt. Kenny Moore: We beat back the attack because we had a listening post, and they alerted us that these guys were crawling up the hill, and as they hit the slope of the hill moving up, they started using illumination, and we did too. We beat back the attack, and I checked for casualties and checked for ammo, and we were a bit low on ammo: we had used about

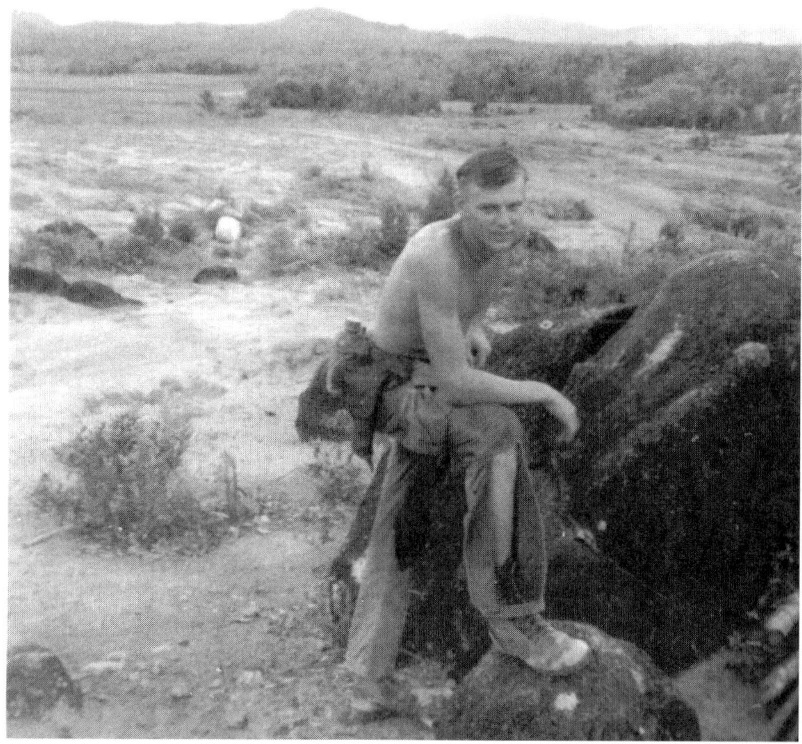

Lance Corporal Earl Heister voluntarily set up a one-man listening post in front of the lines of India Company, 3rd Battalion, 5th Marines, and warned of a vicious enemy attack. He also spotted the enemy mortars so the rocket gunners could destroy them. *Courtesy Roy Bowles*

half. This guy, Lance Cpl. Earl Heister, said, "I am going forward and set up a listening post." So he went out, without a radio, about a hundred meters and dug a hole and camouflaged it. He was looking at what was the enemy line of departure.

Heister remembered going out a couple of hundred meters. At this time there was only a little on-again, off-again light from the flares. He could hear the enemy moving in and setting up. He heard the heavy sound of mortar base plates being slammed into position and the tubes being locked into place and the sound of what he thought were machine gun tripods going down and the guns being mounted on them.

Lt. Kenny Moore: About one o'clock, Heister ran back and told us that they were assembling again, on line, and starting to cross the creek and up the hill again. They came up the hill, and we had our hands absolutely full. We fired almost everything we had. We were out of machine gun ammo. The last NVA that I saw was probably fifteen yards ahead of me and coming into our machine gun position.

They were out of ammo, and this gunner, a black guy named Smitty (Cpl. Ernest Smith), drew his .45 and shot him from about ten feet away just as he was bringing his AK up to fire.

He hit him directly in the chest. He went ten feet back and landed on his back and never moved. The next morning Smitty cut a length of bamboo, tied this guy's hands together, and dragged him around the position, saying, "Look what I did with a .45 pistol last night."

I took a survey, and we were out of ammo. I called back and we got a resupply within about forty minutes. We were distributing it when the three o'clock attack came. We beat that one back, barely. They had just as many men on the third wave as they had on the first wave.

They came up in a ragged line. Just prior to their reaching our position, Heister came back and said, "I have located the 82s. They are about 450 to 500 yards directly in front of the position in this creek bed next to two trees." I sent Lance Cpl. Roy Bowles out. Bowles was an outstanding rocket guy, who could hit targets at 800 to 900 meters.

Cpl. Roy Bowles: Lieutenant Moore yelled, "Bowles, get your tube and as many rockets as you have, and shoot at their CP area, where the mortars and machine guns are coming from." Smitty and I loaded up with all the rockets we had and looked for a good place in the line to shoot from; there were too many Marines in behind us, and we couldn't see our target. We ran out in front of our lines about a hundred meters.

TO SHOOT A 3.5-INCH ROCKET, the gunner stood or knelt, and the assistant gunner loaded the round into the back of the rocket tube, giving it a twist to make sure the electrical connection was good. Then he checked to make sure there was no one behind the tube who could get killed or wounded from the back blast. Finally, he tapped the gunner on the helmet to let him know that he was cleared to fire.

Cpl. Roy Bowles: I squatted down so Smitty could load me, he hit me on the helmet, and I stood and shot right into their CP. We were starting to get

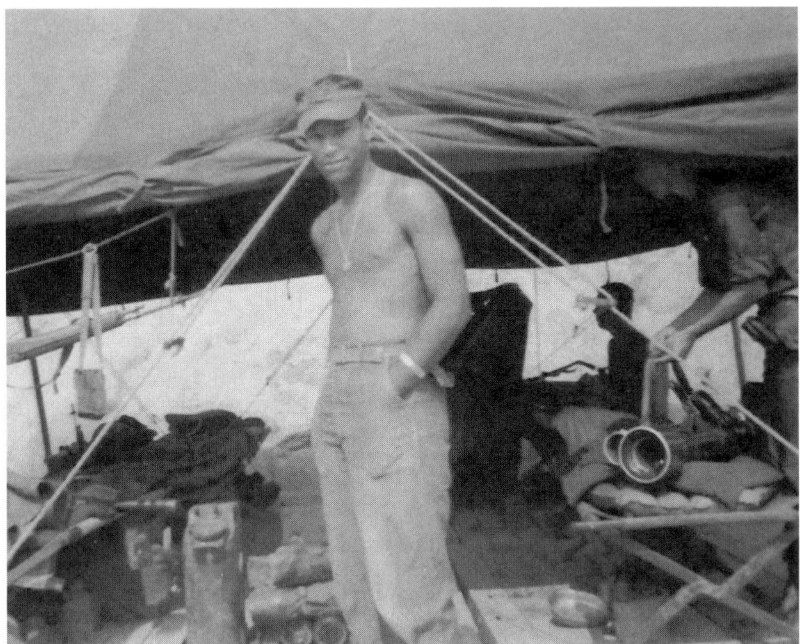

Photographed on Hill 69 in 1967, Cpl. Ernest Smith was assistant gunner and loader for Cpl. Roy Bowles, rocket team leader for a squad led by Cpl. Dale "Gunny" Gunnell. They were part of the India Company, 3rd Battalion, 5th Marines, a rocket section that was highly regarded by the other members of the company. *Courtesy Roy Bowles*

scattered fire as I squatted again for another rocket load. Then I stood and put another round into where their mortars and machine guns were.

Lt. Kenny Moore: He shot two rounds and took out both mortar tubes. The next day we found one of the tubes had a dent in it where he had scored a direct hit. That happened just as the third wave was coming up the hill, and we beat that attack back. I did another survey. We had thirty-seven .45 rounds, thirteen shotgun rounds, and forty M16 rounds. We had a couple of illumination grenades, one thermite, and no high-explosive grenades. I was pleading for a resupply. I starting sending my guys out to pick up the AK-47s that were all over the place, and they started arming themselves with them.

About four o'clock they started with another attack, and about that time we got a flare ship. It was brighter than daylight, and they sent a flight of F-8 Crusaders with 20mm guns only. The fourth attack started as we got about eight hundred rounds of ammo; that's all we got, and we were distributing that as the attack started up the hill.

The fourth wave only had about half as many people as the three previous attacks. The airplanes came in and started strafing the line of departure and did a great job; our FAC was talking to them. The NVA had already left the line of departure, but the air strike must have had an effect on their thinking, because we beat this attack back fairly easily. The airplanes stayed on station for about thirty minutes, although they only made one run. As the fourth attack started up the hill, I gave the order to fix bayonets. Everyone stood up in their holes and started cheering. Everyone was laughing and confident about this time. We beat back the attack. That was the last attack that night, although we didn't know that, and we were prepared for the worst.

Sun was up about 5:30. Left on the battlefield were 175 to 180 bodies and one wounded Chinese advisor, a big guy about six feet four inches. He treated his own wound. We picked him up, and they sent a helo to pick him up. He never made it to Da Nang. Maybe he was thrown from the helo.

We found a body with a flag under his blouse, and he had a journal. The Kit Carson scout looked at the journal, and apparently his regiment was in Hanoi the year before. This squad leader's squad won the division competition for best rifle squad. His award was this flag. At 10:30 p.m. on the eleventh, they were given the order to attack us at midnight. The journal talked about ammo and special equipment, reinforcements, what his objective was, and what his assignment was. It was something like a five-paragraph order (standard combat order). He made the one and two o'clock attacks, so he was probably killed on the two o'clock. He had diagrams of our position and had overestimated our strength, thinking it was a battalion position when it was Mike Company and India. We used much of our machine gun ammo to no avail, firing the gun out to the right to make sure no one got around that end to India.

The next day we could see where they dragged all the bodies off. We sent out a security patrol another five hundred meters and found another twenty-five bodies and an officer, a major. He had been hit through the chest, abdomen, and stomach and was dead. We found a cache of weapons, about one hundred, and trails and the defensive position they must have been in when Kilo stumbled into them. They had two companies along this creek right at the bottom of the hill, and they had another company at an angle of ninety degrees to them in a blocking position that was facing Kilo Company's axis of movement. Kilo was hit with at least three companies, one facing them and two along the flank of the axis of movement.

Lance Cpl. Frank Jurney: I had an ammo can by the hole I was in, and next morning there were six holes in it. After daylight there were bodies everywhere, absolutely everywhere.

Capt. Jim McElroy: We found outdoor classrooms that were spectacular. We got a prisoner who looked like a Korean. He had a high and tight new haircut and was strong, bigger than I was. He was well fed and well exercised and was maybe five feet ten inches and weighed about 160.

When McElroy finally got medical aid in the rear, a surgeon stuck his finger through and through his wound and then flushed it out with a saline solution.

Capt. Jim McElroy: For every six hours you were out there after being wounded, the surgeons would have to cut out an additional quarter inch of tissue. I have a four-inch scar from one bullet twice the size of an eraser.

The Marines spotted more fleeing enemy. On the fourteenth, Mike Company called in an artillery strike and clobbered more than a hundred NVA carrying two mortar tubes and their wounded from the day before. The Marines found twenty-five enemy bodies. Thick pools of blood, bits of brain and body parts, and many drag marks bore witness to the death of another thirty-seven enemy.

The 3rd Battalion, 5th Marines, recovered some M16s, M79s, and M60s lost by Foxtrot Company, 2nd Battalion, 1st Marines on April 21. Captured documents revealed that the enemy units were the 305th and 307th Battalions, an identity that was confirmed by peasants who were questioned the next day. Like another group before them, they were on their way to fight the ARVN at Que Son town, did not want to fight the Marines, and were trying to leave the area in small units.

All told, the Marines of the 3rd Battalion killed a known 239 of the enemy on May 13. The total killed most likely exceeded 500. Twenty-eight Marines died on that day and 107 were wounded.

Lt. Dave McInturff: After the fight, we found that two Marines, Lance Corporal Santos and Corporal Ashlock, were missing. The following December we were up on Phu Roc north of Da Nang and south of Hue, and Santos came walking down out of the hills. We never found Corporal Ashlock.

LANCE CORPORAL FRANK JURNEY speculated that the NVA could rapidly set up ambushes the way they did because they understood the flow pattern of Marine operations, which were "like the flow pattern of a river."

Lance Cpl. John Lobur: I think those bastards were steering us by shooting at us. If you shoot at Marines, they come to you. The NVA knew this.

LIEUTENANT KENNY MOORE GAVE THE NVA CREDIT for a more sophisticated maneuver, a maneuver that he calls a "countersweep." They would set in and then send one or a handful of soldiers out to expose themselves to the Marines' point, to entice the Marines to follow them. The Marines often would do just that, following the NVA into an L-shaped kill zone, where the enemy would fix them in place with small arms, machine guns, and mortars. Then they would send another unit around the Marines and try to get to their rear so they would have them under fire from at least three, and sometimes four, directions. Then they would try to fragment the Marines' position, breaking it up into smaller pieces that they could more easily eliminate.

The last major battle of Union I took place on May 15, when Alpha and Mike Companies, 5th Marines, found another bunker complex. After air and artillery had heavily pounded the bunkers, the Marines attacked against light resistance and found twenty-two more corpses.

The enemy retreated from the valley, and on May 17, Col. Kenneth Houghton, commanding officer of the 5th Marines and operational commander of Union I, closed it down, declaring it a great military and psychological victory for the allies. The Marines lost 110 killed in action, 2 missing in action, and had 473 wounded badly enough to be medevaced. They counted 867 enemy bodies. No one will ever know how many others perished.

The 2nd NVA Division was just catching its breath, and the operations in the Que Son basin grew bloodier and more savage as the year wore on. A captured NVA soldier told of coming down the Ho Chi Minh Trail with a new division from the north. His unit was headed farther south but paused west of Que Son and sent a thousand replacements to the 2nd NVA Division. A few days later, intelligence sources showed that the reconstituted 3rd and 31st NVA regiments were filtering back into the valley.

Chapter 9

Between the Unions

Corporal Lynwood "Scotty" Scott, forward air controller for Lima Company, 3rd Battalion, 1st Marines, recalled that Lieutenant Colonel Esslinger used to get a hometown newspaper that he liked to read in the evening if the battalion was not on an operation.

Cpl. Lynwood Scott: Without the colonel's knowledge, Sgt. Skip Perkins would order illumination missions after the sun went down so the colonel could read his paper. At a reunion many years later, Skip told the colonel, who was put out by the expense of the taxpayers' money so that he could read his paper.

The 1st Marine Division did what it could to replace the Marines lost on Union I, but newly arrived Marines often did not receive even the briefest indoctrination upon reaching their new units. Corporal Art Green describes his experience as an FNG joining India Company, 3rd Battalion, 5th Marines, at the tail end of Union I.

Cpl. Art Green: I was waiting for a bird to take me out when a helo came in with body bags and enemy weapons. Union I was in its final stages. I finally landed at an LZ in the field and went up to report in to the captain, who said, "Get the fuck away from me, you're drawing fire." I didn't even know we were being shot at. A few minutes later, I was told to go with another Marine and was walking on flank when we got shot at, and the Marine I was with was gut shot.

Charlie Company, 1st Battalion, 5th Marines, moves out on an operation from Hill 51. *Courtesy Harold Thrasher*

PRIVATE FIRST CLASS ROLAND MARCHAND'S introduction to Vietnam was typical in a system that used individual replacements in lieu of unit rotation. He arrived as a new mortar man, a stranger to a unit that had already seen a lot of heavy contact. Just a few days after leaving the United States, he found himself on a helicopter on his way to the 1st Battalion, 5th Marines, which was engaged in Union I.

Pfc. Roland Marchand: I had never been in a helicopter, and a guy was sitting there shooting his machine gun. There was a bare spot, and you could see all the smoke coming up; I said to the guy next to me, "What is that?" and he said, "That is the LZ where we are going to land." "What is an LZ?" The guy looked at me, thinking, "Oh, man, this is a boot here. An FNG." My boots weren't dirty, and my uniform was still a bright green.

I landed and got off. There were a couple of guys there, and I told them that I just arrived in Vietnam; what do I do? They said you report to this guy down here. So I went down to this perimeter, and there was a guy in a tent with sandbags all around. It was H&S Company, and he said report to

Gun One. I said, "Where is that?" He said, "They are over there." It was night, but sooner or later I found Gun One, and these two guys came up to me and said, "Do you know how to swab out a mortar tube?" I said, "Swab out a mortar tube, what is that?"

"Well, you've got these big swabs, and we swab out the tubes."

"Why are we doing that?"

"Well, because we are going to be doing H&Is."

Every time I swabbed the mortar tube, they would be laughing. I wondered why, and then later I learned that you don't stick a swab down when you are shooting off mortar rounds. They were just jacking with me.

There are many things we were short of, so stripping the gear from our dead was routine. I learned what food to take. I used a brand of sweetened instant drink mix called Rootin' Tootin' Raspberry to take the bad taste of the Halazone (purification) tablets out of rice paddy water. We ate a lot of peanut butter to control dysentery. We would live on peanut butter and

In the late summer of 1967, John Lobur, attached to weapons platoon, Mike Company, 3rd Battalion, 5th Marines, on bridge security. In the foreground are a 3.5-inch rocket launcher with three high-explosive rockets, an M16, and 782 gear. *Courtesy John Lobur*

crackers and water. We would try to get as many C-ration fruits as we could get. We would collect rice, fill up our canteen cups with it, put them on our belts, and then mix "C-rats" with rice.

Lance Cpl. John Lobur: There were many other things to learn that could keep you alive. You developed an instinct for ambush situations. You could often tell by the way the locals looked at you while on patrol that something was up. There were obvious things, like the fact that most locals went barefoot their whole lives, so the tire-tread tracks in the trail were made by NVA in their Ho Chi Minh sandals. Some less obvious things were never, ever trust a new guy, even an officer. It's just too hard to think the first few times the shit hits the fan, and there is no way to even come close to adequately training for it. Another thing was to close your right eye immediately when you heard the fizz of a pop flare or the pop of an illumination round; keep it closed until the flare burned itself out, then when you did open it, you'd be able to see.

Operations in the Que Son Valley overextended the helicopter squadrons. The pilots got by with four and five hours of sleep each night and then staggered out to their aircraft to fly their missions heroically and skillfully. Some were lucky enough to get an occasional night off to rejuvenate their energies. One of them was Lt. Rick Phillips, Heavy Helicopter Squadron 463 (HMH-463).

Lt. Rick Phillips: We had a night off, our first in quite a while, and the other squadrons were covering for us. All the captains and lieutenants were celebrating, and beer was flowing. Around 10:30 or 11:00 p.m. the flash phone rang, and one of the lieutenants went over and got it and came back with a stupid look on his face. "They have an emergency mission for us in a couple of hours, and all the CH-46s have been grounded." We thought he was kidding. Did you really mean that? You weren't kidding? That changed things quite a bit. We didn't do that much troop carrying, but when we did, we always took it very seriously. They needed a lot of troops in a hurry. All the pilots who knew how to fly that bird, except for the two majors, were right in that hut there. Needless to say, we went down to the mess hall and poured coffee into ourselves. Only three aircraft were up, and we could put experience in both seats in the cockpit. So we did. By the time we loaded up and got down there, it was one or two in the morning, and you could see that the enemy knew we were coming. We put the aircraft lights out. The enemy had fifty-cals, and the tracers looked like flaming beer cans flying by us at five thousand feet.

We made the landings after spiraling down, and no one took hits except for a few small arms. Fortunately, the flaming beer cans did not have any hits on us. It is always very goosey at night to shut all your lights out with several aircraft in the vicinity.[7]

Lance Cpl. Ken Fields: When we got back we had to get haircuts. We had to cut each other's hair with rusty hand clippers. For some reason, Captain McElroy designated me to cut his. With trembling hands I did so. I was lucky that we didn't have a mirror so he could see how I chopped his hair up. I stayed away from him for a few days in case he found a mirror.

The NVA were absolute masters of camouflage. Most Americans would stick a few leaves in their helmets and consider that to be adequate concealment. For the NVA, camouflage was a matter of life and death. When their units had to move in daylight, they were forced to expose themselves to the possibility of allied supporting arms, especially air support, which they feared above all things. Even when they were in areas they considered safe, they rarely moved without camouflage. They worked in teams and camouflaged their pith helmets. And each carried a wire or bamboo frame on his back that acted as a skeleton that another soldier fleshed out with vegetation. As they passed through varying types of terrain, they would immediately stop and change the camouflage to match the surrounding vegetation. For example, if they moved from a light to a dark green area, or if they moved into the brown area of a ripe crop, they would stop and recamouflage each other before moving out. When aircraft flew overhead, they often could escape detection by remaining motionless.

Chapter 10

Union II: The Enemy Strikes Back

After Union I, the 5th Marines wanted a larger permanent presence in the valley. They sent Lieutenant Colonel Hilgartner's 1st Battalion to a new command post location a click south and west of the town of Que Son, near where all the action had taken place on Union I. It was about four clicks south of Hill 110 and five clicks north of Nui Loc Son. The battalion set in on a hill with no numerical designation, so Hilgartner dubbed it Hill 51. His high school football jersey number was 51, he graduated from the Naval Academy in 1951, and he commanded the 5th Marines' 1st Battalion.

The 2nd NVA Division was bloodied, but Maj. Gen. Hoang Thao did not sit in his jungle fastness and brood. He was determined to regain the initiative in the valley, and he received a generous gift that enabled him to jump back into the fight with barely a pause. Just after Union I ended, Thao appealed to his superior, Maj. Gen. Dan Quang Trung, for more regular soldiers. As he had done earlier, Trung intercepted an NVA division on its way to a destination farther south along the Ho Chi Minh Trail. He was able to obtain one thousand fresh troops from this unit and send them to the 2nd NVA Division. Thao carefully wove the fresh new soldiers into the fabric of his battle-savvy units that had fought the Marines. That done, he ran to get back in the fight. The Marines scarcely had time to reflect on their performance in Operation Union when they were rudely interrupted by their own intelligence sources that told them elements of the 2nd NVA Division were seeping back into the Que Son Valley in small groups. Just a week after the

The communications bunker on Hill 51, the command post for the 1st Battalion, 5th Marines. *Courtesy Harold Thrasher*

close of Operation Union on May 19, the Marines set out to meet the enemy in an operation they dubbed Union II.

Major General Donn Robertson, the new commanding general of the 1st Marine Division, called on the 5th Marines, still commanded by Col. Kenneth Houghton, to take charge of the operation. Colonel Houghton had but two battalions, his 1st, commanded by Lieutenant Colonel Hilgartner, and Lieutenant Colonel Esslinger's 3rd Battalion. His 2nd Battalion, under Lt. Col. Mallett Jackson, was the 1st Marine Division reserve.

The Marines alerted the ARVN, and they agreed to have the 6th ARVN Regiment and 1st ARVN Ranger Group attack south and west from their bases at Thang Binh and Tam Ky at the eastern end of the valley.

On the night of May 25–26, Lieutenant Colonel Hilgartner's 1st Battalion, 5th Marines, left Hill 51 on foot at one minute past midnight. It has often been said about the Vietnam War that the enemy owned the night. Under such leaders as Deegan, Hilgartner, Esslinger, and Webster, to use four examples, the Marines very often operated, and operated well, after dark. Well trained, well led, and well conditioned, the battalion marched with a minimum of fuss around the east end of the hill mass that shields Hill 110 from the valley proper. They covered six kilometers in the dark and established blocking positions in the northwestern end of the Que Son Valley near the base of the "thumb," not far from Hill 110, the scene of the bitter fighting on 10 May.

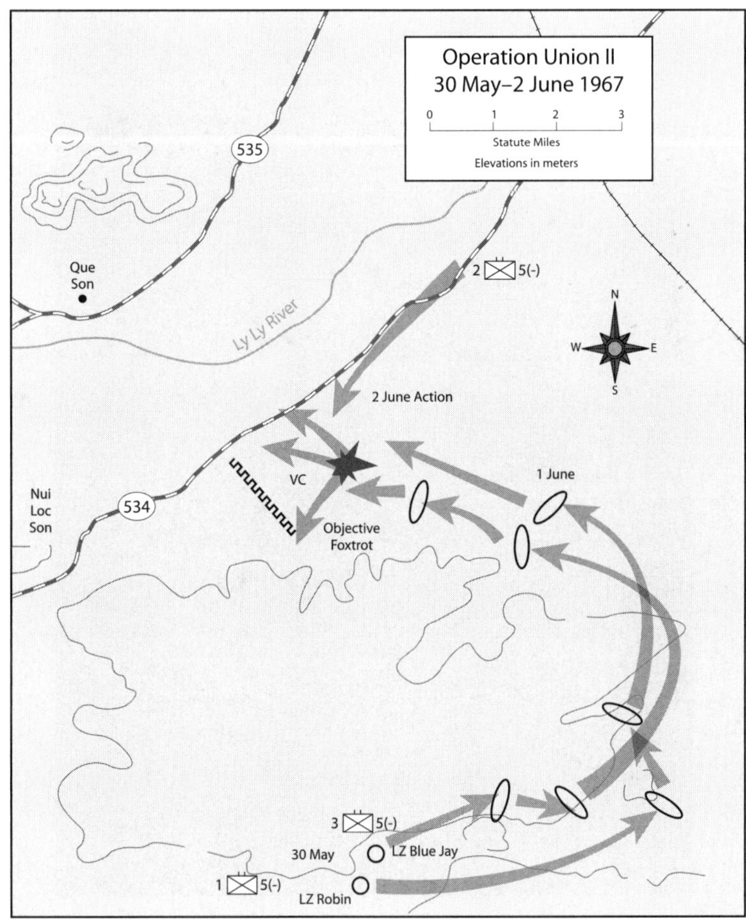

They were in a position to put a stopper at the base of this spur and prevent enemy units from using it to exit the valley floor. Hilgartner's Marines hoped that the ARVN and Lieutenant Colonel Esslinger's 3rd Battalion would drive the enemy into their arms.

At 0945 on May 26, the first of Esslinger's Marines alighted in LZ Eagle, 10 clicks due south of Hilgartner, 1.5 clicks south of Route 534, and but 1.5 clicks east of where Captain Deegan's Foxtrot Company, 2nd Battalion, 1st Marines, was mauled on April 21. Esslinger's Marines attacked north and east, hoping to force the enemy to stand and fight or to drive them either toward Hilgartner's battalion or toward the ARVN.

A Marine from Mike Company, 3rd Battalion, 5th Marines, pours fire into an enemy position during Operation Union II, June 1967. *USMC*

Lieutenant Colonel Esslinger's Lima Company, commanded by Capt. Harold Pettengill, set down in the landing zone first and was greeted by moderately heavy small-arms fire. As Corporal Scott flew toward the objective, he thought about the two unusual treats the troops got the night before, a small beer ration and ice cream. These treats were so rare that many of the Marines were suspicious that this was a grim omen, a "condemned man's last meal" sort of thing. Scott's fears were realized as they

Corporal Lynwood "Scotty" Scott, a forward air controller whose expertise was important during most of the operations. *Courtesy Lynwood Scott*

approached the LZ and enemy bullets punched through the skin of the ship "like .22 rounds through a tin can."

Being shot at for the first time is an unforgettable experience. Having holes shot into a helicopter in which one is riding, like the prospect of hanging, really concentrates the mind. There is *nowhere* to hide, and suddenly one is faced with the prospect of death by gunshot, falling, crashing, burning alive, or any combination of the above. Adrenaline runs hard and fast, heart rate soars, and one suddenly gets a mouth so dry that spit is impossible and no amount of water will ever be enough. One's mind is on a razor edge, and thoughts are redlined at the upper limits of volume and rpm, almost as if one is screaming aloud. The prayer is always some variation of "Get me off this fucking helicopter NOW!" Afterward, one never thinks about helicopters the same way again. Scott's bird landed, and everyone rushed to the rear ramp, trying to get off the chopper and down into the dirt as soon as possible. Fear and frustration piled up when the Marines were trapped by a ramp control that was damaged and went down in fits and starts, slowing their exit from the aircraft. They jostled on the incline of the ramp and squeezed out into the paddy one at a time. When it was Scott's turn to get off, he bounced along with his forty-pound air controller's radio (PRC41) and took up station behind an eighteen-inch-high paddy dike on the perimeter. The first task of the first wave of Marines off a flight of choppers is to set up a 360 degree perimeter to protect those that follow, so the Lima Company Marines fanned out and set up an uneven circle in the flat paddy surrounding the LZ. The paddy was a big one, perhaps a thousand meters across.

The helicopters took off and at 1100 returned with the battalion command group and Mike Company.

Lance Cpl. John Lobur: As we neared the LZ the door gunners were talking on their headsets . . . soon they were shooting almost continuously, and we made our descent. I noticed little dots of light appearing in the wall behind the guys across from me, and I actually thought the pilot was opening some kind of ventilation system. It was bullet holes, and the guy across from me was hit.

Bam, we hit the ground. As we scrambled out of the chopper, I saw the one right next to us get hit by something big, which exploded. Larry Leonard, with whom I'd gone all the way through boot camp, got hit right in the back with a mortar. He was an ammo humper for 60mm mortars, and it hit the pack board with six mortar rounds on it. The rounds did not go off, but the spray of shrapnel got both his hands.

Lieutenant Colonel Esslinger sent Lima into the attack to the north and east where they got into a good fight with a dug-in enemy force. They took the position after hammering it with close air support, but the victory was costly. Lima Company lost 8 killed, and among the 13 wounded was Captain Pettengill, the company commander.

Cpl. Lynwood Scott: We were told to get on line. We could see the NVA about 150 meters away. Lance Corporal Anthony Russo and I put out an orange panel in front of our lines, crawled back, and began running snake and nape. I felt the breeze of something touch my shirt as it went by. It was an M79 round, and it wounded Russo and radio operator Bill Clark.

Cpl. Bill Clark: I was standing there with Captain Pettengill and an FNG, Corporal Schofield. Nearby one of our machine gunners was shot in the head and was struggling to get back on the gun. Another Marine was trying to pull him off so someone else could use it. I fell back a bit, and Schofield was between the skipper and me. An M79 round came and hit Captain Pettengill in the back. He kind of twisted like a pirouette and went down. Two guys from 60[mm] mortars ran over to get him.

Captain Pettengill temporarily lost his hearing, and fragments from the round severed several muscles in his neck, but he stayed in the field, directing air support and artillery fire until the remainder of the battalion landed safely.

Cpl. Bill Clark: Another M79 round landed between Schofield and me, and he went down, and I was hit but not badly. It knocked me out for a brief period, and when I woke up, my first thought was that my candle from our tent had exploded and thrown hot wax on my face. Then Corporal Smallwood yelled at me and asked if I was OK. I had a horrible headache and a bloody face but no serious damage. Marines from 60[mm] mortars came and got Schofield and the two Marine photographers with us, who were both hit.

I was by myself in the paddy, and I looked over and saw Lance Corporal Russo and Cpl. Lynwood Scott behind another paddy dike, so I ran over to see if I could help. Sure enough, Russo had been hit in the chest and stomach. We tried to stop the bleeding. I got up on my knees to try to pick him up to get him farther back.

I told him, "I can't get you up. Can you crawl?" About that time another M79 round landed close to us, and he said, "Crawl, hell, I can run." We ran over to the next paddy dike that was higher, and people grabbed him and toted him off, and Scotty and I got behind the taller dike. Sure enough, we left the heavy air-control radio, the PRC41, back where we had started. We had to go back under fire and get that. Then Scotty left and went back to the CP group with the radio.

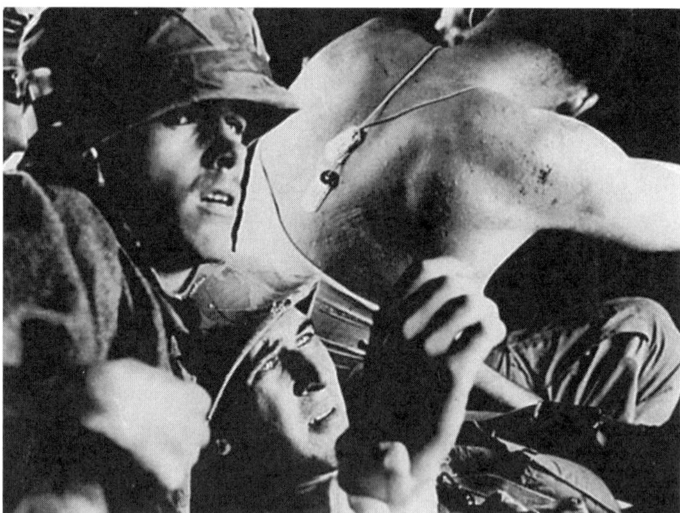

Photos of unidentified Marines and corpsmen taken during the Que Son Valley Campaign. *Vic Perez collection*

AT 1135, A CH-46 SEA KNIGHT helicopter loaded with casualties was just beginning to lift off when it was disabled by fire, but it managed to crash-land in the Marine perimeter. Hospital Corpsman Second Class (HM2) Vic Perez was aboard, desperately trying to keep a Marine alive whose breathing stopped time and again. The chopper smashed into the ground, causing minor injuries. The Marines transferred the casualties to another bird, and this time Perez was trying to keep *two* Marines from dying. He still had the one whose breathing had stopped, and now he had another who was squirting blood through a severed artery.

Just as this second chopper lifted off, it staggered and swung around when a recoilless rifle round glanced off the nose and sent yet another rush of adrenaline racing through the Marines. The pilots nursed the bird into the air, and it got away.

At 1400, Mike Company swept through a village and encountered enemy with small arms, automatic weapons, and mortars. Captain McElroy, who had been shot in the shoulder on Union I, was back in the field.

Capt. Jim McElroy: We landed and were told where to go, and we didn't get very far—fifty meters. A hedge row stopped the whole company. Some guys slipped around to the left, and our mortars went with them, and *wham*, they were splattered with mortars and everything you can think of. There was firing everywhere.

I saw guys from another company running out on this really long paddy, all sand and scrub brush, and they were getting knocked down. I got this one platoon of mine doing what they were supposed to do, and they got waxed, pure and simple. The enemy was just waiting. That was pretty nasty because it was up close and personal.

Lance Cpl. Ken Fields: Mike Company was moving in column when we began to receive sporadic sniper fire from our left flank. Without warning, the order came to assault left. The weapons platoon was in the best position to assault, and swung around to the left, went up to the paddy from a sunken trail, and started across.

A machine gun opened up and sent the Marines to the ground. They lay there in a trough of indecision and taking casualties until Lance Cpl. Gordon Seablom stood up, waving his .45, and urged the Marines on. Fields, being in the gun team, set his gun up next to a mature stand of bamboo and sent bursts of fire into the enemy position. Corporal Charlie Crump was showing Fields where to shoot when a mortar round exploded right next to him, blowing Crump's life away and throwing his body on top of Fields's legs. Sharp, hot steel punched into the ground all around Fields, but good battlefield luck was with him that day, and he was not hit except for a piece that grazed his knee. For Pfc. Fred Riddle, FNG, it was the first time being shot at.

Pfc. Fred Riddle (mortar man): The feeling can't be explained unless it has happened to you. We were given the word to move out, and it really didn't have a lot of meaning at the time, because I still was unaware of what this whole thing was about. When we landed I found out, and very quickly. There was heavy ground fire and mortar fire everywhere.

We moved up out of the paddies to a small house with some trees and bamboo bordering it. Captain McElroy was on the radio, but even though I was around the CP, I had no idea of how things worked. We started to move out, and in a split second everything around me changed. I heard the mortars coming in, but you could not act that fast. Two 82mm mortar rounds landed right in the middle of our group, and Marines were down everywhere. After the initial shock of the event—it seemed like hours, but I know it was just seconds—I got my senses together and noticed the Marine in front of me was holding his face. I asked if he was OK, and he said, "No, I'm not," and that's when I noticed the blood. He got his face torn up and part of his right shoulder. I looked at my right shoulder and noticed that my shirt was torn, and I was bleeding also. I looked around and found several wounded Marines on the ground. I found Rocky, but he was killed, so I looked for Harold. We had become friends, and I had an urgent need to see if he was OK. I saw a Marine that was halfway in an air-raid hole on the side of the paddy dike. He had his arms up holding onto the dirt wall, but something didn't seem right about it, as there was no movement. I yelled to him to see if he was OK but got no response. I pulled him back and removed his pack and started to check him, and it was Harold, my friend, the guy just minutes before I was talking to and sharing my thoughts and my fears about the whole thing, and he was gone. He feared mortar fire more than anything, and almost got to cover, but one small fragment entered through his back and right through his heart. I was in shock.

After we carried the wounded back to the tree line and the dead to another area, we set up a perimeter. We couldn't get the wounded out by chopper because of the heavy fire, so the corpsman had to do what he could for them. Because the rest of the mortar section was either KIA or WIA, it didn't exist any longer. I was all that was left, so I was put in 3rd Platoon and assigned to the perimeter on the left side of the trees.

Private First Class Riddle's bewilderment was short lived. He was no sooner reassigned to the 3rd Platoon as a rifleman than he looked over the battleground and figured out where the enemy mortars were located. FNG or not, he knew enough to leave his position, find the forward air controller, and help him call in strikes on the enemy guns.

Lance Corporal Steve Lovejoy was a radio operator with the 2nd Platoon, Mike Company. He was down in the dirt and hit when burning debris from a white phosphorous round landed on his pack and set it on fire. The pack was full of flares and ammunition, and he was more terrified of the blazing pack than of the enemy gunfire. He was sure he was going to be burned alive and had to stand up in the middle of the fight to get the pack off his back. Lance Corporal John Lobur thought he could smell flesh burning and figured that Lovejoy was dead.

At 1600, India Company, 3rd Battalion, 5th Marines, attacked to come up on the flank of the enemy and relieve pressure on Lima so they could retrieve casualties. The Marines struck the enemy with air and artillery and enveloped the position after much hard fighting.

Cpl. Tim Hanley: We hit a lot of resistance and tried flanking them from the north and really ran into another whole unit. It was a heavier force than we thought it was. India Company was on the point of 3/5 and got pinned down; the gooks were entrenched in the tree line, and we sent 3rd Platoon under Lt. Kenny Moore. He ran into another entrenched NVA unit. We were taking a lot of fire and mortars. We assaulted through this tree line and got the gooks on the run, and it was a Marine's dream come true. There was a down slope on the backside. And the NVA hauled ass down the slope. We could only get a few guys in there to shoot, but there were thirty, forty bodies by the time we finished. We had problems with the M16, so we had our cleaning rods assembled and stuck down the sling swivels.

During a search of the area, an attached engineer, Cpl. David Mollenkamp, peeked into a cave and had a meeting engagement with an NVA whom he outdrew and shot down. He then blew up the enemy ordnance he found in the cave. On his way to rejoin the other Marines he encountered and killed two more of the enemy.

At 1700 Lima fell back, leaving one platoon behind to retrieve casualties after dark.

The NVA had commenced hammering the landing zone at about 1730 with heavy small-arms and 82mm mortar fire, once more taking out a battalion command group, blowing it apart, and killing or wounding nearly everyone. One of the colonel's radio operators and Sgt. Forrest McKay, the chief scout sniper, were the only ones not killed or wounded by the barrage.

Mortar fragments tore Lieutenant Colonel Esslinger's eye out and killed Capt. James Ayers, the battalion communications officer. Sergeant McKay picked up Captain Ayers, slung him over his back, and looked for cover. Esslinger and McKay staggered toward a hole. Esslinger jumped in first, and McKay, with Captain Ayers on his back, landed on top of the colonel. More mortars hit the LZ, and McKay was wounded in the back.

Lieutenant Colonel Esslinger remembers that after he was hit and with the mortars still coming in at intervals, he and several of his Marines dove for the same hole several times. The colonel usually landed on top of the pile, in the most exposed position. He muttered, "Why do I always have to land on top?" A young Marine lying under him said, "That is because you are old and slow, sir."

Cpl. Bill Clark: When the CP group came in and Colonel Esslinger was hit, I started crawling toward them and finally got so tired with the heat and all that I just stood up in the middle of the fire and walked back to where the battalion was.

The first person I saw was Colonel Esslinger with the bandage over his eye. He offered me his canteen. I had just got back to the CP area when we got mortared again.

ONE OF THE MORTAR ROUNDS SCORED a direct hit on Lance Cpl. Robert Daniel, blew him apart, and sprayed the immediate area with a shower of hot, razor-sharp fragments, brown smoke, a pink mist of blood, and bits of flesh.

Capt. Jim McElroy: Down about 150 yards from me, right in the middle of all this fire, were this pilot and a crewman trying to fix their helicopter. They were walking on the top of it like nothing was happening, nonchalantly trying to get it fixed. The aircrew repaired the chopper and flew it out of the LZ at 1800 that evening.

AT 2000 A HELO LANDED AMIDST THE FIRE and managed to get Lieutenant Colonel Esslinger and a few casualties out. The remainder had to wait until the following morning. By the end of the day, HM3 Glenn Glasgow had used every battle dressing in his unit one medical bag.

Marines from the 3rd Battalion, 5th Marines, move out after clearing a hot landing zone on May 26, 1967. *Courtesy Lynwood Scott*

Doc Glenn Glasgow (Lima Company, 5th Marines): We began the day with seven corpsmen. By the next morning there were only four. The senior corpsmen, HM2 John Schon and a friend of mine, HN Mike Carey, were KIA, and Doc Billy Claggett was medevaced to Da Nang.

Cpl. Bill Clark: The M16s were failing. When I was up near the dike, I saw three NVA in the tree line. I got off one round before mine jammed. It looked like the Civil War out there, with all the guys using ramrods. I cleared the jam and fired but only got one round off, and it jammed again. While I was in this exposed position, I could only fire single rounds before having to clear the rifle. I fired a whole magazine that way. I remember thinking that here I am with a single-shot .22, and if they rush me, I'm in trouble. When I got back to the LZ, there was a pile of weapons from our wounded and dead, and I got one of them. It didn't jam as often.

Except for me and Scotty, the Lima CP group was wiped out. I ended up with three radios; I had my battalion net radio, Schofield's company net radio, and the radio that Scotty was carrying before Russo was hit and he took over FAC duties. All of the antennas made a hell of a target. Mel Bellamy casually walked up with rounds flying everywhere and asked if he could have one of my radios because his had a hole in it. He was as calm as if he was on a street at home. I yelled for him to get his ass down, and did he think he couldn't get hit? He took a radio and went back to his platoon. He was completely unflappable. I ended up dragging and carrying that second radio around with me until I got back to the new CP area later in the day.

SCOTT LOOKED OFF TO HIS LEFT and out about 150 meters saw Cpl. Harry White just stand up and walk toward the enemy tree line by himself, firing his machine gun as he went. He just kept walking and spitting leaden death until the enemy shot him down. Scotty thought that White was dead, but he somehow survived and many years later showed up at a reunion.

Cpl. Lynwood Scott: By two or three in the afternoon I was exhausted and out of water, and someone came up on the net and said, "We are going to take over air from you." I said, "Roger." I was so tired and worn out that I just stood up amongst the fire and started walking back like a zombie. I didn't care if I got shot or not. I saw three Marines off to the right who had been trying to evacuate a casualty with two on one side of a poncho and just one on the other. I ran over there to help out, and we took the casualty back.

Captain Ayers had been killed already. He was a real genuine and kind person that everyone respected. A M79 round just touched my arm as it went by, and there were itty-bitty pellets in it. A corpsman came by, and I told him not to bother with me, because there were much more seriously wounded. A Marine came by and said, "Turn Ayers over; half his face is gone." I couldn't do it. I was sitting right by him and had just brought the wounded guy in. I sat there and put my hands over my face and cried. I didn't know before that he was dead. I thought, "What a waste. What a good, good man." Sergeant Marty "Skip" Pickens, Colonel Esslinger's radio man, said, "Scotty, get up and go out there and help bring in the wounded." I thought, "Who made you God?" But I went back out and started bringing the dead and wounded back.

PICKENS LATER TOLD SCOTT that he saw what terrible shape Scott was in and didn't want to medevac him, so he sent him out to carry in the casualties instead. It worked, and Scotty soon regained his emotional balance.

The butcher presented an expensive bill for the day: thirty-eight Marines died and eighty-two were wounded. The Marines found 138 enemy bodies and evidence that they killed many more.

Between 2030 and midnight, Mike Company heard the enemy communicating over the company radio frequency. A Kit Carson scout listened and told the Marines that one of the enemy units was instructed to pick up the bodies in the field. They protested that they had not enough men to pick them all up. Then one of the enemy call signs told another that if he didn't kill an American commanding officer, he would be punished. Yet another transmission ordered a unit to pick up all the weapons on the battlefield so they could be used in an attack later that night. Finally, for a two-hour period, ten different enemy call signs were on the net, making constant radio checks, indicating that the NVA were on the move.

The next morning, Mike moved into the area of the previous day's fighting and found four Marine bodies. Two had been reported as KIA and two MIA. The latter two had been executed. One had an NVA battle dressing on his leg and then had been shot at close range though the head. The NVA apparently tried to patch him up and then decided to kill him. Another Marine, Pvt. Donald White, had been shot in both arms and legs and in the head. His wounds were ringed with powder burns, a sure sign that the rounds had been fired at close range. White had been a happy-go-lucky type. Corporal Scott remembered him goofing around and jumping into a mud puddle the night before when they got their beer ration. The Marines also recovered twelve M16 rifles. Even the enemy didn't want them.

On the morning of the twenty-seventh, Lt. Col. Charles B. "Blake" Webster arrived to take command of the 3rd Battalion, 5th Marines. The company gunnery sergeant sent Cpl. Norm Bailey back to Tam Ky to act as part of the security force. When he alighted he saw dead Marines lying in tents, wrapped in ponchos. He found a dog tag on the ground as he was walking across the landing zone. It belonged to Captain Ayers, the communications officer who was just killed. The tag had a hole in it from shrapnel.

Lieutenant Colonel Webster swept his battalion due north that day, but they found little of interest. For the next three days, the NVA eluded the Marines. After two days with no activity in their sector, the ARVN quit the field and went back to their bases.

But at the 5th Marines' command post, Colonel Houghton was convinced that the enemy was still in the valley, and he decided to move his units back to the south. He sent both battalions to a long, steep valley that extends eastward from Hiep Duc and alongside Route 586, a dirt road that parallels a tributary of the Chang River. Prior to the insertion, Houghton prepped the landing zones with twelve fixed-wing aircraft and four Huey gunships that bombed, strafed, and rocketed the ground. The LZs lay in the shadow of intimidating mountain peaks that soar to nearly five hundred meters above the valley floor on either side. The hills were impassable jungle except where trails went through them. Such terrain was not uncommon in Vietnam and presented a commander with two unsatisfactory options. One was that he could hack through the surrounding terrain on either side of the trail. This method was painfully slow, noisy, and rarely productive. The other option was to use the trails that were often booby-trapped or presented perfect sites for ambush.

On the thirtieth, the 1st Battalion, 5th Marines, lifted out to LZ Robin. When the choppers came back, the 3rd Battalion, 5th Marines, lifted out and landed at LZ Blue Jay, ten clicks west of the 1st Battalion's landing zone.

Lt. Kenny Moore: We were the first company into LZ Blue jay in this little, narrow valley maybe fifty yards wide. The LZ was a paddy and was full of water. The helicopters came down to about ten feet and hovered, and we all had to jump and got stuck in knee-deep mud. It was fifteen yards to the edge of the paddy, and it took ten or fifteen minutes to get there. The NVA were firing 60mm and 82mm mortars, but they were hitting the water and burying in the mud and not going off.

Lance Cpl. Dennis Delaney: We were so deep in the mud that you could lean back in it and rest if you wanted to.

Lt. Kenny Moore: There was an enemy observation post that we found later that had been directing the fire. It was north and a little east of us on a two-hundred-meter hill about a click and a half away. Mine was the lead platoon, and it took us a long time to get through the mud and out of the paddy, and then we had a conflict with a water boo (water buffalo). The animal lowered his head and was snorting and started to charge. My squad leader shot the water boo with the M79 and hit him in the forehead. The round spiraled up about ten yards and went off in an airburst. The boo stopped and was shaking his head, and we fired another M79, and the same thing happened, so we shot him with a machine gun.

We continued the attack about midafternoon and were pinned down by fire from that observation post. Captain Stackpole came up and gave me an order to attack, and I was getting ready to issue my attack order to my squad leaders when he came over and said, "When are you going to attack?" I said, "Captain, I haven't issued an order yet." He said, "Get going now!" We did an impromptu attack and took the knoll very late in the afternoon. We found about ten bodies, a couple of pairs of binoculars, and an artillery range-finder. One of the bodies was an officer. We had a casualty from another unit, and a medevac pilot did the greatest job I have ever seen. There was about a forty-five-degree slant on the hill. This guy came in, lowered his ramp, and hovered there until we loaded the casualty. An NVA shot the copilot through the windshield, and the chopper lost altitude and then regained it as the pilot got it under control. They got the casualty on the ramp, and the pilot got out of there. They did a marvelous job.

We were headed east on a mountain pass and took up a position near where we had captured some stuff, and it was nothing but absolute jungle. I had a night patrol trying to make contact with the enemy. We went east, and there was nothing there except jungle; you couldn't go through that at night, and we couldn't do it.

We were on the edge of this big mountain. A Kit Carson scout started a fire, and pretty soon we were fighting fire like you can't believe. About the time the NVA got in contact with us, we were using two out of every three Marines to fight the fire. We ran a couple of F-8 Crusaders on the enemy and then gave up on them because they were ineffective. We had no casualties, but we knew we were in the middle of something because of the observation post and other signs.

Finding little of interest in his sector, Hilgartner's battalion worked its way onto the Que Son Valley floor and swept in a reverse C-shaped route, quickly overcoming light resistance. Hilgartner had Alpha and Delta Companies from his own battalion and Capt. Jim Graham's Foxtrot Company from the 2nd Battalion, 5th Marines. The battalion's mission was to secure an objective in the Vinh Huy area, where they had reason to believe that a large enemy force had taken up residence.

A Chieu Hoi (a former Communist who rallied to the allied side) told them that the enemy had moved in there, and an aerial observer (AO), slowly skimming the sky above the Marines in a back and forth pattern, reported seeing a stream of Vietnamese civilians evacuating the Vinh Huy village area, leading their water buffaloes and carrying all they could load on their backs and bicycles. This was a sure sign that the enemy was in the area in large numbers and that they expected a big fight very soon. Little did the Marines know that they were going to run smack up against nearly 1,000 soldiers from the 2nd and 3rd Battalions of Colonel Huyen's 31st NVA Regiment, which moved into the village complex the previous night.

In the meantime, the 3rd Battalion, 5th Marines, moved out; Mike and India Companies led off, and Lima Company brought up the rear. At 0830 Mike moved through the village of Dong An, which had been bombed that morning. Not a building still stood.

Lt. Kenny Moore: We continued around on May 31, and on June 1 we continued the movement right around to where we made contact on June 2. We found a couple of NVA sentries in a sentinel post. When they saw us coming up the trail, they moved out like lickety-split. About 9:30 a.m. we came to an area where a trail intersected a creek. My right flank security was on high ground and saw about fifty NVA and two machine guns setting up an ambush. We stopped and went over to the right flank and watched them set in. Then we did an envelopment with two platoons, laying down a base of fire with two machine guns, killing about thirty NVA and capturing about twenty. We had no casualties. It took us a while to evacuate the prisoners. We were out of duct tape, so we used extra bootlaces to bind the hands of the captives.

INDIA COMPANY NO SOONER REACHED the foothills next to the valley floor than they again ran into NVA. Captain Stackpole sent Lt. William Rawson's platoon around to the right flank to try to roll them up. Rawson led the flanking maneuver successfully, dislodged the enemy, and began calling in supporting arms on the retreating NVA. Rawson's attack only lasted about fifteen minutes, but his platoon took numerous casualties. When fire knocked down one of his squad leaders, Rawson ran across an open area and shielded the Marine with his body. An NVA straggler shot the lieutenant through the neck and killed him. The 2nd Platoon under Lt. Fred Smith was ordered to go around on the left side and also got into a fight but overran the enemy.

Lance Cpl. Bob Kreuder: I was walking point on the left flank. I was usually not on point but was two or three guys back. As soon as they opened up from the ville, I ducked, and the fire killed the guy right behind me, where I usually was, and it wounded the next guy.

Lance Cpl. Dennis Delaney: I had just cleared a spent cartridge out of my M16 that wouldn't eject, and I put the bipod down and swung around to see what was in front of me. An automatic weapon walked in some rounds, one of which bounced off the M16 while it was right in front of my chest. It struck the elevation wheel of the rifle sights and shattered them. A quarter of an inch off and it would have drilled me.

AS IT WAS, DELANEY HAD FRAGMENTS from his hand up his arm to his shoulder and his chest.

Capt. Jim McElroy: I could see Captain Stackpole, the CO of India, as we were moving over the foothills. We were moving along, and I heard this scream like you have never heard in your life, and it was Stackpole, who had been shot through the leg. Stackpole stood to lead the assault when he was shot. Both of his radio operators were shot down with him.

Lieutenant Kenny Moore assumed command of the company.

Lt. Kenny Moore: Stackpole moved with the headquarters group and went around to my left to reinforce the attack by the 2nd Platoon. He got shot in the left leg about halfway across the paddy. I got a call from the gunny that a platoon commander was down too, and I was the CO of the company. Stackpole had arterial bleeding, with blood squirting out about a foot when his heart beat. We did an incision there and got the thing cauterized, just inside the left knee. We cauterized it with a cigarette lighter, tied it off with a little piece of string, took one stitch in the leg, and put him on the chopper, an H-34. It went up fifteen or twenty feet, and the pilot was ready to lean it forward and take off when something hit right in front of it. A second round hit the helo right in the nose, a direct hit, and knocked it down.

Lance Corporal James Millirons, a member of the helicopter support team, who directed the helo in, was killed by the blast.

Lt. Kenny Moore: We captured the weapon later that day, and it was a 75mm recoilless rifle.

Captain Stackpole was evacuated on the next chopper.

Cpl. Tim Hanley: We thought we had the area pretty well secured, and two helos came in for medevac. We put Anthony Lajewski, one of our radio operators, on one of them. When they brought in the chopper to get him out, a 75mm recoilless rifle hit the chopper. It was shot down, and we managed to save all but the two pilots.

Lance Cpl. Dennis Delaney: Kenny wanted two guys to go get two dead Marines. I volunteered, although I was all taped up and ready to be medevaced. Kenny said, "No, you aren't going." I said, "You don't have anybody else." Kenny said, "Okay, I am going to throw some smoke grenades out there, and it will be a little bit of cover." He threw the grenades, and two of us went out and brought back two dead Marines.

The enemy left twenty-two dead on the field, and the Marines thought that they killed another forty-five. During the prep fires, a Marine A-4 Skyhawk flew too low on a bombing run, clipped a tree, flipped over, and crashed, killing the pilot.

Capt. Jim McElroy: We called for air, and I had some men in harm's way but not a lot. We wound around some old dikes, and I looked down and saw that we were not getting much air support, because the most air I ever saw in my life was pounding where I later learned Captain Graham was.

Lt. Kenny Moore: We had three platoons with corporals as platoon commanders, a corporal as gunny, and me. That's what we had left after that thirty-minute engagement. I was ordered to continue the attack, and I was down behind a little dike. The VC had moved out in the open. I was trying to figure out what we had left in the company and was peeking over a dike from the chin up with binoculars, when a sniper, the same one that shot Stackpole, shot through my helmet. It severed the webbing on the left and grazed my scalp. We tried to continue the attack that afternoon and didn't make much headway.

Chapter 11

Desperate Delta

In the meantime, Lieutenant Colonel Hilgartner's 1st Battalion, 5th Marines, swept westward with Lt. Dave McInturff's Delta Company out ahead and on the right and the attached company, Capt. Jim Graham's Foxtrot Company, 2nd Battalion, 5th Marines, set back and on the left. Alpha Company, commanded by Capt. Ron Babich, brought up the rear. Contact throughout the morning was light and sporadic. After Delta Company secured its initial objective, Lieutenant Colonel Hilgartner called for a short break, so the Marines set out security, dropped their loads, smoked, and swigged from their canteens. During the pause, the Marines in Delta Company, including Lance Cpl. Wayne Puterbaugh, saw two NVA to their front and dropped them.

Lance Cpl. Wayne Puterbaugh: As we were moving up to take over the point and passed through another company, I ran into a guy I was in boot camp with, Cpl. Victor Driscoll. We chatted a bit as the company passed them on the trail. We only spoke a couple of minutes because the company was on the move. Driscoll was killed later that afternoon.

When the march resumed, McInturff had his Delta Company in a common tactical formation, with the 1st Platoon on the left front and 2nd Platoon on the right front. Behind them was the company command group, which, in turn, was followed by the 3rd Platoon.

They moved westward, along the northern edge of the Vinh Huy villages. Lieutenant Colonel Nguyen Dui Than's 3rd Battalion, 31st NVA

Regiment, was in front of them and had prepared fortified positions along a spur of rough gravel road that runs southeast from Route 534. Delta Company started across a large, 250-meter-wide rice paddy and ran into a fury of enemy fire that struck them from the front and left flank. At the same time, Capt. James Graham came up on the radio to report that his Foxtrot Company had also encountered serious resistance. Foxtrot was about a click and a half southeast of Delta when the trouble started. Try as they might, the two companies never made flanker contact with each other, although both skippers were on the radio trying to explain their positions and popping colored smoke grenades.

Lieutenant McInturff's 1st and 2nd Platoons were completely chewed up. His 1st Platoon under Lt. Larry Chmiel was in the lead when the lieutenant, his platoon sergeant, Staff Sgt. David Dixon, and their radio operator were all killed immediately, and McInturff lost contact with that platoon. He sent Lt. Bill Link with the 3rd Platoon around to the right in an attempt to flank the enemy. McInturff calls Link's effort "valiant but unsuccessful" because the enemy took the platoon under fire from its front and right flank, halting its progress. Link's radio operator, Cpl. Donald Christy, was killed and the radio destroyed, but Link managed to extricate his platoon without help from the company. The enemy machine guns spit grazing fire so close over their heads that it was suicide for the Marines to get up and go to the aid of their downed comrades.

Corpsman Larry Casselman was an FNG who joined Lieutenant Link's platoon the day after Union I ended. New corpsman or not, Casselman was about to become the company's most combat experienced doc after just three weeks in Vietnam.

Doc Larry Casselman: The 3rd Platoon was trying to outflank the enemy to the right. They sent us across a paddy to this high ground, and then we were supposed to assault across a huge, open paddy. We no sooner moved off the high ground into the paddy than we started taking a humungous amount of automatic-weapons fire and mortars from across the paddy and from our right. We hadn't flanked them enough. We took a bunch of casualties right off the bat. There were "corpsman up" calls all over the place. One of the guys, a squad leader named Lance Cpl. Joseph Escobar, had a through-and-through head wound, through his forehead and out the top of his head. He was out in the paddy, and someone called me, and I ran out there to treat him and got pinned down. We had called in air strikes on the ville, and I was trying to protect Escobar from the debris. One of the big bombs went off and lifted all sorts of crap into the air, and I could hear all the whizzing through the air, and a bunch of dirt clods crashed on me. I had to get him out of there. I called for a couple of guys from the tree line, and we dragged Escobar back and put him next to the trunk of a tree. He died later in the afternoon. Toward the end of the day, I responded to a call and found Sergeant Crouch lying in the paddy and grabbing in his groin area. A round had hit him there and stuck in one of his loaded magazines. Except for a little bruising, he was okay. When he realized that, he started laughing hysterically.

Lt. Dave McInturff: The rice paddy was two hundred meters wide but seemed six miles wide when we were trying to get to cover. After calling in some air and artillery, we were able to move over to a covered area where my CP group and 3rd Platoon were.

Doc Larry Casselman: We knew we had to get out of there, so we took off running, across one paddy at a time. Private First Class John Seller jumped up and said he needed to go back and check something; he ran back a bit and was gunned down. We yelled to the guys in some rocks behind us that we were friendly and coming in. We eventually made it to the rocks, where there were a bunch of wounded guys and about ten others.

Toward the end of the day, there were only three or four of us who were alive and could get around on this high ground where the platoon had started their sweep. The rest of the platoon was in the paddy. There was a bunch of guys behind those boulders, twenty-five to fifty meters off in this paddy. We, on the high ground, were getting surrounded.

Lance Corporal Pennington, a gunner, was running out of ammo, and it was late in the day. The NVA were starting to drop mortars, bracketing our position. I was in the back of the rock outcropping and knew we couldn't stay. We had no idea where we were going; we had no radio and didn't know where the rest of the company was. Everyone started moving back, and Bob Warren and I grabbed Charlie LeCrone, another of our squad leaders. LeCrone was shot in both thighs, and both femurs were broken and one rib. We put his arms over our shoulders, started dragging him, got about fifty yards, and were exhausted from the heat and lack of water and food. We heard the enemy jabbering away over on the high ground we had just left. We stopped behind a paddy dike; Bob Warren took off to find the company, and I stayed to take care of LeCrone. I was about thirty feet away from the high ground and could hear the NVA going through our packs. I was trying to keep LeCrone from moaning, but I had no more morphine to give him.

Eventually Warren came back with a squad of guys. I couldn't tell, in the dark, who they were. I told LeCrone to be quiet and that people were getting closer. I still couldn't tell who they were from ten feet away. Just when I was ready to squeeze off a round, I heard the radio say, "Delta 3, this is Delta 6." I said, "Delta 3 is over here." They had a poncho with them. It was about 0200. We were out there at least six hours and were about 150 yards from the company. We got back to the company, and LeCrone was medevaced the next day.

McInturff kept up supporting-arms fire on the enemy positions until most of the enemy seeped out of the battle area after dark, except for a small contingent remaining behind to pick up their casualties and harass the Marines. Small groups of Marines cautiously moved throughout Delta Company that night redistributing ammunition.

Lt. Dave McInturff: When things quieted down after dark, we kept a flare ship up there so we could let our troops see where they were. By that time the gooners were bugging out or had already gone, except for a small contingent they had left behind to drag off or bury their dead.

That night Lieutenant Colonel Hilgartner talked with Lt. Dave McInturff by radio, and the lieutenant told him the enemy was collecting bodies and wounded from the battlefield. Hilgartner saw this as an opportunity to retrieve his own casualties, and he told McInturff to not open fire on the enemy.

The two sides ignored each other in an unofficial truce as each went about collecting their own casualties. Lieutenant Bill Link's platoon drew the casualty detail and brought back all the downed Marines they could find. Delta Company had lost eighteen dead that day and had twenty-two wounded.

When Larry Casselman found his pack the next morning, it had been rifled and the contents scattered about the ground, except for the food, which was taken. He was now the veteran corpsman in the platoon.

Chapter 12

Captain Graham's Last Stand

While Delta Company was fighting for its life, Captain Graham's Foxtrot Company crossed a large, dry paddy to the west. Corporal Harry "Ted" Varena remembers being told that this area had already been swept. In truth, it was infested with hundreds of enemy, and they knew the Marines were moving toward them. At the paddy's edge, a Kit Carson scout named Kinh looked at stacks of straw in the paddy and began shooting at them. The straw concealed spider traps that were occupied by the enemy. The Marines riddled the haystacks with small-arms and machine gun fire, throwing straw, body parts, and blood in all directions. They killed thirty-one of the enemy and started a much bigger fight. On the other side of the paddy, two well-concealed machine guns manned by the soldiers of Maj. Dao Cong's 2nd Battalion, 31st NVA Regiment, rhythmically spat grazing fire into Graham's lead platoon, the 2nd, instantly killing Lt. Straughan Kelsey. Small-arms and mortar fire soon joined the chorus of death. As if that was not enough, another five hundred or more NVA soldiers, these from the 3rd Battalion, 31st NVA Regiment, which had given Delta Company so much grief, hammered Foxtrot Company from the west.

Lance Corporal Roland Legere and his fire team were pinned in the paddy by one of the machine guns to the left and front of Graham's command group. Legere shot four NVA gunners off the gun before they wised up and began firing into the paddy to keep his team pinned. Only two of the four Marines in Legere's fire team survived.

Corporal Ted Varena's squad was also on the left and up front. The enemy decimated his squad, killing and wounding almost everyone. They killed Lance Cpl. Kenneth Endsley right off the bat, and then Lance Cl. Arthur Byrd who was right in front of Varena, and then Lance Cpl. Robert Hernandez, the machine gunner. Finally, Varena was shot in the head. He survived, but he was blind in the left eye for three months.

Private First Class Tom Labarbera was a big, tough kid from Brooklyn who had been assigned as company clerk. Itching to get into a fight, he volunteered to go on this operation as a rifleman. After the initial burst of fire, Labarbera found himself and just one other live Marine isolated on the side of the paddy closest to the enemy. When it all began, there were two Marines, one on either side of Labarbera: Cpl. John Francis and Lance Cpl. John Painter. They were both shot through the head and killed within thirty seconds of each other. LaBarbera's lieutenant, Straughan Kelsey, lay dead, half in and half out of the tree line where the assault had failed, and the paddy was a wasteland of the dead and the dying. The fire tapered off, and an enemy soldier came out of the tree line, saw the slain lieutenant, smiled, and motioned to his fellow soldiers to come forward, thinking all the Marines were dead. Labarbera and Pfc. "Smedley" Butler, the only other functioning Marine at this end of the paddy, opened up on them. Several of the enemy dropped dead in their tracks, and the remainder retreated into the trees. In the brief lull that followed, Butler ran past Labarbera and said, "Let's get the fuck out of here." The two Marines moved back and joined the small company command group. The NVA were regrouping and yelling taunts. "Marine, you die!"

Captain Graham rallied his small headquarters force and attacked through the 2nd Platoon's position. A handful of Marines joined him, including the company gunny, John Green, and Private First Class Labarbera. Graham led his small force into the enemy fire from the front and personally silenced one of the enemy machine guns. When he tried to take out the second gun, he was wounded twice and found that his men were nearly out of ammunition. He supervised the evacuation of the wounded to a slightly safer position and then returned to the paddy to protect Cpl. Marion Dirickson, who was wounded in the chest too badly to be moved. The Marines had tried dragging Dirickson by the ankles, and he shrieked in pain and kept saying, "Leave me, just leave me." Captain Graham ordered the rest of the Marines back, but he stayed by the Marine until the end; his last radio transmission said that he was being overwhelmed by twenty-five NVA.

Pfc. Tom Labarbera: There was a corporal standing there among all that fire before we pulled back. His name was Karl Rische. He said, "I don't know, and I don't care how today is going to work out. I just want you to know that I am as proud as I can possibly be of you guys." Even now I get a chill when I think about that.

Corporal Rische died that day. He was nineteen.

Pfc. Tom Labarbera: By ordering us back when he did, Captain Graham probably saved twenty or thirty lives that day.

Captain Graham was not the only hero of Foxtrot Company. When the initial burst of enemy fire knocked down and killed or wounded many Marines in his platoon, including his platoon commander, Lt. Charles Schultz, Cpl. Lloyd Woods, a radio operator, dodged the intense enemy fire and carried the lieutenant to safety. Then he rallied four other Marines and led them out into the paddy to recover their downed comrades. Enemy machine guns jumped on him, steel predators, preventing further casualty evacuation. Corporal Woods maneuvered to within a few yards of one enemy gun, leapt up, and killed the crew. Then he went after another enemy gun crew and shot them to death or killed them in hand-to-hand combat and, finally, turned the enemy gun on other hostile positions while his companions evacuated the wounded.

Corporal Melvin Long, an African-American squad leader in the 3rd Platoon, led the charge on the left flank of Foxtrot Company's position to try to relieve the pressure. He personally killed six of the enemy in the initial assault. Though badly wounded, he reorganized his squad and continued the attack, overran another enemy position, and held a key piece of terrain. He then led his small force across six hundred meters of fire-swept terrain to relative safety. One witness said that "he looked like a wind-whipped flame, burning brighter and brighter and unquenchable."

It was Gunnery Sgt. John Green's first operation with Foxtrot Company. He placed himself in the forefront of the assault by Captain Graham's headquarters group to relieve pressure on the Marines in the paddy. That done, he attacked with a small force across eight hundred meters of open rice paddy and killed or routed the crew of another enemy machine gun.

Corporal Pat "Water Boo" Haley, rocket squad leader, was in the rear with the 3rd Platoon, which spent most of the day standing watch over the casualties that were brought back. Haley carried no M16, just a .45, and he spent some anxious hours wondering if the enemy would get around to the rear and what he would do if they did.

Lieutenant Colonel Hilgartner's command group monitored the Delta and Foxtrot Company fights by radio and called up air and artillery in their support. As if Hilgartner did not have enough to do, his command group came under heavy mortar, recoilless rifle, and RPG fire. Despite the extensive use of air and artillery by the Marines, the Communist force was too well fortified and too big for the battalion to dislodge by fire. The 1st Battalion command group dug in. The Marines gathered their wounded, but enemy fire drove off the medevac choppers. One Marine was shot through the eye, and the round came out the side of his skull. After he was treated, he got back to his feet and tried to function with a bandage on his head. Another wounded Marine asked for some adhesive tape from a corpsman and taped a letter to his chest because he didn't think he was going to make it out of there.

Lance Cpl. Wayne Puterbaugh: We were low on water, so a bunch of us gathered up all the canteens and went looking for a well. We moved off toward the north. We found a well some four hundred meters away, beside a hooch in a valley. We filled up and did a low crawl back because the battalion was pinned down. On the way back, we passed many dead NVA in spider holes. They were dug in, two rows of them, in a sugar cane field. Most of them seemed to be very big men, 200 pounds or more. They looked more like Chinese.

The Marines pounded the enemy with close air support all afternoon and all night. When the planes came in low to drop their ordnance, the NVA stood up and shot at the aircraft, their tracers seeming to bounce off the jets. While the enemy was exposed, they were easier targets for the Marines who unloaded as much ordnance on them as they could muster. As soon as the aircraft departed, the enemy dropped down into their fighting positions and resumed firing at the Marines on the ground.

Given a brief respite by the close air support, the Leathernecks carried or dragged the dead and wounded into the perimeter. One corpsman staggered toward the lines laden with a dead Marine over his shoulder; blood cascaded down his front and soaked his shirt and pants.

Lieutenant Colonel Hilgartner ordered Capt. Ron Babich's Alpha Company to attack and relieve the pressure on Foxtrot Company.

Lt. Col. Pete "Highpockets" Hilgartner: At about 1400 I had to commit Alpha [Company] to the battle to ward off an enemy attack on Foxtrot's left flank. In the process of moving up to relieve the pressure on Foxtrot, Captain Babich moved to close the gap between Delta and Foxtrot.

Babich had completed his thirteen-month tour in Vietnam, but rather than go home, he volunteered to extend his tour so he could command a rifle company in combat. He always led from the front, and his radio operators fretted because their captain did not seem to know how to duck and would stand up in the heaviest fire. Alpha Company moved down a ravine from a ridgeline to assist Foxtrot, and ran into NVA.

Lt. Paul Kellogg: Captain Babich led the company through terrain in which it was impossible for the Marines to see the concealed enemy because of the vegetation. The Marines got into a heavy firefight with an enemy platoon and scattered them. The 3rd Platoon's lead fire team encountered a lone NVA soldier hidden in a huge rock crevice at ground level, who shot and wounded Babich's point man. The NVA then tried to drag the Marine back to the crevice. When the wounded Marine cried out, two other Marines went to his rescue but were shot and killed by the enemy. Captain Babich ran up to organize an attack on the NVA and was killed while standing and urging his men forward.

One of Babich's radio operators perished with him. The other was seriously wounded. The Marines flanked the enemy soldiers and killed them. The Alpha Company Marines did not reach Foxtrot Company that night. Lieutenant Link, Foxtrot's senior surviving officer, moved the company back and dug in. The next morning Hilgartner assigned Capt. Jerry McKay, his communications officer, to take over Alpha Company. Communications officers do not normally command rifle companies in combat, but Hilgartner had full confidence in McKay,[8] who had also commanded Alpha Company on Union I.

Many young officers, like Babich, felt that they were invincible. Lieutenant Kellogg mused that it was probably best for them to get a nonfatal wound early in a tour in order to erase that feeling of invincibility. Captain McElroy used to tell his experienced NCOs to "get the 'tourist' out of these young lieutenants as soon as you can."

With two of his company commanders dead, the remainder of Lieutenant Colonel Hilgartner's force had their hands full with a determined Communist force that was too dug-in to be dislodged. He asked Colonel Houghton for assistance, and Houghton immediately went to Maj. Gen.

Marines from the 2nd Battalion, 5th Marines, exit helicopters in a hot landing zone on their way to reinforce fellow Marines in June 1967. *USMC*

Donn Robertson, the commanding general of the 1st Marine Division, who authorized the emergency deployment of Lt. Col. Mallett Jackson's 2nd Battalion, 5th Marines, the division reserve. Jackson's battalion was a mishmash of companies and consisted of his own Echo Company; Delta Company from the 1st Battalion, 7th Marines; and Echo Company from the 2nd Battalion, 7th Marines.

Colonel Houghton ordered a ninety-minute air and artillery prep of the landing zone, and at 1900 two companies of the 2nd Battalion, 5th Marines, landed unopposed, just south of Route 534 and about two clicks north of the Delta and Foxtrot fight. Helicopter glitches plagued their movement. Mechanical problems grounded Jackson's helicopter and marooned the colonel in the rear. By radio, he ordered his S3, Maj. Dick Esau, to take command and lead the attack. Two companies of the battalion got on the ground and stood by, awaiting the third company so they could march toward the enemy flank. Night fell, and Jackson's third company had still not shown up. Jackson received permission to begin the attack with just two companies. Colonel Houghton granted them permission to attack. The 2nd Battalion, 5th Marines, ran into a withdrawing enemy force in the dark and fought their way through them, but not without taking some wounded and dead. The Marines spotted a CH-53 Super Stallion helicopter overhead, and the FAC asked for an emergency medevac. The bird landed among impacting mortars, but the pilot sat on the ground until all the casualties were loaded. When the chopper landed in Da Nang, the crew counted fifty-eight holes in the skin of the ship.

Lance Cpl. John Payne (60mm mortar man, Echo Company, 2nd Battalion, 5th Marines): The word came down that Foxtrot 2/5 had gotten into serious trouble. Echo 2/5 staged around lunchtime, but we didn't saddle up until almost dusk. At night we choppered in and staged in B-52 bomb craters for a while, then Echo Company headed up a trail, single file, toward Foxtrot's position. For some reason our 60mm mortar platoon was walking point. Soon after beginning our movement, a squad of NVA ambushed our point and wounded a couple of our men.

Our column swung to the right into a graveyard and set up a perimeter, where I ended up on the right flank. The NVA were mainly located in a tree line several hundred yards away. Small-arms, automatic, and mortar fire came from their position. The firefight was fairly intense. I spotted an NVA forward observer about a hundred yards away, but my M16 jammed when I tried to kill him. My buddy Dennis Curtin's rifle also jammed when he tried. The FO seemed oblivious to it all. The NVA dropped a mortar in front of our 60mm mortar squad and wounded a couple of our Marines. Then a medevac chopper arrived, and enemy fire killed the door gunner as they came in.

The fighting was a stalemate for a couple of hours until two F-4 Phantoms arrived. They roared out of the darkness at low altitude, the sight and sound of them nearly enough to intimidate the enemy. The two pilots had a creative way of pinpointing and destroying the enemy guns. One F-4 with all of its lights *on* flew over the enemy position, and the NVA filled the air with green and white tracers, clearly marking where their automatic weapons were located.

The fire and the roar of the jet masked the sound of the second F-4 flying hard on the heels of the first. It came in at treetop level with all of its lights off, savaged the gun positions and took the starch out of the enemy unit. The Marines felt the heat from the napalm several hundred yards away. As they usually did, the NVA left a few soldiers behind at the fortified positions to cover the withdrawal of the main force back into the hills. Marine supporting arms made short work of these remnants and unloaded artillery and canister after canister of napalm on them.

At 1930 that night, Mike Company of the 3rd Battalion, 5th Marines, moved in attack formation and found the enemy facing them across a 1,400-meter front.

Cpl. Steve Walker/Haygood (3.5-inch rocket man, Mike Company): We hit a bunch of resistance in the ville and got pinned down for several hours in a paddy. The 1st Platoon was on the right flank of an on-line formation. We could not move. If I moved my head up from my position flat on my stomach to look around, I got shot at. In four or five hours, I must have got shot at fifteen to twenty times, close enough to either have dirt kicked up on me, or rounds loud enough and close enough to hurt my ears. We had one guy that no one liked; he was a real whiner, and he just snapped and went crazy. He jumped up in the middle of this, shouting, "I can't take it anymore! I can't take it anymore!" Immediately he got shot a couple of times and was wounded quite seriously. No one could get to him. A corpsman tried and was himself wounded. It rattled everybody a little bit because he started crying and hollering for his mother, and that went on for a maybe an hour or so, and then he quieted down and died.

Lt. Kenny Moore: Late in the afternoon, about 1600, we were ordered to prepare for night activities. I now had two platoons spread across a front and an open left flank. We got the word about 1700 that Mike and India were going to make a night attack. I had India and was the junior guy. McElroy had Mike. We had about four hours to prepare, and we did a classic night attack; sent a patrol out after dark, which crawled up and found the company release points. Mike was behind us as we went to the release points, and India took the left, and Mike took the right. We waited to cross the line of departure. There was a full moon out, and all of a sudden the enemy mortars started up and fired over us, about eighty mortar rounds, and they were landing nearby the battalion CP. I got a call from McElroy, who chewed tobacco, and he wanted to know if anyone had any Red Man chewing tobacco. Any cigars?

We were up to the line of departure, about 100 to 125 meters from the objective. McElroy's end squad, on the right, was too close to the enemy, and his line of departure was nearly into the enemy's forward edge of the battle area. When the NVA activated their final protective fires, we counted thirty-eight to forty machine guns. They covered us on a 180 degree basis, from the right side and on the left, all occupied by NVA. We are down below twelve-inch paddy dikes and trying to get close to the ground. No one was hit, but they were outgunning us. We counted a couple of larger guns that might have been antiaircraft guns, probably 50mms. We called for artillery and couldn't get it, because 1/5 had something going. We were on hold and didn't do anything for two hours. This was between 2200 and 2400. McElroy called again and said, "Do you have any chewing tobacco? If you have some, I'll crawl over and get it." We had a guy who had some Red Man. McElroy crawled over and gave this kid a hundred bucks for the tobacco.

About midnight, artillery came up, and we got a fire mission from 155s. They fired a huge number of rounds into those objectives. The artillery guy told the FO that that was all they had except for three smoke rounds. They fired the smoke, and that was our signal to take the hill. We made the assault at about 0400. There were no NVA that were able to engage, but a tremendous number of NVA casualties. Lieutenant Stan Holmes, the FO, did a terrific job. There were body parts all over the place.

Cpl. Steve Walker/Haygood: We set up for the night, but we didn't dig in. We were told the noise would let the gooks know where our positions were. About 0300, word was passed to drop our packs and keep on our web gear; we fixed bayonets and moved out to a tree line that had us pinned all day. We were on line, shoulder to shoulder, with about five-meter spacing, and about fifty meters from the tree line, the word was passed to put our weapons on full automatic.

Everyone was sure the shit would let loose—just one round of incoming would have been all it took—but nothing was there, nothing. About an hour after sunrise, the villagers and village chieftain returned. The chief told us that the NVA left just after dark the previous night. We had pulled back at the same time that they did.

Capt. Jim McElroy: We moved out really early the next morning, and we finally made it up the knoll, and one of the guys stepped on an NVA doctor's back. He was in a hole and had a tree over him. He was a little short, fat guy and was just kind of laughing, and he pointed out the route they were evacuating their wounded on. He was the only prisoner I ever saw the Kit Carson scouts chat with, not be angry with. They had a ball talking to this guy. About five feet three inches tall, he looked like a forty-eight-year old that had been eating too much. He had on a brand-new uniform, not a spot on it.

The next morning found the living enemy gone from the battlefield. The Marines counted 476 enemy bodies around the Huy Vinh village complex, at a cost of 71 Marines killed and 139 wounded. Colonel Kenneth

Houghton, the commanding officer of the 5th Marines, visited the battlefield that morning and praised the courage and skill of the Marines. He told them they had gutted an NVA regiment.

The Marines also found marks, indicating that the enemy used a travois to transport their wounded. The Marines followed the drag marks, but by the time they tended to their own wounded and dead Marines and counted the enemy corpses, they could not catch up with the main body of the enemy. The Marines' highest priority was evacuating their own casualties from the battlefield, a necessary mission of mercy that always delayed pursuit.

In Delta Company's sector, 1st Lt. Dave McInturff policed the battlefield.

Lt. Dave McInturff: The next day we were picking up our dead and wounded and getting them out, and we found the big, Chinese-looking guys.

Two choppers came in, and I'll be a sonofabitch if they didn't land, and a bunch of goddamned press people got off. I told Gunny Fish to get our wounded on the helos, and the pilot wouldn't let us load the casualties. Those bastards sat there and waited until the reporters finished their interviews.

The gunny never did tell me we temporarily lost a squad, but we linked up with them when they finally found us. I had a couple of guys shuttling back and forth all night, redistributing ammo.

The remainder of Alpha went over and uncovered Foxtrot the next day because Alpha was the least beat-up of Hilgartner's units.

Cpl. Lynwood Scott: We [3rd Battalion, 5th Marines] were receiving fire from the top of a hill where the NVA were, and we had about seven wounded. I sat there and took my helmet off and was eating a C-ration, and a round came in, barely creased my head, and stuck in the tree. Colonel Webster was sitting across from me about thirty yards away, and a corpsman came over and shaved my head. Webster came over, and the doc said, "He is going to have to be medevaced for possible concussion." Webster said to me, "We lost a lot of men on the twenty-sixth, and I need you to stay. Will you stay?" I told Webster, "Alright, I'll stay." As the corpsman was working on my head, the helo lifted off, and a recoilless rifle hit it on the front. It crashed back down. I would have been on that chopper. The chopper burned, but we got everyone out except for the pilots.

Lieutenant Colonel Hilgartner said that Union I and II gave the battalion a sense of confidence that they were the best.

Lt. Col. Pete "Highpockets" Hilgartner: My Marines became cocky bastards who wouldn't take crap from anybody, either on the battlefield or in the regimental beer hall.

Webster's 3rd Battalion, 5th Marines, killed 227 enemy by body count and estimated killing an additional 379. They captured 20 NVA and lost 51 killed and 130 wounded. Hilgartner's 1st Battalion, 5th Marines, suffered 55 killed in action and 74 wounded in action. They killed 458 of the enemy by body count and probably another 425. Air and artillery killed even more.

On June 3, the 3rd Battalion, 5th Marines, patrolled through a cluster of five deserted hamlets a click and a half south of the Foxtrot action of the day before. Used battle dressings and blood spots covered the ground.

There was no more significant contact until the operation was terminated. Once again the Marines inflicted a great number of casualties on the enemy and drove them from the valley. The 2nd NVA Division was, for the moment, ineffective. Major General Thao had not the men, the prospects of immediate reinforcements, or the desire to send what he had left of his units against the Marines in the type of multi-battalion fights that characterized operations Union I and Union II. But he continued to infiltrate small units into the valley, to let the Marines know that he was still in the game. Throughout the summer, these small units and the Marines played hide-and-seek in vicious, intense, small engagements that added to the casualty counts for both sides. Some of these fights were against local Viet Cong units and others against NVA.

Lt. Kenny Moore: About the third of June we were moving, when I heard this commotion and a bunch of firing on the left flank. I only had corporals as platoon commanders. I was the company commander. I called over to the 3rd Platoon and asked what was going on, and they said, "Lieutenant, you'd better come over here."

This Marine had gone over a paddy dike and stepped on a python, maybe ten feet long, skinny and slim. My policy was to carry eighteen rounds in the magazine and one in the chamber. He fired at the snake, all nineteen rounds, and missed him, and the snake bit him near the knee and started to wrap around his leg. It was amazing he didn't blow his foot off. He had the snake by the head and was holding on with both hands. It was wrapping around his leg, and he was screaming for all he was worth. Everyone else was lying on the ground with tears in their eyes from laughing so hard. I got a stick and went over and got the snake off this guy and threw it in the brush, and we continued to move.

About three weeks later, we were on an operation and making a night move from Que Son city directly west about eight clicks and then up into a gap between two mountain ridges. We were going to make an attack at the first light of dawn. We had just made the turn north to go up to these ridges. My flank security discovered the NVA. We put a blocking force on the trail and hit them with the flank security and grenades and rifle fire. We killed about eight, including an NVA paymaster. I passed out the "Monopoly" money, North Vietnamese money, to the platoon.

We started moving again, and we were behind schedule and trying to pick it up. Flank security was ahead of the point about twenty meters on each side. On the left side we heard a bloodcurdling scream. I called the 1st Squad, and they didn't know what was going on. It took me about ten minutes to get over there, and we heard this screaming. We found a crevasse about four feet wide on top and twelve feet deep. It was narrower than that at the bottom. This guy, the same guy who had stepped on the python before, had just stepped off in there but wasn't hurt. He bent over to get his rifle and felt this thing that was alive and moving down there, and he screamed. We got there and shone a flashlight down in the hole, and he had this snake. The huge snake's mouth was clenched on his left shoulder, and it was trying to wrap around his body. The snake was dug in. All my squads carried a rappelling hook with about forty feet of rope. We got the first hook on his pack, and about ten Marines pulled it, and we couldn't budge the guy. We got another hook down there and got into his belt, and we still couldn't move him, with twenty Marines pulling on him. Pretty soon we had three hooks on the Marine and one on the snake itself. We had about forty Marines pulling, and we got the guy out of the hole. The snake was still attached. We cut the head of the snake off, but he was still crushing the guy and still constricting. This corpsman said the snake's muscles are like bands of steel around this Marine's body, and we have to slit the bands. We cut down the body of the snake and got the guy out. We laid out the snake and paced it off, and it was over twenty-five feet long.

Now we were behind schedule, so I had to pull flank security in to pick it up. We got in position for the attack and were due to kick off at 0500 sharp. I was in position, and this corpsman said, "We have to medevac this guy." I said, "He is not in danger of dying. Put something where the teeth marks are, and let's get on with it." The corpsman said, "Would you just take fifteen seconds and just speak with him?" "Ok, doc, get the kid up here." He came up and took off his helmet and said, "Pfc. so and so, sir." His hair had turned

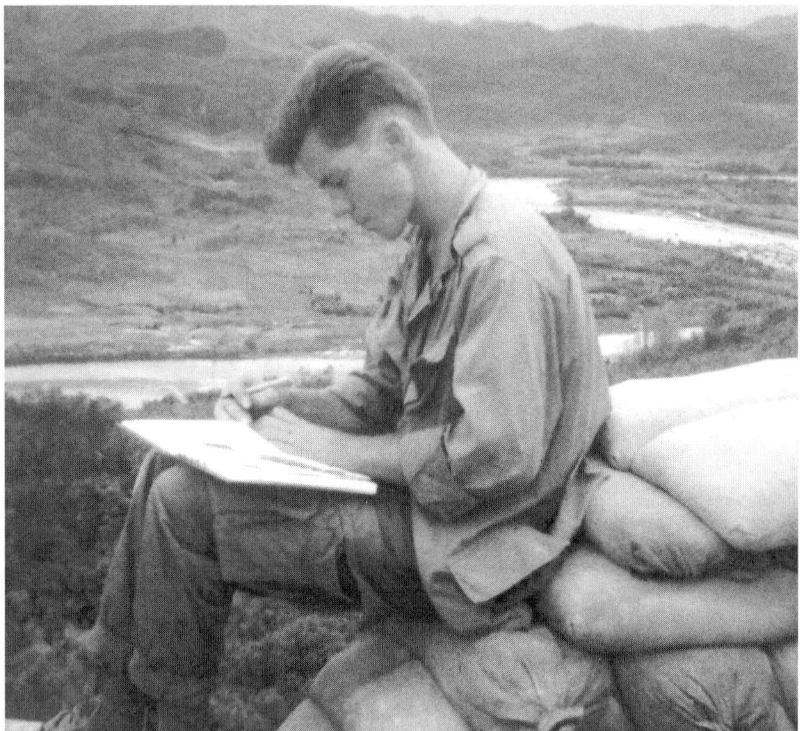

Corporal Luther Hamilton writes a letter home from Nong Son Hill after Foxtrot Company was overrun on the hill, 1967. *Courtesy Harold Wadley*

white, and he was 18 years old. I had the corpsman keep him until the next day, when we medevaced him, and I never saw him again.

In a pause between major operations, eighteen-year-old Pfc. Melvin Newlin, a machine gunner with Foxtrot Company, 2nd Battalion, 5th Marines, defended to the death his position at Nong Son, the only coal mine in Vietnam. He was posthumously awarded the Medal of Honor for his actions.

After two big operations, the Marines began to appreciate the ability of the NVA to dig in and fortify. When their scouts saw a Marine unit on the move, they would often prepare a defensive position with astonishing speed and hope to draw the Marines into an ambush. One way they did this was to send one or a small body of their soldiers out to reveal themselves to the Marines and then scamper in a zigzag pattern back in the direction of where

Charlie Company, 1st Battalion, 5th Marines moving out from Hill 51. Larry Koslowski, with M60 machine gun, facing camera on left. Coonrod, other name not remembered, facing camera on right. *Courtesy John Rusth*

they had set up their ambush. After a few hard lessons in which a few Marines took off after them and a squad got pinned down and then a platoon and then maybe a company, the Marines learned to be careful when pursuing them.

Most military units in combat move with a logistics *tail;* that is, their supplies and support follow them into combat and then are called up when needed. The NVA could not do this, because once they engaged in battle, their logistics train would be exposed to allied supporting arms. Instead, they used what army Gen. Creighton Abrams was to later describe as a logistics *nose*. First they would determine their objectives. Then they would plan their routes of advance and secure these routes by sending small cadres out to convince or intimidate the villagers to help them set up reconnaissance screens. Children were particularly useful for this role. Once that was done, they would press villagers and local VC cadres into fortifying their objective. They prepared extensive trenches, reinforced bunkers, and spider holes; laid communications wire; and strung barbed wire when they had it. As that was going on, they would send their supplies, ammunition, rations, and sometimes their heavier weapons to the objective, moving it in small quantities and at night. Finally, when all was prepared, they would send their main-force units, again in small formations, to recombine near the objective and occupy the carefully prepared positions. Their lightly burdened soldiers could move so rapidly that their sudden appearance in one place or another often confounded the Marines.

The NVA were masters at using combined arms, even though they were often primitive by American standards. Once an allied unit moved into their killing zones, they would stop it with small-arms and automatic-weapons fire. If the NVA had time to put them in, the borders of the route the Marines were taking were sown with booby traps and punji stakes. The immediate instinct when coming under a lot of fire is to hit the deck away from the fire. Very often, especially along trails, Marines did what their training and instincts told them to do, and they tripped booby traps or became impaled on punji stakes and became casualties. Once the allied force was pinned down, the enemy would pound it with mortars and whatever crew-served weapons were available. Very rarely did the NVA stay in a position overnight after contact was made. Not wanting to fall under the heavy fist of allied artillery and air support in broad daylight, they would withdraw before dawn, leaving a few soldiers behind to give the allies pause.

Just after Union II ended, Lt. Ben Drollinger reported in to the 1st Marine Division Headquarters, where they told him to report to the 1st Battalion,

Sergeant Shafer, Foxtrot, 2nd Battalion, 5th Marines, shares his canteen with "Charlie the pup" at Phu Loc (6), 1967. *Courtesy Harold Wadley*

5th Marines. When he asked where that was, an officer pointed generally in the direction of a map and said, "They're down there, and we haven't heard from them in two weeks." After riding around in trucks and helos, he finally ended up at the 5th Marines' command post to meet the colonel.

Lt. Ben Drollinger: The colonel pointed and said the battalion is out there. Just then a Phantom dropped a load of napalm nearby. "Oh, shit!" That's how I was introduced to 1/5.

Drollinger finally found the battalion and met Lieutenant Colonel Hilgartner, who assigned him to Captain Reese's Bravo Company. Reese gave him the 1st Platoon. He quickly gained a great deal of respect for Reese and Hilgartner.

Lt. Ben Drollinger: It's hard for some people to understand that if you keep pressure on somebody and keep moving against them, then they can't hit you. And that is what Hilgartner did. Anytime he became engaged, he pushed and pushed and pushed. If we had resupply helicopters come in, we would move as soon as it got dark to keep from getting mortared. If we had been moving on a north-south axis, he would move us on an east-west axis. Moving at night scared the shit of me, but that is what both he and Captain Reese would do.

The Marines have often been called the "American Spartans" because they always fight with older equipment and expect none of the amenities that U.S. Army units enjoy. Since they are always the last to be supplied with a new item of equipment, they are always looking for ways to improve the "supply system."

Lance Cpl. Ken Fields: We were set in next to an army unit and noticed that they had poncho liners, a piece of gear that had not yet been issued to the Marines. The CO of the army company complained to Lt. J. D. Murray that someone had stolen his. J. D. got the company together and said, "Whoever stole the captain's poncho liner should give it back." When no one answered, the army captain said, to his credit, "Anyone who is slick enough to steal a poncho liner from me can keep it." Soon after that, Mike Company started down the road on a route march and was about a hundred yards away from the army's position, and *everybody* started pulling out poncho liners.

Chapter 13

Operation Adair: The Two-Platoon Fight

After the close of Union II, the pace and intensity of the fight for the Que Son Valley dropped off to its pre-Union levels and stayed that way for nearly three months. The Marines had mauled the NVA, and they kept their large units out of the valley. Instead, they sent squad-, platoon-, and company-sized units forth to let the Marines know that they were still in the game. To keep the NVA off balance, the Marines continued their sweep operations on the valley floor. Nearly every day the two sides clashed in deadly, bitter, but small struggles. Although Marines and NVA continued to fight and die, none of these operations reached the scale of either Union operation or of the operations to follow. Kipling would have called them "penny fights." There were several of these actions; three of them were named Adair, Pike, and Cochise.

Lieutenant Colonel Webster needed to break in his newest company commander, Capt. Joseph "Joe" Tenney, who replaced the wounded Lt. Bob Tilley as commanding officer of Kilo Company, 3rd Battalion, 5th Marines. Everyone expected the operation, which they dubbed Adair, would be a walk in the sun, a routine multi-day patrol. Tenney's 2nd Platoon was providing security for the regimental headquarters, so the captain had to make do with his 1st and 3rd Platoons. The understrength company set out on the morning of June 14.

The terrain over which they were to operate was near the eastern end of the valley and not far from the battalion headquarters, so Tenney's Marines could easily be reinforced if need be. The Marines, the NVA, and the ARVN had fought over this ground in the early months of the war, and it was honeycombed with fighting holes, trenches, and bomb craters that looked from the air like giant acne scars.

Private First Class Bob "Whit" Whitfield, a rifleman, joined the company just after Union II and was assigned to Lt. Wayne Brandon's 1st Platoon. Whit's squad leader was Cpl. Larry Beavers, who Whit described as "super, laid back, and so cool under heavy fire." Whit's mother sent him raspberry instant drink mix, which he hated, and he gave it to Beavers, who loved the stuff.

Whit was amazed at the loads they were required to carry. He thought to himself that he had better be near or next to a tree or a hole when they got hit, because he could not imagine running with all that gear. Indeed, most of the time the Marines wore a flak jacket and helmet and carried three canteens and a pack with an entrenching tool strapped to the back and which contained rations, socks, and anything the individual Marine had the stamina to carry. They also carried gas masks, battle dressings for wounds, many magazines for their weapons, hand grenades, a weapon, and a bayonet.

If he was a mortar man, machine gunner, or 3.5-inch rocket man, his load was even heavier. Because the M16s were unreliable, most company commanders had the troops carry extra machine gun ammo, light antitank assault weapons (LAAWs), and/or extra 60mm mortar rounds, for the company commander's own personal artillery. For many, the load ran to eighty pounds or more.

The company moved out in tactical formation and without incident for the first few hours. Near the end of the day, Captain Tenney sent Lt. Joaquin "Jack" Gracida and a ten-man recon patrol across a brush-covered plateau. Thanks to his two outstanding point men, the Native American "Fearless Warrior" Weahkee and a Hawaiian named Joseph "Momoa" Kamaka, the patrol spotted a large number of NVA hiding in an ambush position. The Marines killed two of them and withdrew. Tenney called up air support and artillery and pummeled an estimated one hundred VC, driving them northward and killing them as they fled.

In the quiet night that followed, a Kit Carson scout monitored VC radio traffic. He reported to Tenney that the VC were planning an ambush but gave no information about when or where this was to take place.

The next morning, June 15, Kilo Company saddled up and moved out and swept to the north. They planned to swing back to the east and return to the battalion command post. The Marines paused in the deserted hamlet of Binh Hoi (2) to draw water from the well. While they filled canteens, the point observed enemy activity in the hamlet of Binh Hoi (3), just under a click away to the northeast. Tenney later admitted that the activity should have set alarm bells off in his head but did not, because of his inexperience. Lieutenant Jack Gracida told Tenney that something looked fishy. He pointed out that the farmers were taking away their water buffalos and were not working the field. "They are worried about something."

Pfc. Bob Whitfield: During the sweep toward this hamlet, Corporal Beavers went, "Oh shit, look at this." And four or five gooks ran from that atoll into the main hedge row. Beavers said, "We aren't going anywhere, the new CO, he's got to get his glory. I guarantee you, we're going to be going right into a trap on this one." It spooked me.

Pfc. Thom Heidtman: I was walking point for Lieutenant Brandon's 1st Platoon. The paddies were bone dry. We walked along, and I passed and ignored three hooches in about one thousand acres of paddy. A little while later there were two more hooches, and I ignored them too. I got to this ville, and there was a tree line running up to the ville in an L-shape, and there was a thirty-yard rice paddy and then a hill covered with brush that rose up very steeply. I stopped and told everyone to get down, and Lieutenant Brandon ran up and said, "What is the matter?" and I said, "Lieutenant, if I was going to ambush someone, this is where I would do it."

I wanted to take everyone over the hill to the left, away from the village that was to the right, with a trail around the outside. The radioman came running up to Brandon and handed him the handset, and he listened and then said, "Yessir." Lieutenant Brandon didn't want to take the company through a cut between the ville and the hill, and I sure didn't want to go there. Orders came on the radio to go back and check out the hooches we had passed. The company turned around, so instead of being point, I was the last guy in line. I had a bag of mixed nuts in my pack and was munching on them as I walked along in the rear. We checked out the hooches, and there was nothing there. I knew that if there were, it would have to be the dumbest enemy in the world.

Pfc. Bob Whitfield: We walked through the hedge row, and when I made a left-hand turn, I looked down, and there was a grenade rigged as a booby trap. Our engineers blew it. Twenty feet on, I found a hole where the gooks had been going in. There was an Indian, Weahkee, who was a tunnel rat and comical as hell and a helluva good man. He went in there and looked around, and there was nothing there.

CAPTAIN TENNEY TOLD THE 3rd PLATOON COMMANDER, Staff Sgt. Paul Orlett, to take his men down a stream bed and then cover the advance of the 1st Platoon, which was to move directly toward the hamlet that was screened by a hedge row. Orlett misunderstood the order, and instead of remaining in the stream bed, he moved his platoon straight at the hamlet across an 800-meter paddy.

Tenney sent his executive officer, Lt. Jack Gracida, after him to correct the situation. In the meantime, Brandon's 1st Platoon and Tenney's command group were about 150 meters out into the paddy when he decided to recon the tree line in front of them by fire (that is, to fire into a suspected enemy position and see if anyone shot back).

Pfc. Thom Heidtman: They put us on line, and I was on the left. We are about a thousand meters from this other ville and were told to recon by fire, which was hard to do when the M16s weren't working.

CAPTAIN TENNEY TOLD ORLETT'S PLATOON to move back and lay down a base of fire while Lt. Wayne Brandon's 1st Platoon enveloped from the left. The Marines sent fire at the tree line, and that set off a violent reaction from the NVA. The Marines found themselves on the receiving end of mortar, machine gun, and small-arms fire.

Pfc. Bob Whitfield: As soon as we started moving out toward the main hedge row, with the ville on the left, they stopped the column, and a guy named Jack Ross, a machine gunner, opened up. We started toward the village when Jack began shooting, and I was so scared I thought I was going to piss myself. I had seen nothing like what was about to kick off.

I was looking at Jack Ross, and I was at twelve o'clock, and he was at two o'clock to my right but up ahead about 150 yards, and he started raking the hedge row with the M60. He disappeared in a cloud of dust because of the AK fire that was being fired back at him. All of a sudden you wake up and think, "Holy shit, that was a round that just went by." Snapping and cracking past me like I was pulling butts on the rifle range. I'm getting shot at!

Most of the fire was coming from our right. I started running to get down and get on line. The paddy was dry as a bone and like concrete, and where the water boos had been, there were holes. My foot went into one of those and went down. My helmet went off, my entrenching tool that wasn't secured hit me in the back of the head, and I thought I had been shot.

I crawled up on a three-foot embankment the guys were lining up on. I was the next-to-the-last guy. The shit was really hitting the fan. Explosions were going off. As we were lying there, something kicked up behind my leg, and then it kicked up again and sprayed little pebbles on me. I looked over, and we were taking fire from our left rear.

I tapped the Marine next to me, and we started shooting over there. Somebody hollered, "What the hell are you shooting over there for?" and I told them that the fire was coming from over there.

Brandon's platoon swept through Binh Hoi (1), an intermediate objective, and was headed toward Binh Hoi (3), flushing the enemy before them. They no sooner had the enemy on the run than the M16s began to fail, and many of Brandon's Marines fell to their knees, trying to clear their rifles. With the diminution of fire, the NVA stopped retreating, reversed course, and came right at the Marines.

Pfc. Bob Whitfield: The guy next to me and I turned back, and the other guys were going up over the bank and at the hedge row. We were about half a step behind. When I came up and stopped to help the guy next to me up, the wind had billowed out my shirt, two rounds went right through it and hit my cigarettes and a brand-new Zippo. I was really pissed. We assaulted on line, and it was really creepy. The dirt was kicking up around. I saw half a dozen guys go down. I remember training for this stuff but never thought I would do it.

They started lobbing 60mm mortars on us. I think the CO was trying to move us up to connect with the 3rd Platoon, but the assault kind of fell apart. Everyone was running for cover when the mortars started going off, and I dove over a paddy dike and got hit. And I remember looking up, and there was a radioman and Captain Tenney.

Tenney was lying about thirty feet ahead of me with his left side up against that dike. We were taking rounds right directly down that dike. He got hit in the back of the head, and it blew his helmet off. A corpsman jumped over the dike and came to me and said, "Hang in there," and I said, "Go take care of the CO." As long as I could shoot, I was happy. I kept shooting, and the next thing I remember is medevac choppers coming in.

Lance Cpl. Richard Byrne (60mm mortar man.): When we were hit, I began firing mortar rounds into the tree line. We were getting so much return fire that Staff Sergeant Orlett, I, and a corpsman moved into some bamboo. Suddenly, a squad of NVA appeared, moving from left to right just a few feet away on the other side of the bamboo. I drew my .45, and just as I was about to shoot, Orlett put his hand on my .45 and pushed it down.

Pfc. Thom Heidtman: We get to this village, and I was on the extreme left next to my squad leader, Sgt. Willie Davis. Davis had extended his tour in Vietnam and went back on leave to see his new baby in Chicago, and came back to Kilo. We were about forty yards from the village, and Davis was shot in the thigh with a Thompson submachine gun. I crawled over to him and started to bandage him up. It appeared to be a flesh wound because it wasn't bleeding enough for the femoral artery to have been hit, and he wasn't in enough pain for a bone to have been hit. I told him he would be fine. The NVA sprayed us again; two rounds went through my pack, and one round went through my shirt and creased my chest, and the blood ran down to my belly button. It hit my plastic cigarette case in my pocket, knocked a button off, and hit my squad leader in the belly. I screamed for a corpsman, and nothing happened, so I screamed every obscenity I could think of.

Doc Clinton Caszatt (corpsman, Lieutenant Brandon's platoon): We got separated because some guys went to the right and some to the left. The guys who went to the left [would appear] on the KIA list except Ernesto Sanchez, who was off to my right. We had no radioman. Mortars and machine guns were coming in, and we were trying to get into the tree line. Don Lehuta from Missoula, one of my best friends, went down with a through-and-through wound to the chest. I lay on top of him and patched the holes and put him up so the injured side was down. A machine gun kept shooting at us from the tree line. They were hollerin' for a corpsman, so I went down there. We had no radio, so we couldn't get a medevac. The next guy I went to was Sergeant Davis. He was still alive and complaining about his legs. I slit his trousers with my KA-BAR and looked at the wounds on his legs, which weren't that bad, and I knew something was wrong. Then he started talking about how thirsty he was, and I pulled up his shirt, and he had been shot in the stomach.

I looked at Lance Cpl. Jerry Forehand, and there wasn't anything I could do. He was shot through the head from the front side. A Polish kid we called "Ski" carried a LAAW, and he fired it while lying on his side, caught the back-blast, and had to be medevaced out. I carried a pistol, grenades, and a rifle. Tom Haugen wanted my rifle, but I wouldn't give it up, and my pistol was so full of sand that I didn't think I could crank a round in the chamber.

Lance Cpl. Paul Malboeuf: I volunteered to be a machine gunner. We could tell when there was something wrong with a village. We were reconning by fire and moving though the paddy and trying to get to the tree line. Tenney called up air support and artillery under the direction of an AO. The ordnance landed in the midst of an estimated one hundred VC and drove them away.

Whoever was reconning by fire tripped the ambush. We were about thirty or forty yards out from the tree line. Then it hit: withering fire. To my front was a well, and I had my gun set up. There was a gook with a weapon that had a bipod, firing at me with a light machine gun or BAR, and we were trying to put each other down. I fired across a 180-degree arc across my entire front. I put a lot of fire into that well area, trying to suppress the NVA. And then all of a sudden my a-gunner [assistant gunner] said the rounds were falling out of the barrel. We had cooked the barrel. The a-gunner was hit, so I changed the smoking-hot barrel with my bare hands and didn't really give a shit if I burned them, since I was trying to survive. We got the other barrel in and got some more ammo in, and I got hit with a concussion grenade that blew me up in the air and off the gun. I thought I was full of holes. My ears were ringing, and someone came to my aid and started stripping me to see if I was hit. I thought I had bought the farm, but I didn't have any holes. We moved all the wounded into a hooch where Doc Caszatt was working overtime. We were all trying to give first aid, even me. I was trying to take care of Lance Cpl. Ernesto Sanchez, who was hit with small-arms fire and got a sucking chest wound. I put some plastic over his chest wound. He asked if he was going to make it, and I told him that he was, and he died in my arms. The medevacs came in, and the doctors put a tag on me.

There was a cave in the ville, which provided some cover for the Marines when the mortars hit. Inside the cave, Lieutenant Brandon looked around and said, "Where is Retisik?" Someone stuck his head out and hollered for him, but no one answered. After the mortars quit, the Marines found him outside the cave lying on his poncho sound asleep.

Pfc. Thom Heidtman: Flynn, a corpsman from Wyoming, Michigan, came running over, and the same guy that shot Davis shot at Flynn. I saw a small puff of smoke come out of the tree line. It didn't dawn on me what it was. I yelled at Flynn, and he was face-down. He lifted his face up and opened his eyes, and he had so much dirt on his face that he looked like he was in blackface. I had to laugh among all this horror show. We turned Davis over, and Flynn shook his head and gave me some morphine and told me to dope him up. I looked over, and there were two FNG corporals with a guy who had been shot in the ankle. I yelled to these two corporals to ask the wounded guy if he could walk, and he said, "I'll try." On the count of three, they grabbed him and made it over to the bomb crater. We got off a single shot each, and I shoved the morphine in Davis's thigh, and five minutes later he died.

The air strikes were coming, and jets were right over my head. I looked up, and it said "Navy" on a jet, and he was about fifty feet over my head. He put the napalm in as well as if he had put it in with a forklift. It was about a hundred yards away, and it was the only time I ever felt like running away. But I didn't; I stayed there with Davis. It was hotter than hell.

During the air strike, I was lying on my back with my rifle. I put my towel on my belly and started oiling my weapon, taking the magazine apart and carefully oiling and reinserting the rounds. I cleaned the chamber, douched everything down with oil, put everything together, and told these two corporals to come with me. "We are going up to the village." I thought about that puff of smoke and my squad leader getting killed. We crawled up along the edge of the village and were about to go through the gate on the count of three. One guy said, "Let's throw grenades." So on the count of three, we all threw a grenade. Two grenades went into the ville, and the other one bounced off the bamboo and came down like a pinball. It exploded and slowed us down and might have saved our lives. I got up and was covering these two guys. Just then I saw an NVA head pop up about fifteen feet away, and I had to stop these two Marines because we were supposed to go through the gate on the count of three, and I had two fingers in the air. I stopped and waved them down, and as soon as I put my finger back on my trigger, the head popped up, and I shot him right in the eye. I knew that I got him although he disappeared. All three of us ran through the gate and sprayed the area. Then we went back a bit and set up in a bunch of saplings on the enemy flank.

The company was engaged to my right. There was an enemy automatic weapon next to a stone well that was shooting at the Marines. We fired a few rounds toward the well and where we could see bodies moving around. We had flanked the NVA but, with just with the three of us, we had little chance of rolling up their flank. We went back to the hole and hauled the body out, and then I reached down and got hold of this homemade bandolier with Thompson magazines in it. The gook had six or seven magazines, and I couldn't lift the damn thing, it was so heavy. I got a better grip and changed my body position and hauled it out. Then we hauled the dead guy out and his brand-new Thompson. It was very well cared for and had a whole lot of oil on it and was probably the source of the puff of smoke I saw earlier. It occurred to me that I had known where the guy was, but it didn't register, and he could have killed us all from fifteen feet away.

Our platoon sergeant, Tom Haugen, from Arizona, was a big, John Wayne sort of guy, about six feet four inches, with big shoulders and very gung ho. He appeared, grabbed the body in one hand and the Thompson in the other, ran to the gate of the ville, held them up like trophies, and gave a rebel yell sort of thing. Then he dropped the body and ran diagonally across the firefight to where he had come from. He took the Thompson with him, and that was the last I saw of it. He had thrown the body down, and the other guys came over and said he was still breathing, so I moved the muzzle of my rifle about three inches and shot him again. The FNGs had never fired their weapons when the shooting started. When I shot the NVA again, he splashed blood and whatever on these guys and they shrunk back a bit. Then someone took a LAAW to the well and blew it up. We were moved back to where the tree line met the village and found that someone had taken the gook's body away. They said they could see his face through the back of his head. A Marine lost his eye, and his face was swollen like a watermelon, and you couldn't see the battle dressing because his face was swollen.

It was at this point that Brandon made Heidtman the squad leader. It didn't last. Heidtman admitted that he "had a problem with officers," but he was an outstanding Marine in a fight.

Tenney's radio operator was on the air with the regiment and advising them of what was going on. Tenney grabbed the radio, and Colonel Houghton came on the other end and told him to hang on, help was on the way. Lieutenant Gracida assumed command of the company from the wounded Captain Tenney, who needed to be medevaced.

When the fight broke out, Lieutenant Colonel Webster lost no time mounting out Mike and India Companies and the Alpha command group. Helos lifted them out of the landing zone at Tam Ky and put them down about three clicks north of where Kilo was in contact. They moved rapidly toward the fight, but by the time they closed Kilo Company, it was over. The Marines and their supporting arms drove the enemy out of the village and back into the hills. The day cost Kilo Company 9 killed and 20 wounded. They killed 30 of the enemy.

One Marine remembers loading thirty or more M16s in ponchos and throwing them on a chopper. Many of them had cleaning rods in the barrels.

Lance Cpl. Harvey Newton: We thought the fight might have been avoided. We saw the farmers taking the water boo out of the field and couldn't understand why we were being sent down there toward a tree line with no prep fires.

WHEN THE MARINES GOT INTO THE VILLAGE, they found a dead Vietnamese with a BAR, chained to a well, possibly an innocent villager that the enemy had forced into service to cover their retreat.

Pfc. Thom Heidtman: That night, when we sat down to eat, Tom Haugen was sitting next to me, and he was pulling out C-ration cans that were shredded. He looked at his pack and it was full of holes. He had been wearing that pack, crawling behind these dikes. I pulled my lighter out, and there was a big dent in it. A round had hit it. I had it in my left pocket over my heart.

Chapter 14

Pike and Cochise

The 3rd Battalion, 5th Marines, with the attached Lima Company, 3rd Battalion, 1st Marines, ran a small, three-day operation called Pike beginning on August 1. Lieutenant Colonel Webster's battalion was sent to the far northeastern reaches of the valley to look for enemy activity north and east of the junction of Routes 534 and 1. The operation yielded little in the way of enemy activity other than constant encounters with small enemy units, usually Viet Cong guerrillas, rather than NVA. The operation kept enemy heads down and their units off balance and unable to consolidate into battalion-size formations.

On the first day, five snipers found the courage to shoot at the 3/5 command group and were rewarded with an air strike that mercilessly pounded their position. While policing up the battlefield, the Marines captured a badly wounded VC paymaster named Nguyen Van Ba, from the 40th Battalion of the 1st VC Regiment. Some of his comrades had attempted to carry him away, but in the face of an advance by the Marines, they abandoned him and fled. As an enemy combatant, he could not be medevaced by helicopter and could not be carried by the Marines as they moved out in pursuit of the remainder of the enemy force. They took his money and left him with food, water, and some medical supplies in the care of a Vietnamese woman.

Later that day, Marines from Lima Company, 3rd Battalion, 1st Marines, observed a junk in a nearby river. They sank the boat with 3.5-inch rocket fire and killed two VC in the water. The remaining four enemy were gunned down as they reached the riverbank.

Major General Donn Robinson was determined to keep the pressure on the NVA and prevent them from regaining control of the valley. He formed Task Force X-ray under the command of his deputy, Brig. Gen. Foster LaHue, and sent it off on an operation that the Marines called Cochise. Reacting to intelligence sources that pinpointed elements of the 3rd NVA Regiment and the 1st VC Regiment back in the Que Son Valley, the operation jumped off on August 11, with two battalions under the operational control (opcon) of the 5th Marines, now commanded by Col. Stanley Davis.

The special landing force (SLF), battalion landing team (BLT), 1st Battalion, 3rd Marines, now commanded by Lt. Col. Alfred Thomas, was ordered ashore, and Lima Company, 3rd Battalion, 1st Marines, was attached to the battalion that had become one of the real workhorses for the division that year, the 3rd Battalion, 5th Marines. Their mission was to destroy the enemy that had ventured into the valley or send them packing back to the far west. The operation plan for Cochise called for a two-battalion sweep, from Hiep Duc in Antenna Valley to the village of Que Son.

The 2nd ARVN Division simultaneously launched Operation Lien Ket 112 with two ranger battalions that were lifted into an area southeast of Hiep Duc and swept to the east. The three battalions of the 6th ARVN Regiment occupied blocking positions west of Tam Ky. The ranger battalions went out first; choppers lifted them into their area of responsibility, and they began sweeping eastward, while the 6th ARVN Regiment settled in.

Marines are trained to be warriors, even those who fill supply, administrative, and other support functions. Many of them who were assigned to support roles often went out of their way to make sure they were on the point of the spear, as riflemen. Lance Corporal Raymond "Bud" Eckart, Lima Company, 3rd Battalion, 1st Marines, was one such Marine. He wanted to do something different with his life, so he had joined the Norwegian merchant marine when he was just seventeen. After the Vietnam War started, he returned to the States and enlisted, determined to be a Marine rifleman. Upon completing his infantry training regiment course, he was assigned to be a 0351, rocket man. But when he reported in, he told the first sergeant that he was a 0311, rifleman, and no one checked, so he happily reported to Lima Company in the only job he wanted.

Eckart remembers another Marine, Lance Cpl. Gene Ward, who volunteered to be an office pogue right before they were sent on Cochise. Ward could type and was assigned to the company office.

Lance Cpl. Raymond "Bud" Eckart: The next day the troops were saddling up and getting ready to go. Ward was watching us, and all of a sudden he said, "Screw it. I never wanted to be a pogue anyway." He got his gear ready and went on the operation as an infantryman.

CH-46s flew Lima Company into a landing zone where the choppers could not set down. Helicopters almost never landed in mud. There was a genuine fear that the undercarriage might be so mired that the helo could not lift off. The Marines had to jump out while they were hovering. The Marines took a little fire but soon cleared the LZ and headed out toward their first objective.

It was hotter than blazes as usual, and the Marines humped over one hill after another in the first few days, frequently running out of water. Lance Corporal Eckart found himself in a muddy paddy under fire one day and was so desperate for water that he scraped a film mud off the paddy with a bayonet and into a canteen. Then he drained the mud from the canteen into a sock and put the moist sock to his lips.

The ARVN Rangers made the first significant contact on the morning of August 12, when they clashed with all three battalions of the 31st NVA Regiment, and heavy fighting continued throughout the day. Night fell, and the rangers were dangerously low on ammunition, with no sign of letup in the fighting, and they requested an emergency supply. A CH-46 from HMM-165, piloted by Lt. Jack McCracken, loaded up with ammo and flew to the landing zone but was unable to set down because of the intensity of enemy fire. However, McCracken, aware of the urgency of the situation, had his crew chief, Cpl. James Bauer, stack the ammo on the ramp. He brought his bird over the ARVN position and, ignoring hits on his chopper, hovered at thirty feet while Bauer kicked out the ammo. As the last box went out, his helicopter was severely damaged, but McCracken limped back to base, trailing smoke and fluid as he went. McCracken was unharmed but found a 7.67mm bullet that had come through the skin of the aircraft and lodged in the heel of his left boot. The ammo kept the rangers in the fight, and before midnight the enemy withdrew, leaving 197 bodies behind. Ranger losses were also high, with 81 killed and 153 wounded.

The Marines continued to watch and patrol the valley vigorously and found signs that all three enemy regiments, apparently rejuvenated, were pumping men and materiel into the area. As was their custom, the NVA lessened their exposure to artillery and air strikes by moving in small-unit groups, usually platoon size or less, and then reassembling at their destination.

The Marines first found the enemy not far from Nui Loc Son and a click or two from Route 534, around which so much blood had been shed that year. They chased the enemy from that area and followed them into the valley of the Nha Ngu River, which runs through the very steep and rugged terrain south of the Que Son Valley proper.

On the night of August 16, enemy units tried twice to infiltrate and then attack Lima Company, 3rd Battalion, 1st Marines' night position, but the Marines turned them back by fire, killing thirty-six of them. The next morning, Lt. Col. Joseph Nelson, the ever-alert commanding officer of Marine Observation Squadron 6 (VMO-6), was flying a Huey gunship as escort for resupply choppers, when he spotted more than fifty of the enemy in the open. He expended all his ordnance and then directed fixed-wing aircraft against the target. Meanwhile, Lieutenant Colonel Webster's 3rd Battalion, 5th Marines, moved into position, and Webster sent Capt. Joe Gibbs's Lima Company, 3rd Battalion, 1st Marines, into the assault.

Capt. Joe Gibbs: We were stopped, and I sent my 2nd Platoon back to the rear to make sure no one was following us. We got the word from Lieutenant

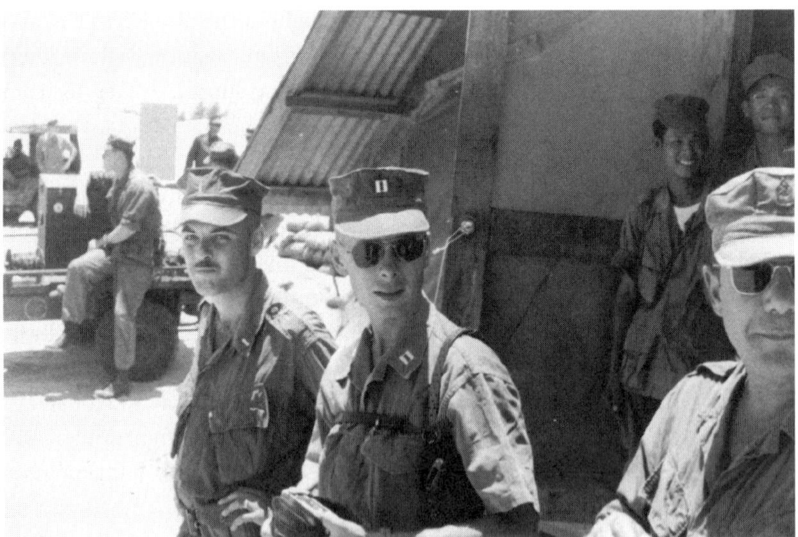

Captain Joe Gibbs, center, with two of his Marines from Lima Company, 3rd Battalion, 1st Marines. Gibbs's company made a classic attack against an enemy force in the open and killed sixty-five of them without taking a single casualty. *Courtesy Andres Vaart*

Lieutenant Andres Vaart was one of Capt. Joe Gibbs's platoon commanders in Lima Company, 3rd Battalion, 1st Marines. *Courtesy Andres Vaart*

Colonel Nelson, and he gave me the coordinates, and we took off after the enemy. I put the 2nd Platoon into a blocking position, and we moved off to push the enemy into the 2nd Platoon. It was pretty dense terrain.

While we were moving to this position, Lieutenant Colonel Nelson kept his eye on the enemy and told us to move faster. I had a disciplined company that was used to moving fast, and I had good officers. We were probably moving faster than we should have but were moving well. I talked with Nelson the whole time, and he called in fixed-wing close air support on the enemy with my permission. When the air ran out of ordnance and I asked for strafing and dummy runs to fix the NVA in place, Nelson recommended artillery, which I rejected since I didn't want to slow us down. We got the dummy runs and strafing, and all this time, Nelson was urging more speed. We finally found the enemy on a slight rise, a flat piece of ground on an embankment. We quickly formed a two-platoon assault line, went right and left, and spread out as we lifted the dummy runs, and we charged up the hill when the last airplane went over.

It was a perfect example of a rifle company in the attack, just like the officers were trained to do at Quantico. The two lead platoon commanders, Lts. Victor Burlingame and Andres Vaart, shouted their orders, and the squad leaders passed them on and led from the front. The Marines completely surprised the enemy. Lieutenant Alex Wells said there were "Charlies running everywhere in mass confusion."

Capt. Joe Gibbs: We had hand-to-hand combat and killed every one of them in that position. We caught them with their heads down. There were about forty bodies there. We only had one walking wounded and no medevacs and no KIAs.

Cpl. Santos Salinas: It makes all the humping worthwhile when you hit them like that.

Capt. Joe Gibbs: Our movement to the LZ for pickup took us through Brigadier General LaHue's command post. The general was standing out in front of his tent when we passed by. I felt so good I started humming the Marines' Hymn, and all the troops picked it up and started humming too.

The main phase of Cochise ended on August 18 as Task Force X-ray withdrew the 3rd Battalion, 5th Marines. There was little contact between then and the twenty-eighth, when the operation officially ended. Enemy casualties were 156 killed and 13 captured. Marines lost 10 killed and 93 wounded.

Chapter 15

Operation Swift: Desperate Delta Again

For most of the summer, the 2nd NVA Division licked its wounds and stayed in its far-western sanctuaries, only occasionally sending small bodies of regular troops into the valley to let the Marines know that they were still in the fight. Operations Union I and II crippled the NVA so badly that their forays into the valley that summer were tentative and unsuccessful.

In mid-August, Major General Thao received new orders; he was to march into the valley in force and seize as much of the autumn rice harvest as he could and disrupt the nationwide South Vietnamese elections scheduled for September 3. After that, his division was to prepare for a major offensive in 1968; they would support Viet Cong units that would invest Da Nang in the General Offensive, General Uprising, which the world would call the Tet Offensive. Thao ordered his units to infiltrate the valley, reconstitute themselves into battalion and regimental formations, and go to work immediately, seizing rice and disrupting the polling places. He withheld from his commanders the details of their subsequent mission—preparing for the Tet Offensive. He closely held this information to prevent leaks to the allies.

Allied intelligence knew that the enemy was on the move and sent out a general alert to Marine units in the valley. The Marines responded by increasing the number of small-unit actions near polling places, and they enhanced surveillance along expected routes of advance from the mountain

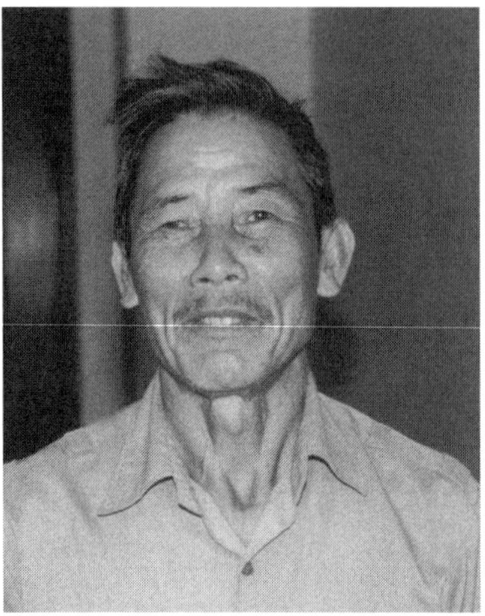

Lieutenant Colonel Tranh Ngoc Trung, retired, 1st Viet Cong Regiment, commanded the 60th Battalion during much of 1967. *Otto J. Lehrack*

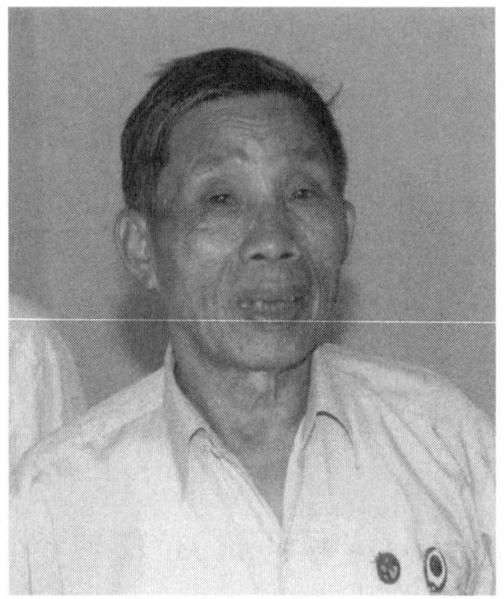

Major Dinh The Pham, retired, 1st Viet Cong Regiment, enlisted in the Viet Minh in 1944 to fight against the Japanese. He was present at the iconic battle of Dien Bien Phu in 1954. By the time he retired, he had thirty years of continuous combat. *Otto J. Lehrack*

range in the west. Operation Swift was the outgrowth of this harvest-protection and election-day screening.

On September 3, two platoons of Capt. Robert Morgan's Delta Company, 1st Battalion, 5th Marines, about ninety men, moved out toward the village of Dong Son (1), just north of Route 534, to provide a screen for the harvest and the elections. As they dug in that day, they heard the villagers banging pots and pans. The Marines wondered if the peasants were signaling their presence to the enemy. Captain Morgan set his men in a defensive perimeter near the village to spend the night. Delta Company had been busy that summer. Their biggest fight was the desperate action on June 2 during Operation Union II, and since then they were continuously going at it with small groups of VC and NVA. Little did they suspect that about six thousand enemy soldiers, most of the 2nd NVA Division, had infiltrated the valley in small groups and reassembled, ready to take another shot at the Marines. Silently in the night, a battalion of Quach Huu Hop's 1st Viet Cong Regiment moved up to within a hundred meters to the west and northwest of Delta's position and prepared their attack.

When they had time, the NVA painstakingly organized their assaults. They sent three or four men, dressed in dark clothing, each carrying wire cutters, to recon the enemy position. The team crawled up to the defensive position, usually about five meters apart in a line. If they thought they could do so, they would infiltrate into the position itself. In all events, they took maximum advantage of the terrain, keeping to low spots as much as possible. After their reconnaissance, they would gather at someplace well outside the perimeter and compare notes about where the Marine crew-served weapons were located and where the strong and weak points were. They drew crude maps for their commander, who then studied them and issued the attack orders. Part of their attack preparation was a decision where to place their machine guns. Once positioned, they drove aiming stakes into the ground to restrict the traverse of the guns and to create lanes of fire. These lanes were routes of advance, illuminated by tracers, within which their assault troops would attack, allowing the guns to hammer the Marine positions right up to the very moment when the assault hit the perimeter.

At 0430 on September 4 they struck. Machine gun and mortar fire pounded Delta Company as a tidal wave of NVA soldiers crossed the line of departure and came at the Marines. On they came, running behind the fire and the smoke of their mortars and within the attack lanes marked by their green tracers. They punctured Delta Company's perimeter and drove hard to the right and left, trying to widen their foothold. At the cost of his life, Captain Morgan led a force that ejected the enemy from his perimeter and reestablished his lines and then attempted to counterattack the NVA. Overwhelming fire stalled the Marines, and they withdrew. The enemy pursued them back to their broken perimeter.

The sun soon cracked the horizon, but the morning brought no relief. The wounded executive officer, Lt. William Vacca, took temporary charge and called in air strikes as close as he possibly could and told his battalion commander, Lieutenant Colonel Hilgartner, that he needed help. Vacca's wounds were too severe for him to continue in command, and the responsibility fell on the shoulders of Lt. Carlton Fulford.[9]

At 0530 an air observer in a Bird Dog spotter aircraft and an armed Huey came on station. The Marines of Delta Company tried using a strobe light to mark enemy positions, but the enemy, in turn, used it to mark the Marine lines and intensified their fire.

The Marines fought for their lives. Lance Corporal Thomas Driscoll took over the duties of the wounded artillery forward observer and stood among the fire, adjusting artillery, trying to break up the enemy advance. At the

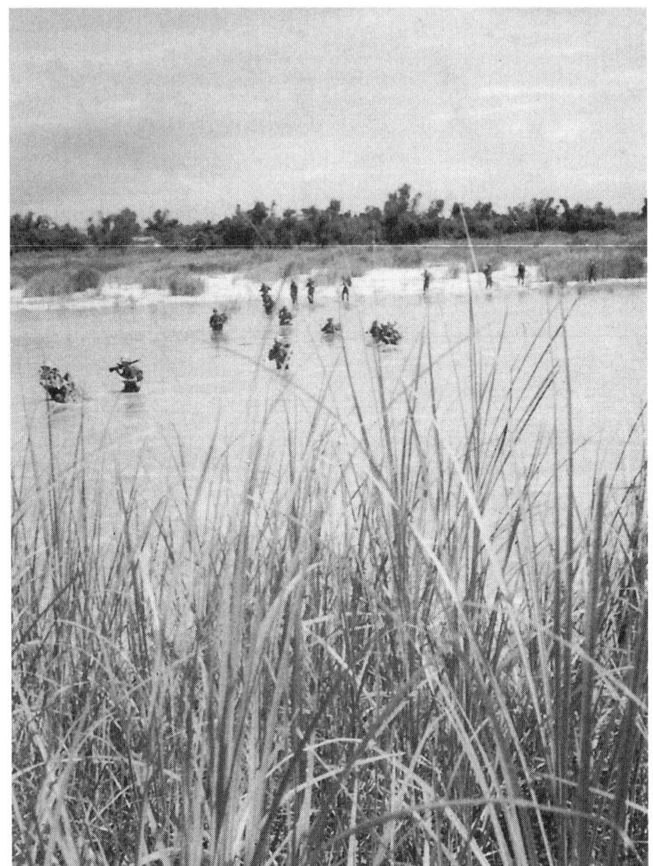

Marines cross a river. *Courtesy Lynwood Scott*

beginning of the fight, when the enemy fractured Delta Company's lines, Lance Cpl. Ernest Huron became separated from the remainder of his company. As he worked his way back, he jumped into a hole to avoid fire, and found a wounded Marine. He put a bandage on the man's injury, and as the two stood up to leave, an NVA popped up from a hole three feet away. Huron tried to shoot him, but his M16 did not fire. The NVA lunged at him with a bayonet. Huron parried the bayonet with his rifle and clobbered the him with a vertical butt stroke. The two Marines hurried back to the perimeter.

At 0600, Lieutenant Colonel Hilgartner ordered Capt. Thomas Reese's Bravo Company of the 1st Battalion, 5th Marines, into the fight. These Marines had their work cut out for them. To get to the battle, they first had to cross the Ly Ly River and then fight their way through the enemy to Dong Son (1).

Lance Cpl. Lonnie Henshaw: We didn't have any idea why we were going, even though Delta usually got beat when they went out. They were having an unlucky streak, and we thought this was part of it. We moved three or four clicks and crossed the river once and were going to cross again at a fork when we saw a helo go down. When we went across the river, we didn't have time to find a shallow place to cross, and most of us were under water and bobbing along trying to stay up and keep moving.

Some of the shorter Marines had to swim with their heavy gear and in Cpl. Gregory Crandall's case, he was laden with a radio and floated himself across as best he could, bouncing his feet off the bottom.

Captain Reese's Marines could hear the Delta Company fight in the distance and were trying to hurry. Some of the Marines were in the river when the NVA hit them. Automatic weapons from a nearby village took out many Marines of Bravo Company's point squad. Corpsman Larry Casselman yelled at the Marines down in the paddy to see if anyone was alive.

Lance Cpl. Lonnie Henshaw: My squad was the point squad. I was lucky not being in the first fire team. We had guns in the middle and the rocket man, John Di Domizio, my best buddy.

Helicopters in Vietnam always acted as mortar magnets, and this case was no exception. Choppers from HMM-363 flew toward Delta Company's position to take out casualties. The helicopter the Bravo Company Marines saw go down was an H-34. Lieutenant Jack "Screw" Warner had only been in Vietnam about three weeks when Operation Swift began and was flying as copilot for Capt. Don Engel. Warner had served as an enlisted man and got the nickname "Screw" from his drill instructors in boot camp.

He out-shot and out-physically-performed all the other recruits in his platoon, and the drill instructors told him that he was as "tight as a screw." The name stuck with him after he was commissioned and sent to flight school.

When Engel and Warner got word that Delta Company, 1st Battalion, 5th Marines, needed an emergency resupply, they landed at a Marine position on Hill 55, kicked off a courier who was on a routine mission, loaded up two thousand pounds of ammunition as fast as they could, and lifted off. On the way to Delta Company, they heard that the company commander was dead, the executive officer had been wounded, all of Delta's machine gunners were out of action, and the Marines had been involved in hand-to-hand combat on the perimeter. Lieutenant Warner knew that if the machine gunners had been taken out, then they were dealing with an experienced enemy, and getting the two M60 machine guns he had on board the helicopter to the Marines was urgent.

They descended through the fire. Enemy bullets cut their tail rotor control cable just as they were about to touch down, and the helicopter spun in the landing zone. Engel and Warner slammed it down hard and shut it down, hitting the rotor brakes and stopping everything.

An enormous amount of fire peppered their aircraft, and their crew chief and gunner, Corporal Price and Private First Class Muszynski, both yelled that they had been wounded. Warner and Engle jumped out and dragged their wounded crew to cover. Then Lieutenant Warner took one of his M60 machine guns and two boxes of ammo and headed to the perimeter where the fire was the heaviest. Captain Engel went to the command post to see what he could do as the senior Marine on the ground.

After placing his guns on the perimeter, Warner got out his hand-held emergency radio and contacted Maj. David Ross in a Huey gunship that was flying cover. Ross made several runs, suppressing enemy fire until fixed-wing aircraft came on station. Delta Company got a brief chance to stabilize parts of its lines when A-4 Skyhawks and F-4 Phantoms showed up with napalm, dropping great billows of orange fire and black smoke, Halloween colors at their scariest, vaporizing the enemy among whom it landed.

There were plenty of enemy soldiers left, and when they crippled Ross's helicopter, the major made a controlled crash within the Delta Company perimeter. Once on the ground, he helped direct air strikes, changing his radio call sign from "Deadlock" to "Deadlock on the Deck," and also lent his M60 machine guns to the defense of the perimeter. Seeing the desperate situation the company was in, Major Ross made his way through the fire to find the company command post, where the situation was rapidly deteriorating. He called in flights of armed Hueys, repeatedly exposing himself to hostile fire as he stood to identify targets.

Bravo Company was still trying to punch its way through the enemy to Delta. Captain Reese ordered a tear gas drop on the enemy, who broke contact, withdrew about a kilometer to the northwest, regrouped, and attacked once more.

Cpl. Gregory Crandall: After we got across the river, the 1st Platoon went out on point along the side of the small ville, and when they got into the paddy, they started receiving fire from their right flank. Captain Reese sent the 3rd Platoon around in an enveloping force around to their right flank by the ville. As the 3rd Platoon passed a small and very narrow island in the rice paddy containing about three hooches, they got sniper rounds from their left and figured out that the enemy was between the 1st and 3rd Platoons. Captain Reese responded by sending his 2nd Platoon right up the middle. We moved into this small ville, which was a very narrow island with paddies on both sides.

Lance Cpl. Lonnie Henshaw: When we moved out, the enemy stopped firing, and my fire team leader, Lance Cpl. Robert Sadler, saw an NVA stick his head out of a hole. We threw a grenade and wounded him, and we ran up, Lance Corporal Call and me, and filled the NVA full of rounds. We pulled his body out and took his gear. We were amazed at their great uniforms and how well they were equipped for combat. They had lots of grenades, both Chicoms and M26s. We captured three M79s and eighteen M79 rounds. We were at the other end of the ville when we saw another large body of NVA crossing a paddy toward another ville about three hundred meters away. We fired and they kept on running.

Cpl. Gregory Crandall: We had just come off the trail when we noticed a small, bunker-like hole. It had an NVA pack and a helmet in it. There was nothing else but the gear. We radioed back and were told to leave all the gear and move on toward Delta Company. We started trying to check every small hole and bunker-like object we came to. We saw someone in the next hole, threw a grenade in, and fished out the body of an NVA with an AK-47. This continued on for another forty-five minutes, throwing grenades in these holes and pulling out bodies and weapons. We accounted for thirteen bodies and nine weapons. During this action we took two casualties. One was shot in the side by an NVA, and Lance Corporal Langham received shrapnel from an enemy grenade. One of the NVA got out of his hole and started running, and we shot him down. By the time we checked out this area, it was almost getting too late to reach the objective.

Just as choppers came down to take out their casualties, the Bravo Company Marines heard the thump of a mortar from a nearby ridge, and the first of about thirty rounds impacted among them. Then the machine guns started their deadly chatter, laying grazing fire across the Marine ranks. Most took cover in a small trench and lay there with bullets passing inches above their heads, some rounds creasing the ground and throwing up sand and dirt all around them. Corporal Crandall had a radio on his back that stuck up past the edge of the trench, so he wiggled out of its harness, laid it alongside of himself, and became as flat as he possibly could. The Marines had captured one NVA and had him tied up and leaning against a rock. Shrapnel from his own mortars killed him, and then he got a round from an NVA machine gun on the ridge. After about an hour, the heavy fire slacked off a bit, and the squad leaders began to reorganize their men to repel an expected assault from across the paddies.

A machine gunner and his assistant gunner were down and wounded, and the gun was lying there unattended. Private First Class John Di Domizio reached down to pick it up and was shot in the head, dying almost immediately. Lance Corporal Henshaw, Di Domizio's best friend, yelled, "Corpsman up," but there was nothing the corpsman could do.

First Lieutenant John E. Brackeen and Corporal Crandall went up and down the trail trying to locate the heaviest fire. Amidst the din, the danger, and the chaos, Lance Corporal Askin singlehandedly carried four or five casualties to the rear all by himself. Somehow he got through the day without being hit.

An enemy machine gunner in a bunker on the high ground overlooking the Marines shot Private First Class Phillips in both legs. Besides the dead, there were wounded lying all around, including Pfc. Curtis Mitchell, an African-American member of Lance Cpl. Oswaldo Miranda's fire team. The machine gun shot Miranda; first he was shot through the leg, and he said, "I'm hit but don't know where." While they were trying to patch him up, he took another round through the side of the neck.

Private First Class Mitchell was the only one left in his fire team after the other Marines were killed or wounded, and he decided to go after the gun. Somehow he got to the enemy bunker without being hit, reached inside, and yanked the machine gun right out of the NVA gunner's hands. He then ran back and gave it to Corporal Reyes, and they put it to work. It was an unknown type, but it worked well, and they used it for the next twenty minutes, as long as the ammo lasted.

Lance Cpl. Lonnie Henshaw: Lance Corporal Townsend was trying to get his men organized and together. His squad had been unlucky. On Operation Cochise his had been the only squad to lose anybody, three men. And now he was losing man after man in his squad. He was upset and trying to make decisions all at the same time.

We set up a perimeter along the river, while the other two squads behind us moved around to envelop the trench line where the NVA were. Mitchell was one of them. He, Lance Cpl. Fernando Foote, and Pfc. Bobby Kinkle got the idea to assault another machine gun bunker. Foote was the first one to get hit, was hit in the chest and died almost instantly, drowning in his own blood. Once more, Mitchell ran for a machine gun bunker, and while the gunner was firing, Mitchell got his hands on it [the gun], but his luck had run out, and the gunner must have put fifteen rounds into his stomach. Lance Corporal Kinkle was killed trying to put a bandage on Mitchell after he got wounded. Kinkle got hit in the stomach, looked down and saw a little bit of intestine loose from the hole in his belly, and went into shock and died.

Private First Class Mitchell gave us time to get our wounded and dead back before he was killed. I was about the third man in a column going up a trail, and when we saw the enemy at all, we could see that they were well camouflaged; the only way you could see them was if they fired and you saw the smoke and the muzzle flashes. They had an ambush set up all around, covering all sides. It took quite a bit of fighting before we finally broke into their lines and drove them back across another paddy.

During this fight, a navy corpsman demonstrated yet again why the Marines love their "docs." During the fight, HM3 Gerald Strode moved to the point of initial contact, undaunted by the heavy volume of fire, and began administering first aid to the casualties. He was attacked by a small group of NVA but killed them or drove them off with a pistol, grenades, and hand-to-hand combat. Then he went back to tending the wounded. He carried several casualties to a protected area and worked continuously throughout the night trying to save lives. He finally acknowledged his own wounds and allowed himself to be evacuated only after all the other casualties had been cared for.

Lance Cpl. Lonnie Henshaw: When it was all over, we regrouped and moved back and started to search the ville. We found several pigs, which the NVA had left there, and then we set up a perimeter and ate chow. After a while we moved back and picked a few men, including myself, to take the dead over to the LZ. We carried them across the rice paddy where the firing had been, and all the time we were carrying casualties, we were not fired upon at all.

Cpl. Gregory Crandall: We were in this firefight for two to three hours and had five killed and seven wounded. We got the wounded back where they could get medical attention and set up a perimeter. Once we were sure that the NVA had left the area, we picked up all the enemy gear. We found fifty-two NVA bodies, AK-47s, Chinese rifles, machine guns, and rocket launchers. We started the gear over to a helo zone that Delta Company had secured. After the choppers collected our killed and wounded and the gear, they had to lift out a chopper that had been downed.

There were only four of the heavy-lift CH-53 helicopters in Vietnam at this time, and their primary mission was to lift out downed aircraft and evacuate them to Da Nang for eventual repair and return to service.

Bravo Company finally fought its way through the enemy and linked up with Delta. The two companies consolidated their positions on the western end of Dong Son (1).

Lance Cpl. Lonnie Henshaw: We moved up to a tree line, and snipers began shooting at us. Lieutenant Brackeen told us to pull back to the LZ and set up a hasty perimeter. It was getting dark, and we knew we were going to get mortared. A few minutes later, the enemy hit us with a heavy volume of automatic-weapons fire. I was sitting up, loading my magazines; I should have been lying down, and I was lucky because the rounds were very close. Then we heard the thump of an enemy mortar tube firing, and they shot about twenty-five rounds into our CP. Many men, especially in the 3rd Platoon, were hit, and they had at least nine WIAs and some KIAs. Then we got some incoming M79 rounds too. After the mortar barrage, the squad leaders checked the perimeter and tightened it up. We were 100 percent alert that night; no one slept. We were afraid the NVA would overrun our position like they had with Delta.

The night sky was illuminated with flares as a C-130 hosed down the area with gunfire, forestalling any further enemy attacks.

The next morning a Huey gunship from VMO-6, once again piloted by the sharp-eyed predator and squadron commander, Lt. Col. J. A. Nelson, spotted twenty to thirty NVA in bunkers and raked them with fire; then he called for fixed-wing support. Two Phantoms from VMF-115 responded.

The aircraft were on their way to a mission over North Vietnam, which had just been cancelled because of weather. With little fuel remaining, they flew down to the Que Son Valley. Leading the attack were Capt. Tom Fisher and his radar-intercept officer (RIO), Capt. John Day. Lieutenant Colonel Nelson marked the enemy position with red smoke, and Captain Fisher, followed by his wingman, Capt. Fred Tenner and RIO Bob Butterman, dropped twelve thousand pounds of steel and high explosive onto the target. The explosion was so violent that it threw several large trees a hundred feet into the air. The aircraft were low on fuel, and they did not have time to make a second pass to assess the damage.

When the situation developed with Delta and Bravo Companies at Dong Son (1), Col. Stanley Davis, CO of the 5th Marines, sent a battalion command group and two more companies into the fight. He ordered Kilo and Mike Companies of the 3rd Battalion, 5th Marines, to be chopped opcon* to Lieutenant Colonel Hilgartner's 1st Battalion, 5th Marines, and for them to be inserted into the battlefield immediately.

The CH-46s, the only helicopters available for such a big lift, were all grounded because of mechanical problems that sometimes caused crashes and killed passengers and crew. Because it was an emergency situation, the commanding general of the 1st Marine Aircraft Wing authorized their use for Operation Swift.

By 1130 both Kilo and Mike were in the landing zone waiting for pickup. Kilo and the command post of the 1st Battalion, 5th Marines, went first and debarked at a position about two thousand meters northeast of Dong Son (1).

Then they moved westward on the north side of Route 534, which all summer long had been a highway of death and destruction. As Kilo moved along, they apprehended a Vietnamese male, who told them that he had seen a group of enemy soldiers with seven mortars nearby. The Marines pressed on without locating the mortars, and when they got to an area south of Dong Son (1), Lieutenant Colonel Hilgartner sent Kilo into the attack to the north. The attack helped to relieve the pressure on Bravo and Delta but contributed very little to the survival of Mike Company, which was headed for the fight of its life.

Lance Cpl. Harvey Newton: We went through several villes, and I saw a fourteen-year-old in white shirt and black pajamas. I thought he was too young to be a VC, but the next morning he was standing in line with other prisoners.

---

* *Chopped opcon* means to assign operational control of a unit to a headquarters that is not normally that subordinate unit's parent.

Pfc. Patrick Mosey: We were humping to help Delta, and a guy was badly wounded by a water boo, which slowed down the column that was trying to save Delta's ass. As it got dark, Lieutenant McCool told us to cross this paddy, "but don't stop, there is a machine gun on your right." John Strunk and I ran across the paddy and jumped into a bomb crater with four other guys. We were the last guys from the tail end of the column.

I was lying against the side of this crater, looking at ground level, and I saw these curved green backs hopping around toward us. I asked a lieutenant in the crater if he had anyone out there, and he said, yes, two guys. I thought it must be them. But they came right up to the hole, and they were NVA. One of them ripped off a bunch of rounds from his AK, and one threw a grenade in the hole. I shot one round at the gook, and then my M16 jammed.

I heard the spoon [of the grenade] go, and I was grabbing my nuts. The grenade went off, and I caught a piece just under my rib cage. I shot that single round with one hand, and I don't know if I hit him or not, but he was three feet away, and his sandals were in front of my face. Brush was belly-button high. John Strunk finger rolled a grenade under the NVA. He tried to pull the pin from the grenade, but he had his weapon in one hand, and he couldn't get it out with just the other hand. So he bit the ring and busted a tooth when he pulled the pin. He did a finger roll under the enemy, and then he put his hand on my helmet and pushed me down. The crater saved us.

There was a Hispanic guy there with a bad, bad wound; one leg was blown off. Strunk dragged him to the rear. I looked across sixty or eighty yards and saw four NVA on a mortar by the light of their muzzle blast. I only had a .45, and John had an M16, and I thought, "No way." We had to shoot them dead or not. There was no middle ground.

Lance Cpl. Harvey Newton: I was with Wayne Brandon's 1st Platoon, and we set up a CP in a hooch and had nothing to do for several hours. We were monitoring Mike Company's situation. Our 1st Platoon was in a trench line around a ville where a Marine named Baird got into a grenade-throwing contest with the NVA. I was sitting up in the center of the hooch in a family chair eating a can of peaches and feeling safe when I got hit. A mortar came in, wounded an engineer in the throat, and hit Sgt. Tom Haugen above the knee. I was hit above the hipbone on the side and the right hand. Two of my mortar guys got hit and had minor wounds.

Lance Cpl. Larry Mazurkiewicz: An officer was hit in the knee, and I was one of the guys that carried him in a poncho. It was becoming dark and I lost

Sergeant Tom Haugen, a gung ho member of Kilo Company, 3rd Battalion, 5th Marines, aboard a hospital ship. *Courtesy Gerry Haugen*

my squad on the way back. We were getting mortars and machine gun fire, and I had no idea where I was. I started shooting, and some Marines yelled at me to stop, that I was shooting over their heads.

I stopped shooting and still had no idea where the perimeter or my squad was. A mortar came in and blew me up. I thought my leg was blown off, and I lost my hearing and was trying to feel my leg. It turned out that it hit me in the leg and the arm. I thought, "Now I am wounded and bleeding and freaking out, and I don't know what the hell to do." I crawled along and got behind a big, black rock. I still couldn't hear very well, but I heard, "Gas." I put my gas mask on. I yelled for a corpsman, and a voice near me, a Marine who was tending to another wounded, said, "There are no corpsmen." A second mortar came in and blew my gas mask off my face, and shrapnel nearly ripped my finger off. I had a grenade and my rifle, but I wasn't John Wayne anymore. The machine guns were firing, and all of a sudden Puff came up and completely stopped the enemy fire. I was bleeding and didn't know what to do. I could hear a Marine gasping for air all night long. Morning came, and it turned out to be Lance Cpl. James Nicholls, one of my best friends, who had been on his knees all night and had taken one in the lung. Everywhere I looked there were Marine bodies.

Kilo Company had no shortage of outstanding Marines in the fight that night. Corporal Robert Herrera, a seemingly indestructible machine gunner, was in the thick of it once more. Anytime there was a fight, he was there, and he always volunteered to go out on any sort of patrol and with any squad or platoon.

Many times the enemy shot his assistant gunners and ammo humpers out from under him, but he never got wounded. Every single night, his wife back in the States said a rosary for him. His ability with a machine gun was well known among the Kilo Company Marines.

Then there was Weahkee, the Fearless Warrior from the Pima tribe. He was one of a type of almost legendary proportions—the Marine whom everyone wanted to be near in a fight but who was always in trouble when his unit was in the rear. Every time he got a stripe, he was sure to get busted back down to private. But he volunteered for the dangerous jobs that no one else really wanted. No one wanted to be in his squad, because he volunteered for everything, but everyone wanted to be near him in when the fighting started.

The helicopters returned from inserting the 1st Battalion, 5th Marines' command (or CP) group and Kilo Company, 3rd Battalion, 5th Marines, and lifted out Mike Company, commanded by 1st Lt. John "J. D." Murray. Corporal Larry Nunez of Mike Company was squad leader.

Cpl. Larry Nunez: While waiting for helos, Father Vincent Capodanno came down to the LZ and was conducting some sort of service for the Catholic members of the company. He gave away rosaries and Saint Christopher medals, and I wanted one of those medals, so I got in line, and before I got to him, he had given away his last one. I talked to him and said something about wanting one, and he took his own off of his dog tag chain. I just wanted one as a keepsake since I was a Protestant, and Capodanno said, "Son, I want you to have one." I put it on my dog tag chain.

Father Capodanno, a Maryknoll priest from Long Island, was in every way a Marine's chaplain and was universally respected and loved by them. He somehow seemed to show up near the center of every fight, and he asked for nothing for himself except to be able to serve his Marines.

Lance Cpl. John Lobur: Father Capodanno was extremely charismatic and was instantly very popular among all the men, Catholic and otherwise. He had a kind of serenity about him that I thought then was my idea of Christ-like. I don't remember him saying much; he mostly listened and empathized.

Cpl. Norm Bailey: We used to hide our cigarettes from Capodanno because he smoked like a chimney. He'd give you a Saint Christopher's medal and then bum a cigarette. The guy thought he was bulletproof. If you had to provide bodyguard for him, you were in deep shit because he wouldn't listen to you and get down. I was a corporal and he was a lieutenant, so he didn't have to listen to me.

On another occasion, two Marines were digging a hole, and Capodanno came by, got out his entrenching tool, and went to work helping them dig. The two Marines took a smoke break, but the chaplain was still digging when the gunny came by.

Chapter 16

Life and Death on a Very Small Knoll

John Lobur, rocket team member with the 2nd Platoon, Mike Company, didn't like the way things were shaping up.

Lance Cpl. John Lobur: They told us we were going into a hot LZ, and I didn't see any of the other companies saddling up. We were in the same area as Lima and India, but we were going without them. My feeling was that if a company of 180 to 200 Marines were saying they needed help, there were probably a whole hell of a lot of bad guys out there. The enemy did not mess with us casually on a day-to-day basis. They only hit us when they had the big odds. There wasn't much time to worry about it though, because the choppers were there right away.

As the helicopters flew Mike Company toward the battle, the pilot told Lieutenant Murray that the Kilo landing zone was hot, and he would drop Mike Company off in the alternate. No one had briefed Murray on an alternate LZ, and he had no idea where they were going to drop him. It took him a few minutes after touching down to determine where Mike Company was. Lieutenant Murray quickly figured it out, but it took a while longer to convince the staff of the 1st Battalion, 5th Marines, of his correct whereabouts. Apparently Lieutenant Colonel Hilgartner had not been briefed on an alternate LZ either. Once Murray convinced the 1st Battalion, 5th Marines' command group where he was, he moved Mike Company in a southwesterly

Marines from Mike Company, 3rd Battalion, 5th Marines, move through the Que Son Valley on Operation Swift, September 1967. *USMC*

direction, just north of and parallel to Route 534. The terrain was slightly hilly, covered with low vegetation, and surrounded by rice paddies. There were a few scattered houses.

Murray's Marines moved in a wedge, with Lt. Ed Combs's 1st Platoon leading the way, followed by the company CP group. Behind them on the left was Lt. Ed Blecksmith's 2nd Platoon. To the right rear was Lt. Randy Cernick's 3rd Platoon. Bringing up the tail end of the company formation was the Weapons Platoon, commanded by Lt. Mike Hayden, the only officer other than Murray who had any combat experience to speak of.

Mike Company had walked over this same terrain before. Corporal Chuck Cummings, in the right rear with Cernick's platoon, remembered it from Operation Union I.

Lieutenant Murray was well aware that Bravo and Delta Companies of the 1st Battalion, 5th Marines, were engaged in a bad fight, and he moved his company as fast as he could and still maintain tactical security. Despite the vicious firefight ahead of them, the terrain over which the Marines moved was tranquil, and they noted a few Vietnamese calmly working in the fields. The Marines later decided that this was a ruse, designed to draw them into the jaws of an ambush.

After moving about 2,500 meters and stopping for a short break, the Marines walked through a shallow draw and then up over a small knoll and through a scattered cemetery near the hamlet of Chau Lam (4). They were less than a kilometer from the Marines in the 1st Battalion, 5th Marines, and the command group. The knoll is a gentle one, about a hundred meters across and less than five meters above the surrounding terrain. It is so slight that it does not even show on the map as an elevation. Except for a few large black rocks, and old bomb craters for those who could find them, the knoll would offer the Marines no natural cover or concealment.

About the time the Mike Company Marines started down the western slope of the knoll, they got word that Kilo Company, 3rd Battalion, 5th Marines, was in contact with the enemy. Murray told his Marines pick up the pace.

The point man for the company, Pfc. Jack "Swannie" Swan, often walked point, and point men don't like being rushed. Nonetheless, he moved as fast as he could and kept his eyes and ears open. He headed down the far slope of the knoll and started toward a paddy. To his front, he saw what he believed to be a young couple, civilians, loping along with buckets suspended from poles over their shoulders. The sight reassured him. But as he stepped into the paddy, he thought he saw a bush move on the other side. Swannie had been in the field for four and a half months, much of it walking point, and knew more than just a little bit about how the enemy moved. He yelled back to his squad leader, Cpl. Bill Vandergriff, that he saw something move across the paddy that did not look just right. Vandergriff yelled back that if Swan saw something move again, shoot it. When he thought he saw the bush move again, he fired an M79 high-explosive round. It detonated just short of the hedge row where he had seen the bush, and it was the shot that set the fight in motion.

Private First Class Howard Haney was to Swannie's left rear. He saw the puffs of smoke from the enemy weapons as he dove for a paddy dike to his front. A bullet struck him in the chest while he was in midair, and he landed still clutching his M16. When he yelled for a corpsman, blood sprayed from his mouth, and he could hear the blood gurgling in his chest. Swannie yelled over and asked, "Are you okay?" Haney told him that he was hit. "Can you move?" "No I can't." Swan told him that he would not leave him and for him to hold on, and they would get to him as soon as they could. Haney lay there crying in pain and asking God to let him live. Later, when the air strikes began, every one of them looked like it was heading directly for him.

Five battalions of NVA had waited for Mike Company in an L-shaped ambush. Directly to their front were two of Col. Quach Huu Hop's four battalions from the 1st VC Regiment. Arrayed along the Marines' right flank were his two other battalions and a battalion of Colonel Huyen's 31st NVA Regiment.

Lance Cpl. John Lobur: The roar of the firing and explosions for that first five minutes of that battle was continuous and overwhelming. If you haven't been in combat, you can't really imagine what its like; but if you have been in combat, you probably can't imagine what that battle on September 4 was like. It was like a volcano was erupting or something. It was stark terror. First platoon had gone over the top of the hill, heading for a small ville, and right into the middle of hundreds of tough, professional, straight-shooting and hard-fighting NVAs.

Cpl. Chuck Cummings: We were marching along in the rear of the column when we heard one shot, and then the firing picked up. Then a gunship came in. I remember seeing Capodanno at that time, since he was the oldest-looking person out there. Later I saw him running around with something white around his hand. Just as we got on a line with the gun team, we got mortared and mortared again and then saw the enemy coming at us. The lieutenant sent one of my fire teams, led by a guy named Pete Dye, to support the other end of the perimeter. That is when the first jet showed up.

THE FIRST AIR OBSERVER (AO) ON THE SCENE was Lt. Tom Redmond, who was flying with Capt. Tom Nowak. Lieutenant Murray was on the radio, explaining his situation to Redmond and saying, "Get them off me! Get them off me!" The first thing that Redmond did was run in a flight of A-4 Skyhawks with tear gas in an attempt to break up the enemy attacks. The aircraft discharged the gas at too high an altitude, and it rapidly dissipated without having any effect on the enemy advance. Lieutenant Redmond then mustered a flight of Hueys with the same mission. One of the Hueys mistook some of Mike Company for the enemy and loosed several bursts of machine gun fire at them. Luckily the rounds hit no one.

Lance Cpl. John Lobur: The chopper hovered in the same place again, and it's evidence of how close they were that we easily recognized our boy the door gunner. This time he wasn't manning his gun; he was fiddling with some contraption about the size of a large backpack. It was tilted toward us, and I could see that the top of it revealed rows of open tubes like you see in golf bags. He yanked on some sort of lanyard and fired at least fifty gas grenades right at the side of our hill.

Struggling with the effects of the gas, which stings skin as well as eyes, nose, and lungs, Lobur was handed a gas mask, which he donned and just as quickly tore off because it fogged up his glasses. A machine gunner named Bert Watkins yelled at Lobur to go get the machine gun ammunition that was draped across the chest of one of the dead Marines, Lance Cpl. Jack Berry. Lobur recalls that he just did not have the spirit to do it. Just then an air strike came in and caused the NVA to get their heads down. Watkins only had a few seconds to get out and get Berry's ammo, but he did it.

The gas helped buy time for the Marines of Mike Company, who donned gas masks. This, according to J. D. Murray, was the most important support he received that day. In accordance with NVA doctrine, whenever gas was used on the battlefield, they were to fall back a thousand meters, wait until the gas dissipated, and then resume the attack. This gave Murray the briefest respite before the onslaught continued.

Just when things were at their worst, the air observer saw a large mass of troops moving rapidly toward the fight. There were three separate columns of them moving down rice paddy dikes toward Mike Company's position from the north. Redmond told Murray, "You have three columns of Marines closing with your position on the north." Murray replied, "We don't have any Marines to our north." Redmond made a low pass over the oncoming troops and, sure enough, they were NVA soldiers wearing camouflage. As if Murray did not have enough on his hands, the enemy threw the other two battalions of the 31st NVA Regiment at him. Lieutenant Redmond quickly called for fixed-wing air support and got two F-8 Crusaders, each carrying two one-thousand-pound bombs, which they dropped at the head of the NVA formation, savaging the enemy and throwing bodies and body parts all over the landscape, slowing down but not stopping the columns. That done, Redmond told Murray that his fuel tank was nearly empty and he had to return to base.

In April 2009, retired North Vietnamese Army Col. Tran Nhu Tiep took J. D. Murray, the former commander of Mike Company, to a spot three hundred to four hundred meters north of the knoll to show him an underground position for the 31st NVA Regiment. The entrance was very small, so small that an American would have found it very difficult to enter. And it was well concealed.

Lt. J. D. Murray: A flower pot would have covered it up.

THERE WAS A LARGE NUMBER OF SOLDIERS in this position, and it was they who came out of the north and right at Mike Company.

Cpl. Chuck Cummings: When the jets came over, they were very, very close to us. They dropped bombs, and green tracers went up, and you could see smoke coming out of one of the airplanes as he turned tail and left. The bombs killed a lot of NVA. About that time we knocked out a gook machine gun in front of us, but not before it shot one of my fire team leaders, Billy Moy, in the shoulder. He yelled that he was hit, and a corpsman and I ran out to get him. Why the gunner didn't get us—I think he may have been the NVA who was wounded in both legs that we captured the next morning—I don't know. This machine gun was to the east, toward the South China Sea, indicating that they were trying to surround us. Somebody yelled, "Here they come!" and the gooks came out of this tree line.

We shot all of them down, about thirteen to fourteen of them, before they got to us, except one, and we killed him inside the perimeter. There was an engineer with an M14, and he put out some pretty good fire. That was the only assault we had in the rear of the company where I was. I am guessing that the jets took out the others who may have followed up on that. All this time we were getting mortared. A mortar round landed right on Dominic Duca's 60mm mortar team, but they came running through the smoke, apparently unhurt. By this time there were about twenty to thirty dead NVA in front of the lines.

STAFF SERGEANT CRAIG SULLIVAN and his radio operator, Lance Cpl. Ron Mercurio, were up front with the 1st Platoon and dove for a nearby crater when a cauldron of fire erupted all around them. Almost immediately, Murray's entire formation was under attack. All three of his platoon commanders bombarded him with radio traffic, all of them trying to report to him at once; all said that the enemy was hitting them very hard; all requested immediate help. Murray patiently and calmly settled them down and got them to report one at a time.

The enemy attack nearly overwhelmed the Marines. The NVA came at Murray's men by the score: in a whirlwind of violence, hard on the heels of mortars that mushroomed across the knoll, throwing hot, sharp steel in every direction; within lanes, marked by tracers of Soviet-made machine guns and small arms that chain-sawed every bush, sapling, and blade of

Colonel Tran Nhu Tiep, retired, North Vietnamese Army; and Lt. Col. John "J. D." Murray, retired, U.S. Marine Corps. Tiep's soldiers and Murray's Marines clashed in the violent battle on the knoll in the bloodiest day in the Que Son Campaign, September 4, 1967. *Courtesy Lynwood Scott*

grass to stubble; in platoon formation, firing from the hip; in squads, firing and maneuvering their three-man fire teams; singly, men orphaned by the Marines' return fire but still on their feet and attacking. The NVA kept coming at the Marines in a flood, like water from a burst dam, flowing around the strong positions, threatening to carry away the weak and then trying to come together on the far side, attempting to isolate and surround small clumps of resistance, and they nearly succeeded. Had it not been for the outstanding courage of the individual Marines and their close air support, the entire company would most likely have been butchered on the knoll.

Cpl. Bill Vandergriff: I had one man on the left flank who took three rounds of machine gun fire through his back as he dove for the deck. My point fire team was pinned down in the paddies—there was no way we could get to them, and I was pinned in a bomb crater. My other fire team was on the left flank, pinned down almost entirely in the open except for a few shrubs.

My platoon commander was about twenty-five meters behind the bomb crater next to some small trees, which gave him a little cover. We tried to adjust mortar fire and knock out Charlie's position. The lieutenant would holler up to me and tell me where our mortars were hitting, and I would relay from the bomb crater up to the two men back up on the knoll, and they would tell our 60s.

It was not the most effective way of adjusting mortar fire. About three hundred meters separated Vandergriff's squad from the mortars. The information had to be passed by several Marines in sequence, all of whom were in a firefight.

Enemy machine guns and small-arms fire still skimmed the knoll, and most anything that stuck up more than a few inches above the surface was quickly chopped down. Much of the automatic-weapons fire seemed to be coming from Hill 63, to the southwest and halfway between Murray's Mike Company and the Marines of Delta Company at Dong Son (1).

The fire wrapped around the Mike Company front to the Ly Ly River to the north. Additionally, enemy skirmishers were sniping at the Marines from their left and their rear. The enemy tried to execute their countersweep maneuver and surround and then fragment the Marine formation so they could deal with one small group at a time.

Cpl. Bill Vandergriff: Lieutenant Combs, the platoon commander, stopped calling me, and I didn't know what was going on, except that mortar rounds were landing all around where I was, and I kept hearing, "Corpsman up, corpsman up," and I knew people were getting hurt pretty badly. I didn't know how badly, because I couldn't raise my head out of the hole without getting shot myself. I was in this bomb crater for about two and a half hours by myself, and finally a corpsman made it down to my position.

I don't know how he made it. Shortly after, another man came down, and I don't know how he made it either. There was a gun team out in front of me. They made it back, and now there were five of us in the hole, and there were the three men out in front in the paddies whom I was more worried about than us in the bomb crater, because they had one wounded man and we had medical aid right here, but we couldn't get to them. Someone started yelling, "Pull back, pull back, bomb strikes are coming in!"

I didn't know what to do then except to try to figure out a way to get to the wounded guy. At this time, the perimeter was set up about a hundred meters in back of us, and they were trying to bring in the dead and wounded and calling for us to pull back because of the air strikes. I made the decision to get these four other men and myself back to the perimeter and leave the other three out there.

Corporal Chuck Goebel, the forward air controller, stood in another bomb crater running air strikes when the badly wounded Lt. Ed Combs staggered up the knoll and slid into the crater with him. Combs wanted water, but he had a chest wound, and Goebel knew better than to give water to someone with a chest or stomach wound. Instead, he tried to patch him up. Goebel got the word back to Lieutenant Murray that Combs was seriously wounded. Murray tried unsuccessfully to reach Combs's platoon sergeant, Staff Sgt. Craig Sullivan, on the radio, so he went looking for him. In what Sullivan described as the bravest act he ever saw, Lieutenant Murray raced through the fire to his position. The lieutenant knelt beside Sullivan and said, "Sully, Lieutenant Combs is hit. You take command of the platoon and get them organized." Sullivan replied, "Aye, aye, sir" and got out of the crater as Lieutenant Murray turned and ran through the bullets back to his command post in another crater. Sullivan and his radio operator made a dash for one of the big rocks that dotted the terrain, where he had a little cover and could see his platoon and try to turn the situation around.

The situation on the knoll was touch and go. One platoon commander was down, and there were dead and dying Marines everywhere and corpses of dead NVA all around and within the position. Yet, the enemy kept coming.

Lance Corporal Thomas Fisher, one of Sullivan's fire team leaders, stood among the fire and pointed out concentrations of NVA for his team. First, he directed fire onto two NVA automatic-weapon positions that his Marines quickly engaged and knocked out. Then an enemy round smacked into Fisher's rifle, damaging it and wounding him in the arm. Though without a weapon and wounded, Lance Corporal Fisher ran out to help another fire team bring in a casualty. He refused aid for his wound and stayed in the fight, directing his unit's fire until he was killed.

Murray's Marines were tautly stretched and he began to wonder if his company could hold under the continuous enemy assaults. At this point the company was strung out about three hundred to four hundred meters, from Swannie's position in the rice paddy in the front, to the 3rd Platoon and mortars in the rear.

Lance Cpl. Kevin Kelly (radio operator): I was with the Lieutenant Hayden in the rear with 3rd Platoon. The 60mm mortars were with us, and we put out as much fire as we could. After we expended most of the rounds and were getting ready to move out, a Huey dropped a smoke near our position and strafed us twice. The rounds hit all around us, but no one was wounded. We moved out again, and we took a lot of mortar fire from the rear, but no one was hit, because when the rounds started coming in, we moved out ahead of the mortars, and they landed behind us. The helicopters dropped the gas, and we had to use our gas masks for five or ten minutes. We finally reached the CP. The 1st and 2nd Platoons were under heavy fire, and the skipper was trying to set up a perimeter. He told two squads from the 3rd Platoon to dig in, and he sent one squad to assist the 1st Platoon.

A THOUSAND METERS TO THE WEST of the knoll, the 1st Battalion, 5th Marines' command group and Kilo Company were also under fire. In a post-operation evaluation, J. D. Murray believed that much of the fire that rained on Kilo Company was fired at Mike Company but was high and went over their heads and landed among Capt. Joe Tenney's Kilo Marines. Tenney was aware of Mike Company's precarious position and tried to move his company in support, but they did not get very far before they encountered a group of NVA in an open paddy and shot down and killed some of them. The enemy regrouped and tried a halfhearted and futile counterattack. Two 60mm mortar men, Cpl. Steve Ortiz and Lance Cpl. James Sheafer spotted NVA mortar and antiaircraft crews setting up on the other side of the rice paddy. The two Marines only had two rounds left, so they moved their weapon to a better location, took careful aim, and knocked out the antiaircraft gun with the first round and scored a perfect hit on the mortar position with the second.

Back on the knoll, the NVA tried again and again to fragment Murray's company by moving troops into the draw behind him, encircling the main body, and preventing the Marines in the rear from reinforcing their comrades. Three or four NVA machine guns laid down a grazing fire, and they sent more of their troops into the attack. Lieutenant Mike Hayden reported large numbers of enemy pouring into the gap between his position and the bulk of the company on the knoll.

Lance Cpl. Kevin Kelly: Before the 3rd Platoon could get their holes dug, the enemy started coming from the rear; one man would dig and one would shoot. We set in and began bringing in the 1st and 2nd Platoon Marines who were still out there. I was with Lieutenant Hayden still, and when the 1st Platoon commander was hit, the skipper appointed him as the 1st Platoon commander. They told us where the 1st Platoon was and told us to go there with a squad from the 3rd platoon. Before we could get there, the lieutenant and I were cut off, and we got down in a hole because we began getting a lot more small-arms and mortar fire. I don't know how many NVA had us zeroed in, but we couldn't move. We lost contact with the squad that was sent to help 1st Platoon, and I still don't know how many of them made it. While we were in this hole, Lieutenant Hayden and I spotted bushes moving twenty to twenty-five meters to our right. We had two choices, drop them or to let them on by. I had an M16 and he had a .45. He took my M16, laid it on my back, and dropped the first bush. Another man dressed as a bush moved up to help him, and more bushes rapidly moved in. The lieutenant told me to follow him to the CP, and when I stood up, the radio fell off my back, and I dropped the .45. The lieutenant still had my rifle, and I had to go back to the same hole to get the radio back on. When I finally got it, the lieutenant was already at the CP, and I was out there by myself, about fifty meters away. I picked up the pistol and looked around to make sure nothing was real close, and as I started to move, I spotted bipods and a muzzle about twenty meters away, sticking out of a bush near the CP. I aimed the pistol and shot two rounds, and I made my way back to the CP. At this time the 1st Platoon was just starting to bring back their wounded. The company CP was in a bomb crater, which was about the best thing in the area.

Sgt. Forrest McKay: I knew when we fixed bayonets that we were in trouble. An NVA ran from behind us, between us, and back to where he originally came from. We were so shocked that he ran between us from behind that no one shot him.

Cpl. Chuck Goebel: When we got the word to load up for [Operation] Swift, we immediately staged in the LZ. We could not have loaded weapons at our rear area unless we had guard duty, so I carried my .45 without a magazine, and in the rush to check radios for the operation, I forgot to put rounds in it. In middle of battle, with enemy running around, I took out the .45, cocked it, and tried to shoot an NVA running through the position . . . nothing happened.

Years later, the Marines gave Goebel an empty .45 shell with a note in it that read, "*This* is what they look like after you cap a round."

Corporal Goebel was one of the keys to survival that day. He worked two radios, calling in artillery and air, and tried to keep a hand on Lieutenant Combs's wound.

The next AO on station was Lt. Rob Whitlow in an aircraft piloted by Capt. Bob Fitzsimmons, who was flying his first mission of the war. They came over the battleground and peered down at the fight between clouds of gun smoke and tear gas that drifted about. Whitlow called for more air support and soon had A-4 Skyhawks and F-4 Phantoms stacked up over the battleground.

Pinned down out in front of the company, out of ammunition, and with everyone around him dead except for a severely wounded Marine to his left rear, Pfc. Jack Swan lay on his back, wedged against a dike, and spent most of the afternoon watching the AO moving back and forth over the battleground and thinking, "Stay up there, you bastard. I don't know who you are, but I love you."

Cpl. Ron Pizana: The NVA moved in closer, utilizing camouflage and holes that had already been dug farther down the hill. They had forest green uniforms with different types of bushes and leaves tied on their backs and legs and arms and helmets. The camouflage was so well done that it appeared that a bush would just pick up and move. If you didn't have a good eye, you would not have seen the movement at all. The camouflage was the main reason they were able to get so close to us.

Cpl. J. E. Fuller (machine gun team leader, 2nd Platoon): Some NVA were dressed in khaki colored uniforms, and some of them were VC that were dressed in black pajamas and coolie hats. They had a lot of camouflage on them, and it was the same type of vegetation as the area we were in. It was hard to see them coming up.

Someone spotted a group of NVA closing on Fuller's flank and shouted to warn him. It was only then that he saw them for the first time. Three of the Marines in Fuller's four-man team were armed with M16s, and all three rifles jammed just as an NVA fire team came directly at them. The Marine got the machine gun into action and killed them. While the gunner and assistant gunner manned the gun, the other two Marines tried to clear the jammed M16s. They would ram their cleaning rods down the bores to eject the stuck cartridges and then try to fire them.

Time and again the weapons jammed after a round or two. Fuller's squad leader ran from machine gun to machine gun, distributing ammo. On one of these trips, his part of the perimeter was pulled back while he was at Fuller's gun position. When he ran back to where he had come from, he found himself outside the perimeter and face to face with four NVA carrying a mortar. He loosed a burst in their direction and hurried back to the new lines. The 2nd Platoon had casualties that were caught outside when the

Lieutenant Rob Whitlow, an air observer, provided support critical to the survival of Mike Company, 3rd Battalion, 5th Marines, on the knoll on September 4, 1967, and also to Golf and Hotel Companies, 2nd Battalion, 5th Marines, during Operation Essex. *Courtesy Rob Whitlow*

perimeter was set up, and the Marines had a hard time getting to them and bringing them back.

Cpl. Larry Nunez: Before the fight began, the column stopped for a break, and Cpl. Bill Young and I sat with our backs to a well. When the gunfire started, a lot of rounds clipped very close to that well. Soon they gave us orders by radio to move up to the crest of the little knoll to our right front. Our 2nd Platoon was to position itself just over the high point on the knoll. We no sooner got in place than Young was struck by a light machine gun round in the lower pelvic area; I did my best to treat him. Corpsman Armando "Doc" Leal came along and looked at the wound and indicated that there wasn't anything we could do. I patted Young on the shoulder and went on with my squad to the crest of the hill.

We usually carried three hundred to four hundred rounds of M16 ammo, and it didn't take long for us to expend it. We took a tremendous amount of mortar and gunfire out of the tree line, and right at the edge of the trees was a group of NVA with a mortar. Corporal Ron Pizana's ammo was gone, and when he saw the crew setting up the mortar, he yelled for a grenade from

On patrol in the fall of 1967 south of Da Nang, Steve Lovejoy is carrying a PRC25 radio and M16 and is wearing a flak jacket. *Courtesy Steve Lovejoy*

another Marine. I was on my way up the knoll with my people when I saw him . . . he stood up and took an M26 grenade, pulled the pin, let the spoon fly, let it cook right beside his head for a couple of seconds, and threw it like a baseball. I would guess that he threw that thing thirty yards. The enemy spotter, who was ahead of the mortar team, turned around, and the grenade struck him high on his back, and when the grenade was still in the air it detonated. And when it did, it took out that guy and the entire mortar team. I don't know if it killed them all, but it put them out of action. I watched Pizana as that happened . . . it was very heroic for him to *stand* up and throw it like he did.

I moved up the knoll. There was a group of Marines on my right. I put my squad to the left, crossed over to the military crest, and passed an old bomb crater. About the time I took up position, the enemy made a concentrated attack out of the tree line. We had one man down, Sgt. [Harold] "Red" Manfra, to our right front near the bomb crater. We began taking a lot of wounded, and we dragged them into that bomb crater. Some guys stayed in there to direct defensive fires, and Sergeant Peters was there with a machine gun.

Lance Cpl. John Lobur: I saw Red Manfra trying to crawl toward me on his hands and knees. He was right in front of the NVA machine gun, and he kept getting shot and getting back up and hit again. I was screaming at him to stay down, but I don't think he could hear me over the constant roar of the battle. I figured he was dead. Steve Lovejoy was there with his radio, but he'd lost contact with the platoon commander. Fred Tanke was there, and there were a few wounded guys. They were all clearing M16s and handing them to Tanke and me, who were on the rim of the crater. There were gooks everywhere, so we had no shortage of targets.

Staff Sergeant Sullivan, now commanding the lead platoon, told Lieutenant Murray that his situation was critical. Murray ordered Lt. Ed Blecksmith to send a squad from his 2nd Platoon to reinforce Sullivan. Blecksmith sent Sgt. Lawrence Peters's squad. As Peters and his men left the lines of the 2nd Platoon, Father Capodanno joined them. Ignoring the intense fire, twenty-year-old Sergeant Peters maneuvered his squad around the backside of the knoll until he reached a position where he could support the 1st Platoon. With bullets snapping all around him, sounding like drops of water hitting hot grease in a skillet, Peters stood upright in the open, firing a machine gun and pointing out enemy positions until a bullet slammed into his leg and knocked him down. He pulled himself back to his feet and with a great deal of effort led his squad forward, advancing behind the fire of his gun. Limping from his wound, he inched toward the enemy until their fire pinned his squad and halted their assault. He struggled to his feet once more and stood in the open, directing his squad's fire. Seconds later a mortar round impacted near him, and fragments tore up his face and neck. Still in action, he stood again and directed fire toward a group of NVA that was trying to infiltrate behind him and cut the company position in half. He was wounded twice more and killed.

Cpl. Larry Nunez: When Sergeant Peters stood up with the machine gun and began to fire, he had this long-sleeve green shirt on, and I saw what appeared to be a puff of dust that was a bullet passing through Peters's torso. Peters did not quit work; he dropped down as the assault slowed down, and as it picked up again, he would stand and direct fire with his machine gun directly into the face of the North Vietnamese.

Lieutenant Murray did not know that Father Capodanno had boarded one of the Mike Company choppers at the last minute. As soon as the fight

Sergeant Lawrence Peters, Mike Company, 3rd Battalion, 5th Marines, was posthumously awarded the Medal of Honor for incredible heroism in the savage fight on the "knoll" on September 4, 1967, the opening day of Operation Swift. *USMC*

started, and there were dead and dying Marines all over the knoll, Capodanno ignored the fire and moved from wounded Marine to wounded Marine. Some he gave medical assistance to. For others, all he could do was administer last rites. When Sergeant Peters's squad rushed forward, Capodanno joined them. He was severely wounded by a mortar round that caused multiple wounds to his arms and legs and tore off part of his right hand, but he refused aid from others and kept administering to his Marines.

Lance Cpl. John Lobur: There Capodanno was, standing straight up right in the area where the machine gunner was on top of the hill. There were bullets flying everywhere, constant mortars falling right on us, and there he was, the only guy standing up on the whole field of battle.

When Father Capodanno saw the badly wounded corpsman Doc Leal lying some fifteen yards away, he disregarded an enemy machine gun that had the range on his position and attempted to reach Leal. A burst of machine gun fire cut him down before he reached his goal. Leal tended the wounded for over two hours under intense fire after he himself was hit. While treating wounded Marines and trying to get them into protected positions, Leal was hit a second time and immobilized. Despite this, he continued to try to render aid to Marines within arm's reach. A Marine tried to drag him to safety, but the Marine was shot in the hand, and Leal pushed him away and told him to take cover from the fire of advancing NVA soldiers. Leal was probably killed with the same burst of machine gun fire that fatally wounded the chaplain. They both saved many lives that day.

Lance Cpl. John Lobur: I saw plenty of fearless and reckless acts performed by the enemy, but I never once saw them risking their lives for one another or even tending to their wounded. I wonder what they thought when they saw Father Capodanno exposing himself to their fire, the stole and lack of weapons signifying he was a man of God, actually trading his life for the sake of assisting an obviously dying comrade on his own journey from this world to the next.

Lieutenant John "J. D." Murray, the heroic commander of Mike Company, 3rd Battalion, 5th Marines, is seen here around the time of (although not during) the savage fight for the knoll, September 4, 1967. *USMC*

The side of the knoll where Sergeant Peters's squad attacked was completely open to the enemy; it had no Marine positions. If Peters's squad had not been there at that exact time, and if he had not been the courageous Marine that he was, the reinforcing battalion of NVA that streamed in from the river might have swept onto the knoll and overrun all Marine positions.

Cpl. Larry Nunez: Guys were getting hit all around. Because of the casualties we were taking, I pulled my people fifty or sixty meters back over the knoll onto the reverse slope to get just a little bit of cover.

It soon became apparent that we were going to have to retake the military crest because if the enemy reached it, we would be in real trouble. I had what remained of my squad and a few Marines from other squads. I ordered them to fix bayonets because we were very low on ammunition, and I knew if we went back up on that knoll, we might have to engage in hand-to-hand. We had some grenades left, and I ordered each man to throw one or two, whatever he had left, on my signal. When I pulled the pin, I let the spoon fly and waited a second or two for the grenades to cook and then threw them up on the crest of the knoll; they did the same.

Tony Martinez was two Marines to my left and had a jammed M16, which meant he did not have a weapon. He was looking at me with these big eyes and had a grenade in his right hand, just as I had ordered him. I hollered at him to get a weapon and get some steel [a bayonet] on it, and he said, "I don't have one."

I said, "Pick one up," but we had to go then, and he didn't have time to look for one. So we threw the grenades, and he did too, and he assaulted the top of the knoll along with the rest of my squad even though he had no weapon. I often wondered if he intended to beat the enemy to death with his fists. I suppose he would have. That was a very courageous act. He could have stayed behind.

Lance Corporal Keith Rounseville also made the assault with me. When we reached the crest, the grenades had done their job, the enemy was knocked back off of it, and we retook it, but the enemy was very close, just a matter of yards. Then the fire actually increased, and Rounseville was struck and had a spurting blood wound in the neck. I said something to the effect, "Are you okay?" and he indicated that he was fine and continued to fire his rifle and fight that battle until it was finally over. Rounseville could have easily gotten into the bomb crater with the other wounded. It was an extremely courageous act.

Lance Corporal Blackwood took a round in the chest. It was a lung wound, and I took a piece of paper and put it over the wound. He would not go into the hole either. We had received an ammo resupply, and he lay there and faced me as I was on my knees firing. We were like a T. He lay there and loaded magazines, with his back toward the enemy with a bullet in his lung, and would hand them up to me, and I would fire directly into the enemy force, which was only yards away. I do not know why we were not killed by enemy automatic-weapons fire. Lance Corporal Blackwood never faded . . . a tremendously courageous act. We stayed on the crest of the knoll for the rest of the battle and the rest of the night.

During the fight, a bullet clipped Nunez's ear, a second hit his shoulder, and yet another grazed his back. When Nunez was pulling pins on grenades, he waited a second or two and then tried to bounce them off the ground so that he would get an airburst, and the enemy would not see where they were coming from.

Cpl. Larry Nunez: The next thing I knew, here came a Chicom, and I didn't have my helmet on: I couldn't throw grenades with a helmet on. I said, "I'm dead." I ducked down, and the grenade exploded, and I took some shrapnel in the head and blew an eardrum.

Aloft, Lieutenant Whitlow continued to muster more air power against the flood of enemy. The three advancing columns, although savaged by the one-thousand-pound bombs, still had plenty of soldiers who were full of fight. They were loaded down with weapons and gear, and they were camouflaged, and they were trotting toward Mike Company.

To Whitlow it looked like battalions of Marines on the move. He ran napalm strikes on the area where the one-thousand-pound bombs had been dropped.

Between air strikes, Cpl. Fred Riddle, a Mike Company forward observer, called in as much mortar fire he could. The groups of NVA near the knoll continued to throw troops at Mike Company from the tree line. Mike Company's 60mm mortars, in the rear with Lieutenant Hayden, fired in support of the company, although they too were under continuous assault.

The groups of enemy who penetrated Lieutenant Murray's lines tried time after time to fractionalize his command even further and made Murray's struggle to consolidate his position more difficult. Whenever supporting arms created brief windows of reduced fire, Murray brought his

Lieutenant Rob Whitlow, aloft in a spotter plane, runs these air strikes to help break up the masses of enemy soldiers who are closing on the desperate fight by Mike Company, 3rd Battalion, 5th Marines, on the knoll, September 4, 1967. *USMC*

lines together wherever he could and brought some order to the chaos. Air support ringed his position ever closer with bombs and napalm.

Corporal Chuck Cummings, squad leader in Lt. Randy Cernick's 3rd Platoon, was told to place his squad facing the tree line north of the knoll and slow down the enemy enough for the rest of the platoon to get across. Cummings and a corpsman were tending to one of his fire-team leaders who was just wounded when another Marine yelled that the enemy was coming out of the tree line. The enemy came on, but the Marines shot all of them dead except for one who got into the perimeter. Someone killed him with a .45.

Cpl. Chuck Cummings: About forty-five minutes later, Lieutenant Cernick told us to get up and start moving. As we started moving toward the knoll, we could hear the mortar rounds coming toward us. They were adjusting on us, probably because they thought we were reinforcements. My squad got up to a bush line, and the word came to report to Cernick. He was in a hole with a lot of bullets going around, and he told me to turn my squad and my gun around. At the same time, we had all these mortars coming in, but luckily none of my guys were hit. Our 60s, run by a kid named Dominic Duca from Philadelphia, were mixed in with us along with some headquarters guys.

When we started going to where Cernick was, a tall, skinny, badly wounded Marine ran up and said, "They're taking away our bodies." He had bandages all over him and was all shook up. I pushed him to the ground and said, "Save yourself." That really got my attention when I saw him full of blood and bandages, and he said again, "They're taking away our bodies." I don't know who this guy was, but it got my attention for two reasons. One, this guy was in such shock, and, two, if they were carrying away our bodies, I wondered how many of them there were if they had the ability to do this. I pushed him to the ground by his shoulders as a corpsman moved toward him.

At dusk, enemy fire and ground assaults slackened off but did not cease. Lieutenant Whitlow, in the air, had an increasingly difficult time picking out the Mike Company lines on the ground. As a parting gift to his infantry brethren, Whitlow called in an A-6 Intruder flight that dropped a full load of five-hundred-pound bombs on a large NVA mortar position, eight to ten tubes, that had caused the Marines a lot of grief all afternoon. The gathering darkness may have obscured the enemy lines, but the flash from the mortar's muzzles enabled Whitlow to pick them out. Whitlow plotted the location of the mortar battery on his map and saw that it sat just a few meters south of Route 534. It was most likely these weapons that were reported to Kilo Company on their march from the landing zone. These were also most likely the mortars that set up the rolling barrages behind which the NVA attacked Mike Company.

After dark, the Marines retrieved most of their wounded that had lain outside of their lines. They dragged a severely wounded Lance Cpl. Richard Guerrero into a bomb crater. One of the Marines yelled to Staff Sergeant Sullivan that Guerrero had stopped breathing and was turning blue. Sullivan tried to give him mouth-to-mouth resuscitation but when that did not work, took out his knife and made a small incision in Guerrero's throat. Then he took apart a ballpoint pen and inserted part of the barrel into the incision to act as a breathing tube. Finally, he started blowing air into the tube and got Guerrero breathing again. Later that night, enemy fire again hit Guerrero, and this time it killed him.

After dark, Lance Corporal Lobur was sitting on the back edge of his hole, and two Marines, Lance Corporal Blackwell and a new guy named Boone, were digging-in nearby. An NVA casually strolled into their lines with his AK-47 at port arms. Lobur had nothing to shoot him with, so he yelled at Blackwood to shoot him. Suddenly, Boone jumped out of his hole, ran right up to the enemy soldier, stuck him with a bayonet, pulled it out, and ran back to his hole.

That night, a voice came out of the dark, crying for help. Staff Sergeant Sullivan got ready to leave the crater, when one of the Marines shouted, "That's not one of ours." They listened carefully until the voice cried out once more. Sure enough, they detected a Vietnamese accent.

Cpl. Bill Vandergriff: About an hour later after the last air strikes came in, they sent a rescue party out to pick the men up who were stranded in the paddy out front. All through the night we took an occasional mortar round, just a few. And you'd hear the men on the lines firing and Charlie sneaking around out there, and he threw a few grenades at us, and we threw a few back at him. We had Puff upstairs working out for us. If it had not been for the illumination, I don't think most of us would be here right now. Puff was guided by a little spotlight that Corporal Goebel had and was firing 150 meters in front of our perimeter. This and the illumination kept Charlie off our backs.

Cpl. Larry Nunez: The enemy was dragging dead and wounded off most of the night. Even though we had been resupplied with ammo, it was a long, laborious process getting it out of cans and getting magazines reloaded. Rounseville and I went out a few meters in front of the lines to check on the situation, and the enemy had pulled back most of their dead.

There were very few that we could see in the night. We saw no more attacking NVA after dark, but some of them tried to infiltrate until sometime much later.

An NVA came up between me and Jim Raines where I was trying to scratch out a depression in the ground. I looked up and saw the sandals of this guy, and I looked up and saw this smiling NVA with an SKS carbine slung over his right shoulder. Jim had a .45, and I didn't know where my weapon was. I told Jim to shoot him, but Jim was so surprised that the guy walked past. I hollered, and someone else shot him.

The next morning we looked at him, and he was young, as we all were, his uniform was clean, and his weapon was covered with Cosmoline and had obviously not been fired, nor did it have any rounds in the magazine. I do not believe the weapon would have fired because of the Cosmoline in the receiver.

Cpl. Chuck Goebel: We could not get wounded out that night. I brought a resupply helo down in the dark, and he put a skid mark across my helmet cover when he came down. He threw off ammo but couldn't land to take out wounded because of fire. It was not the pilot's fault. They were too big a target.

Several Mike Company wounded Marines who otherwise might have lived bled to death; other casualties were not found that night and lay outside the lines until morning. The next day one badly wounded Marine told of being given some rice and water by an NVA who crawled among them in the dark. Mike Company lost seventeen dead and eighty wounded.

As the day wore on, Bravo, Delta, and Kilo Companies continued to trade punches with the enemy a click west of the knoll. The Marines from Bravo Company began setting up a perimeter for a landing zone when the enemy hammered them with fire from their direct front. The company took shelter behind a dike except for the 1st Platoon, which was sent off to sweep the hill and push the enemy back or wipe him out. Stanley Darius was a rifleman with Bravo Company.

Pfc. Stanley Darius: The enemy was uniformed and well trained and equipped. While the 1st Platoon was sweeping the hill, I was running around picking up gear that we had captured from the NVA.

Lance Cpl. Harvey Newton: At dusk we [in Kilo Company] pulled back to form security for the 1/5 CP group. The NVA were firing fifties in our lines. We lost a corpsman that day and the XO was wounded. I was trying to help another corpsman whose ears were shot from explosions. He was taking care of casualties and administering morphine, and I was yelling at him, trying to remind him to put an M on their foreheads so they wouldn't be given another, maybe fatal, dose of morphine by another corpsman. There was total confusion. I passed out, and when I came to, it was in the middle of a lot of shooting. I spoke to the Marine next to me only to find out he was dead. I made it over to a trench line and crawled the length of a trench. I lost my helmet and was reaching around the trench trying to find one, but they were all attached to living Marines, and there were a few words exchanged. I lay there and spread out, as flat as I could to the side so the bullets wouldn't take off my toes. The fire clipped leaves off of branches, and they fell in my face.

When Puff came overhead, they accidently put some of their rounds inside our perimeter. One H-34 got into Kilo's position that night and took out a guy who was hit in the throat, an engineer. The NVA lit up the area with fire as the chopper took off. I got off on the first chopper in the morning.

THE DELTA COMPANY 60MM MORTARS fired counterbattery against a pair of enemy mortars and knocked them out. Singly and in pairs, NVA circled the perimeter in the dark, tossing in hand grenades and wounding a few Marines.

Pfc. Stanley Darius: That night, Puff was giving very close support, and the flare ship was up. A few of the enemy tried to get into our lines but didn't make it. We called artillery where we thought they might be, in a ville about two hundred meters away.

That night we were on 100 percent alert, but it was too hair-raising to sleep anyway. We had twenty Marine dead and a lot of wounded. Some were medevaced that night and some not. That morning we moved out to our objective, Hill 63.

Pfc. Patrick Mosey: That night I was on a listing post, and we heard movement to our front. "Halt! Who goes there?" We challenged a squad of about ten NVA and got into another grenade-pitching contest, the grenades passing each other in the air. Another LP heard movement in front of them and reported it to the company command post.

They were told to stay put. Then they spotted moving shadows in the paddy and heard splashing noises. An M79 man fired two rounds into the paddy, and the splashing stopped. We were ordered to return to our lines, and we popped a green star cluster to signal we were on the way back. The flare was about to burn out when one of the guys dimly made out an NVA who was very close and was looking right at him. The Marine popped off four quick rounds and ran back to his lines.

The NVA were yelling, "Marine coming in," trying to infiltrate our position, and we were afraid we were going to be shot by our own guys when we came back to our lines. One of our guys was a Hispanic Marine and yelled in Spanish, and a friend of his yelled back in Spanish.

I was crawling back with this little black Marine named Moses when a grenade landed between us and blew three of his fingers off his left hand. I was blinded and couldn't hear for about twenty minutes and got a chunk of shrapnel under my right eye. There were small groups of enemy all over the position. We finally crawled into a ragged perimeter. I ran over one of our officers that I believe was dying.

As the sun came up over Delta Company's position at Dong Son (1), the Marines found some enemy stragglers who were still within their perimeter. Staff Sergeant Charles Jenkins walked down a trench, clearing the enemy before him with grenades. After it was all over, he found a little space for himself, sat down, and cried.

Staff Sgt. Charles Jenkins: There were thirteen bodies lined up for the medevac birds, one of which was shot down within the company perimeter.

On September 5, India Company, 3rd Battalion, 5th Marines, arrived on the scene at first light to take over area security from Murray's weary Marines. Mike Company was down to a field strength of fewer than a hundred men.

Staff Sgt. Craig Sullivan: My platoon began with forty-five men and one officer. When we returned after the operation, I had nineteen men and one corpsman.

Close to the Mike Company perimeter, scores of NVA bodies littered the ground, and the area was covered with drag marks where others had been carried off. In their search for bodies, the Marines walked through puddles of blood and stepped on pieces of flesh and chunks of bone. An interrogation report of a captive confirmed that the enemy gave greater precedence to carrying their wounded away than they did retrieving weapons. It was part of their psychological warfare plan to not let the Americans know how badly they had been hurt in a particular battle.

Every NVA squad had one or more members who carried wooden hooks with which they could snag their fallen comrades and drag them away. The Marines of Mike Company could hear the noise of the NVA retrieving their dead all through the night, and their patrols on the fifth found many mass graves between the knoll and the Ly Ly River. The enemy were getting better at retrieving their dead. They were generally successful in getting and dragging away all they could find from as close as twenty meters to the Marines.

Very often they would hit the Marines with machine gun and mortar fire to give their soldiers cover while they retrieved the corpses. They got a lot of practice doing this in the Que Son Valley that year, and the better of them could retrieve all the bodies they could reach and drag off within an hour of the time they decided to withdraw. A farmer named Truong Dinh vividly

A Marine stands guard over a wounded enemy soldier, captured in the bitter fight on the knoll by Mike Company, 3rd Battalion, 5th Marines, on the opening day of Operation Swift, September 4, 1967. He had been shot through both legs. *Courtesy J. D. Murray*

A few of the enemy weapons captured on the first day of Operation Swift, September 4, 1967, by Mike Company, 3rd Battalion, 5th Marines, are displayed. *USMC*

remembered that night and told the author that he was pressed into service to help the NVA dig graves.

Lance Corporal Lobur remembers 137 bodies lying next to the Mike Company position. He thinks this is far too conservative because he reckons the air strikes killed more than that.

Lance Cpl. John Lobur: There was a little tangle of bodies there, one of them with everything gone from his midsection to his spine. A little further to the right I came across an NVA who was still alive, although his guts were in a pile next to him like a bunch of rope. He was lying on his back, not moving, but following me with his eyes. He looked like he was fourteen years old. He was fading in and out, his eyes rolling back momentarily. I went to get some battle dressings to patch him up. Just then he kind of squinted a few times, then his eyes closed and opened a little bit, and he stopped breathing.

Capt. Joe Tenney: September 5 was spent resupplying and licking our wounds from the fighting on the fourth. India was fresh. Mike was chewed up. I had one killed, the corpsman from the 2nd Platoon, and several wounded, including my brand-new XO of one day, Lt. Ed Easton. The company had fought well, but the men were tired. We had been on the move since early August, with less a day off the line or out of the field.

The fatigue experienced by a combat infantryman is indescribable. There is nothing any civilian has ever encountered that even remotely approaches it. It exceeds that of marathon runners after a race or basketball players after a hard game or firefighters working on short sleep rations as they fight a huge fire. Day upon day and night upon night, month after month, they face drudgery, fear, trauma, filth, inadequate food and water, working in steambath heat, all of which contribute to a physical and emotional stress not found elsewhere.

Lance Cpl. John Lobur: We were exhausted and beginning to experience a familiar phenomenon. After the stress is relieved, darn near everybody falls asleep, no matter what the continuing danger is.

When Kilo continued the operation that evening, they were heavily laden. Because they could not trust the M16s, even the lieutenants carried extra machine gun ammunition.

Lieutenant John "J. D." Murray, CO of M/3/5 and hero of Operation Swift, eats chow the day after the battle on the knoll. Note the NVA helmet on his right knee. He was later awarded the Navy Cross. *Courtesy J. D. Murray*

Lance Cpl. Kevin Kelly: The next morning we [in Mike Company] went around and retrieved all the enemy and Marine gear that was left out. We found a lot of enemy bodies, and most still had their weapons. During the day, we got our gear squared away and then had all our KIAs taken out.

We went on a patrol, my squad and a gun team, with Lieutenant Cernick, and we found pieces of gooks all over the place. The patrol went toward the river, northeast of us. We saw a lot of NVA holes, packs, and body parts. We got to edge of the river, and Lieutenant Cernick was ordered across the river, but the Bird Dog saw lots of gooks across the river, and Randy [Cernick] wouldn't go, because there were only eighteen of us.

Corporal David Jones of Bravo Company, 1st Battalion, 5th Marines, was among those who went down the next morning and helped retrieve WIAs and KIAs.

Cpl. David Jones: We gathered up all the 782 gear. In the ville we found NVA corpsman gear, like morphine, and we found boxes of 250 rounds of .30-caliber link ammo that was buried; it looked like the NVA had been there for a while. They had trenches dug in way back and big caves in the rocks.

The next morning we got resupplied with chow and ammo, and the choppers went out one by one. Before we moved out that day, we sent out a patrol and found fresh graves in the area. The CO told us to dig them up, and we found fourteen more bodies. Our company saddled up for our next objective and continued to it without contact whatsoever. That night about midnight there was an explosion in our position. Corporal Townsend was checking lines at the time and caught fragments in both legs. They took him out in the morning before first light. Lance Cpl. Sadler took over as squad leader, and Lance Cpl. Lonnie Henshaw moved up to take over his fire team. As we saddled up and moved out, we heard the arty landing in the distance: that was for Delta 1/1, which was calling in arty on the objective to which we were moving. We received a round from our own arty in our midst, slightly wounding the gunny and blinding Sgt. Varde Smith, who died two days later.

Chapter 17

The Fight for Hill 43

Corporal Tim Hanley was with India Company on September 5, the day before they went off to take Hill 43.

Cpl. Tim Hanley: We moved up a ridgeline and found a great many trenches. Lieutenant Corr told me to take out my reinforced squad and set in an abandoned village about five hundred meters in front of us, as an early warning for the Marines on the ridge.

There were trenches and fighting holes in the village, and there was "Commie" written all over the place and a lot of propaganda laying around. The NVA had a habit of stuffing the pockets and mouths of our dead with that stuff.

I came back and reported to Lieutenant Corr, and he said, "You looked over the village damn good?" and I said, "Yes, sir, not a soul." It was spooky. I sensed that they were there, but we couldn't find them. We went all through the village, throwing grenades into the many tunnels, but found not a living soul there.

The 3rd Battalion, 5th Marines, command group took to the field in the early morning hours of the fifth with India Company and Capt. J. M. Gallagher's attached Delta Company, 1st Battalion, 1st Marines. Lieutenant Colonel Webster regained control of his Kilo and Mike Companies early on the sixth. Then his battalion set out with India on the left, Kilo on the right, and the battered Mike Company in reserve.

Lance Cpl. Kevin Kelly: We moved over to the 3/5 CP group, about eight hundred meters away. We stayed there for the night and received sporadic fire but nothing real bad. The next day we sat around the CP while they sent other companies out to new objectives. When we did move out, we moved in front of the 3/5 CP group, and we got to the objective that India had taken without a fight, relieved them, and started eating chow. India moved on. While we were sitting there, two arty rounds landed in our perimeter but didn't cause any casualties.

BY 1400 LIEUTENANT COLONEL WEBSTER'S 3rd Battalion, 5th Marines, seized Hill 48 with only a smattering of resistance. Then Webster ordered Capt. Francis "Stoney" Burke's India Company to move forward and seize Hill 43, about a thousand meters away. The company made its way toward the western slope of the hill, at the base of which thick vegetation grew along the paddy dikes. At 1530, Burke ran into an entrenched NVA battalion on the western slope of Hill 43, just two clicks southeast of Route 534 and four clicks from the site of the fights on September 4. Yet another NVA battalion sat less than a click south of Hill 43 and was in a position to support their comrades on the hill with mortar and machine gun fire. The fight that erupted was just two and half clicks from the Vinh Huy village complex, where Captain Graham made his last stand on June 2.

When Burke's company was about two hundred meters from the base of the hill, his Marines spotted and fired at two camouflaged NVA soldiers. Automatic-weapons fire came at India Company from the left front, but initial enemy resistance was light, and the lead platoon pushed through. As resistance stiffened, Captain Burke ordered his two other platoons up, one on either flank. They did not get very far. Within a few moments they were heavily engaged, Marines were down, and it was only with great difficulty that the company consolidated its position.

Lance Cpl. Bob Kreuder: We stopped in the paddies before we got to the first hill. I was carrying a radio, and we tried to get the hill prepped, but we couldn't get anything but 60s. We went over the first hill, and there were freshly dug positions all over the place. When we got on the other side, we found a ditch and brush line, and we got to that, and I somehow was no longer the point; I was back eight or ten people. And I was down in some brush just before you dropped off into the paddies. I saw this guy camouflaged with banana leaves run across the paddy. I couldn't fire because of

Corporals Al Campos, radio operator, and Gary Peterson, squad leader, with India Company, 3rd Battalion, 5th Marines, were key members in their company in the Que Son Valley Campaign. *Courtesy Roy Bowles*

the Marines in front of me, and I was thinking, "Why didn't you shoot this guy?" He was about a hundred feet from the point.

LANCE CORPORAL KREUDER AND SERGEANT RUSSO were on their hands and knees right at the edge of the paddy and could see that all the Marines that had gone before them were dead or wounded. A bullet furrowed the earth right under Kreuder, and he dropped flat. The noise from the enemy fire and a nearby helicopter gunship drowned out the sound of an order to pull back. Kreuder looked around and discovered that he was alone with the radio. The Marines behind him poured fire into the enemy position. The helicopter made another pass at the enemy, giving Lance Corporal Kreuder the bit of cover he needed to move back. "Why did you leave me out there?"

They told him that when he suddenly dropped to the ground, they thought the round hit him and he was dead.

Lance Corporal Kreuder looked back and saw that the NVA were at the edge of the paddy, where he had been just moments before. The lieutenant's radio operator, Al Campos, came running up and said that his radio had been shot up, and requested to use Kreuder's. Kreuder gave it to him, and a short time later, in the fog and confusion that reigns on the battlefield, Kreuder again found himself alone, this time in a graveyard.

Lance Cpl. Bob Kreuder: I was in this graveyard when another company showed up, and four or five guys came into my position, and I told them to spread out so they didn't get a rocket or something. They didn't move, so I got out of there and no sooner left when they were hit by a rocket.

CORPORAL ROY BOWLES, THE UNCANNILY ACCURATE rocket man, had been promoted to rocket team leader and was traveling with a squad led by Cpl. Dale Gunnell, whom they all called "Gunny." Bowles had just sent a couple of Marines out to recon the area to their front when suddenly the whole brush line exploded with AK-47 fire. Corporal Ernest Smith moved up alongside, and he, Bowles, and Gunny each went through several magazines of M16 rounds trying to suppress the fire. The berm they were behind was a low one so the three Marines, on the count of three, rose up to move behind a higher berm. As they did so, Gunny went rigid and fell back. Bowles caught him in his arms and lowered him to the ground. He had a small, nearly bloodless entry wound in the front and a large exit wound in the back.

Cpl. Roy Bowles: I started mouth-to-mouth, and Smitty was trying to stop the bleeding. I shouted, "Gunny, don't die. You'll make it." Fifteen minutes later he slipped away. I can still taste the salt on his lips from giving him mouth to mouth that day.

INDIA COMPANY WAS FIGHTING a larger force than one rifle company could handle, and at 1700 Captain Burke requested help. Lieutenant Colonel Webster ordered Capt. Joe Tenney's Kilo Company to assist. In the rear, the Mike Company Marines heard the sounds of the fight far to their front and wondered what it meant for them.

Cpl. J. E. Fuller: About a half hour after they moved out, we heard a heavy firefight begin just out to our front where India Company had gone. We were

Corporal Gary Peterson, squad leader with India Company, 3rd Battalion, 5th Marines. *Courtesy Gary Peterson*

waiting for word on what was going on when four arty rounds pounded in on us and hit inside our perimeter and about forty meters from where my gun team was set up. If it hadn't been for the big, flat rock we were set in behind, I know they would have got us.

It seemed like nobody knew where these rounds came from. Our arty FOs said there wasn't supposed to be anyone firing over there. So nobody knew where they came from, but everybody knew that they did come in.[10]

India was about one and a half clicks away to the north and east. Kilo Company moved as fast as it could, but one platoon carried a man wounded by a charging water buffalo. This platoon kept up with the rest of the company but only with great difficulty.

While Kilo was moving, a Huey gunship reported a large number of NVA immediately south of the perimeter. The pilot cut his report short, saying that the enemy was "swarming all over the top of this hill, and I've got to get to work." He killed twenty-three of them before leaving to refuel and rearm.

In the meantime, India Company still had a hot fight on its hands. Corporal Gary Peterson's squad, on point, was cut down nearly to a man.

Cpl. Roy Bowles: There were bodies of Marines piled on each other. It looked like the Civil War, where a whole regiment would march up to the front, stand and fire, and the return volley would drop the whole line on top of each other.

Cpl. Gary Peterson: Within thirty seconds all but three of us in my squad were killed. My point man, who had been shot in the face, was screaming, "Help me! Help me!" When the screaming stopped, I knew he had died.

NEAR CORPORAL PETERSON, ANOTHER MARINE was hit with mortar fragments in the head.

Cpl. Gary Peterson: I put some field dressings on him and told him we had to get the hell out of there.

THE DRESSINGS COVERED THE CASUALTY'S EYES, so Peterson had to crawl backwards holding the hands of the wounded Marine, who kept asking where they were. It was a slow, painful process, and Peterson and the two men passed numerous dead Marines.

Cpl. Gary Peterson: There was a pile of Marines, all killed. It looked like someone had piled them on top of each other.

PETERSON NEARLY REACHED HIS DESTINATION when a sniper found their range and put two rounds through the casualty's legs. Roy Bolwes and Al Campos ran out and helped Peterson get the man over a paddy dike. Despite Peterson's valiant efforts, the Marine died.

About the same time, fire from the other NVA battalion in the north smashed into Kilo's right flank, wounding several Marines, among them Lt. Dave Blizzard.

Pfc. Thom Heidtman: I was walking point again along this trail next to some foothills, with rice paddies to the right. I had walked the same route about two weeks ago. It was about 5:30 p.m. when India was hit badly. We were on a path that led between two hills and through some evergreens. All of a sudden we were surrounded, and by this time it was jet black. Part of the company was cut off. We got to a steep hill but with a plateau on top. There was another trench where the NVA had a machine gun duel with one of our guns later that night. The guns were offset about fifteen feet, and there were red tracers and green tracers that fired for fifteen or twenty seconds, and they were about forty feet apart. Both guns traversed, and each tried to knock out the other. Someone threw hand grenades at the NVA, and that was the end of that. They put me by a row of bushes in a ditch-like area. "Where is India?" I asked. A Marine answered, "They are out there somewhere, but nobody can make contact with them, so fuck 'em; they're on their own."

At 1830, heavy machine gun fire hit the 1st Platoon, India Company, on the left. The forward observer, Lt. Dennie Peterson, ran toward the firing until he found a position from which he could bring supporting arms to bear on the enemy guns. The enemy went after him with machine guns, but he kept moving from one position to another to gain a better vantage point to adjust his artillery. Fearing for the life of his radio operator, he told the man to stay back, and he took the radio, put it on his back, carried it himself, and moved into contested ground beyond the company perimeter to a position where he could better observe and continue to adjust artillery. He rained artillery fire on the NVA machine gun positions. Five or more enemy automatic weapons spotted him and tried to take him out. They wounded him, but he stayed in place for two hours adjusting artillery until after dark, when he crawled back to his own lines. Despite his own wounds and the heavy volume of fire, he assisted another wounded Marine into the perimeter. After a corpsman patched him up, Lieutenant Peterson called a temporary halt to the artillery fire, organized groups of Marines, and led them through the enemy lines on three occasions, recovering casualties and carrying them to protected areas in the company area. By this time he had been hit four times, but he went back to work bringing in artillery. He paused once more to get his wounds treated and was killed by a burst of automatic-weapons fire.

Sergeant Thomas Panian took over the lieutenant's section of the line and organized a defense. During eight hours of heavy contact, he led his men in repulsing three attacks on his position on the company flank. Though wounded three times, he consolidated the platoon within the company position and evacuated his casualties. Only after it was all over and all of his men were accounted for did he allow himself to be evacuated.

It took until well after dark for Kilo Company to close India, and even then, the latter had to fire some flares for guidance after sundown. Had it not been for the courage and initiative of twenty-year-old Cpl. Billy Bolton, it would have taken longer for Kilo to reach India Company. The NVA forces were all around India, but somehow Bolton managed to get through their lines in the dark, find Kilo Company, and lead them to the beleaguered India. Bolton, a fine Marine, was later killed on the first night of the Tet Offensive.

Pfc. Thom Heidtman: At 9:00 at night I was smoking, and a guy I went through boot camp with named Hargraves, who had been a smoke jumper in civilian life, came up and asked for a cigarette and said, "Will you bandage me?" I looked, and he was creased across the back of his neck, and it looked like lips on the back of his neck, and I cracked up laughing. Then I said, "You don't smoke," and he said, "I do now." I tried to bandage him, but if I put it around his neck right, he couldn't breathe, so I put it as tight as I could so he could still breathe. It was the only cigarette he ever smoked in his life.

Lt. Dave Blizzard: On the sixth of September my life changed forever. We were coming to the relief of another company on the top of a hill.

BLIZZARD'S PLATOON WAS IN THE LEAD, and Blizzard was with the lead squad as they approached the open area that circled the entire hill. He set up a base of fire with one squad and attacked. As they fired and maneuvered, a machine gun opened up on their right. Blizzard was hit twice in the legs and went down.

Blizzard's grenadier killed the enemy machine gunner as his corpsman and radio operator dragged him forward under heavy fire into the lines of India Company. His platoon was the only one that initially made the India lines. Later in the evening Captain Tenney and another platoon made it through. As Kilo moved up, the NVA attacked its rear elements and cut off Lt. Jim McCool and two squads from his 3rd Platoon.

Tenney and Burke struggled to get a perimeter formed in the dark and while under attack. Kilo dug in behind a shallow bamboo hedge row. Tenney placed his troops under Burke's command since Burke was the senior commander.

After dark the two companies fought off two enemy assaults supported by heavy machine guns. The first enemy attempt was more like a probe in force but was not very well organized, and the enemy was quickly repulsed.

Corporals Roy Bowles and Gary Peterson lost their way trying to move back to their lines in the dark. They decided not to take a chance on running into the enemy's lines by mistake, so the two Marines sat there all night, back to back, rifles at the ready, and waited for the sunrise.

When Kilo reached India, Lance Cpl. Robert Christian, Captain Tenney's FAC, discovered that the India FAC had been killed. Christian immediately moved into the fight and began calling in air strikes against the enemy, some as close as fifty meters from the Marines.

During a lull, Captain Joe Tenney moved through his lines to check on his Marines. He asked each one if he was wounded. Nearly every man who had been hit replied that they were, but that they could still fight.

Before the second attack, Tenney came up on the radio and asked Staff Sgt. Paul Orlett, who still commanded the 3rd Platoon, what his situation was. Orlett knew that the NVA had captured one of their radios and correctly figured that the NVA were listening to the Marines' transmissions. He told Tenney that he was strong and ready for a second attack. The opposite was true; Orlett's side of the line was sparsely populated and very shaky. The enemy sent fewer soldiers against Staff Sergeant Orlett's side of the line, which may be what saved it.

The second enemy ground attack was much stronger, and the sky lit up with red and green tracers. The NVA again advanced, with the tracers marking their lanes until they went into the assault. Tenney yelled at his men to hold their fire until they had a target and then fire at the tracers' source. Tenney had the center of the line with his new executive officer, Lt. Bob Hawks, on the left and the company gunny on the right. A two-man listening post was overrun to the company front. Lieutenant Hawks ran out and found one Marine was still alive and tried to drag him back. As he did so, an NVA shot him in the chest. Then the enemy overran a Kilo Company machine gun team on the left of the line and captured the gun. The twice-wounded Lieutenant Hawks staggered back down the line, but he stayed on his feet until he reached Tenney and reported; then he collapsed.

Suddenly, the firing increased as the enemy once more laid down a base of fire, and there was a loud blast right in front of Captain Tenney. The NVA blew a hole in the bamboo with a Bangalore torpedo and poured through the breach. Tenney ran right at them and fired his .45 at the enemy from a range of five yards until it was empty. Then he threw it at the nearest NVA soldier and reached for his KA-BAR. More of his Marines moved up and took on the NVA in hand-to-hand combat. Lieutenant Wayne Brandon's men from the 1st Platoon caught the enemy attackers in a crossfire, felled them by the dozen, and savaged their mortars and machine guns.

During the fight, Lance Cpl. William Baird volunteered to go out with a small team to retrieve casualties. They soon spotted the location of an enemy mortar tube. Guns up! Before they could open up on the mortar, they were hit by fire from two NVA machine guns. Lance Corporal Baird picked up two LAAWS and went after the guns. He got both of them, and the other Marines picked up the casualties.

When the second attack came, Sgt. Cecil Huff, a forward observer attached to Kilo Company, took charge of his section of the line, organized the Marines around him into defensive positions, and told them to hold fire until the enemy crossed the open area to their front. Minutes later, someone yelled, "Here they come, open up!" Huff was administering aid to a wounded corpsman when the attack came, and the enemy set up a machine gun just a few yards in front of his position. Huff rose up and silenced the gun with a grenade. He was wounded in the arm and after putting a dressing on it, moved among the Marines distributing ammo. The NVA came again, this time behind a rolling mortar barrage, their lanes once more marked with green machine gun tracers. Again, the Marines waited until they were close and then opened up with everything they had. Their fire was at point-blank range and murderous. Huff killed two NVA personally before he was wounded in the hip and back. The Marines broke the attack and killed or threw back those who penetrated their lines.

Pfc. Bob Whitfield: We were ass deep in NVA everyplace you looked. They knew their shit. I was just worried about running out of ammo. They came at us in waves, shoulder to shoulder and barely visible in the light of our pop-up flares. I stitched a guy in the chest and he kept coming.

Some of the NVA would appear out of nowhere and jump up and shoot at us. When the fire subsided a little bit, three or four of us crawled out to bring in a couple of wounded guys who lay in a small ditch to our front. My light bulb lit up. No wonder they got so close and we couldn't see them: the sonsabitches were crawling up and sliding into the ditch, and then they popped up and shot at us.

We took casualties left and right, and Orlett stood up and was hit. I looked over my shoulder when we were taking heavy rifle and mortar fire, and Orlett was standing up and directing mortar fire and directing gun crews and directing our redeployment to set in tighter. I remember tracer rounds going by him so close that a frog hair wouldn't measure it. If it weren't for Orlett, that side of the line would have folded.

I was hit badly when a mortar round exploded on my left. It picked me up and threw me twenty feet and knocked the wind out of me. I was totally numb on the left side. My pack was shredded, and all of a sudden I could feel that warm blood flowing down my body. It went in the side of my jaw and the top of my left eye; there was what I thought was my eyeball; but it was my eyelid; and it was hanging down. Joyce hollered over and said, "Are you all right?" and I said, "I don't know, I think I am blind." I took my canteen and poured the water over my face, and my sight started coming back. I felt this chunk of meat on my face and thought it was my eyeball. I said "fuck it" and ripped what was left of it off and poured some more water, and my sight came back. That fleeting moment of happiness didn't last long. They were still mortaring us, and the lines were collapsing in certain areas. They were passing the word down that the NVA were breaking through the lines, and there was hand-to-hand fighting. Someone dived on top of me when the mortar rounds started flying, and it was Corporal Beavers, and he dragged me behind a bush and a rock. A corpsman came over and wrapped a poncho around my ribs because I had a broken rib and a collapsed lung. I was okay as long as I could lie on my left, and I wasn't going to just lie there, so I was still shooting. The corpsman came back to check on me, and I fell asleep.

Pfc. Thom Heidtman: Pretty soon we got Puff, and it was bright as day. Five or six Marines came through this row of evergreens, and I was sitting there, leaning back against a big rock. These guys were standing there wondering where to go, and all of a sudden a mortar round hit right in the middle of them, and they are rolling around calling for their mother and "Oh Jesus." The corpsman ran up and started to bandage *me* up, and I said, "What the fuck are you doing?" He told me I was wounded too, and he said he would take care of them next.

Slattery from Ohio was on the rock on the other side, and an RPG or mortar hit the rock, and he started yelling that his arm was gone. I could see his arm, and his tricep was up where his bicep ought to be. He was carrying on, and I shook his hand in his face and told him, "Here is your arm, shut up." He shut up and went into shock. I took his tricep and slapped it back on his arm, and a corpsman came up and began putting big bandages on him. Our XO, Lieutenant Hawks, was shot in the shoulder, and it came out his chest. Lieutenant Wayne Brandon put the cellophane from his cigarettes on the wound. I helped drag him up and laid him between two rocks. I lay down beside of him.

IT WAS A VERY LONG NIGHT for the wounded. Those whose wounds were life threatening were taken out first. The triage process was painful for those who had to make the decisions on who to treat, who to send back to duty,

Lieutenant Wayne Brandon was a platoon commander in Kilo Company, 3rd Battalion, 5th Marines. The photo was taken on Operation Swift, where Brandon earned the Silver Star. *Courtesy Gerry Haugen*

and who to let die. There was no real way to treat wounds in a landing zone except to stop heavy bleeding, throw on battle dressings, treat for shock as best they could, and administer morphine. Just as the wounded Lieutenant Blizzard thought things could not be any worse, he leaned over to talk to another wounded Marine and when he got no response realized that the man had died. Blizzard was not medevaced until fifteen or sixteen hours after he was hit, and infection set in, seriously hampering his recovery.

When he finally reached Charlie Med, they wheeled him in and gave him a spinal injection to cut the pain and then began cutting away the bad flesh. As they were finishing up, one of the surgeons leaned over and asked if he was an officer or an enlisted man. He replied for some reason that he was a second lieutenant. The surgeon tuned to his colleague and, with gallows humor, said, "Sam, put the stitches closer together, he's an officer." After Blizzard was hit, the senior Marine standing in his platoon was Cpl. Greg Rossof.

The battle in the field continued. Lieutenant J. D. Murray, summoned to report to the battalion command post, returned with orders to move his Mike Company across two thousand meters of unknown terrain at night and join the fight. "And by the way," he told the men, "wear your gas masks because India and Kilo are having it dropped." Murray huddled with his platoon commanders under a poncho with a flashlight, briefed them, and gave them fifteen minutes to start moving. At 2300 Lieutenant Murray's much-depleted Mike Company went into action once more.

Lance Cpl. Kevin Kelly: Earlier, after India moved out, we could hear firing. Kilo was out somewhere with them, and they were taking a lot of casualties. By this time it was dark, and the skipper was called over to the CP group. When he came back, he said we were going to have to move out on a night march to India's position.

The march to the battle was not without great difficulty. Lieutenant Cernick's 3rd Platoon, leading the Mike Company advance, surprised an unknown size enemy force as they closed the other companies. Cernick led from the front and punched through the enemy resistance to reach the two-company perimeter, although he was severely wounded.

Cpl. Ron Pizana: After dark we got the word that Kilo and India were hit heavily, and their casualties were so severe that we would have to reinforce them. We moved over a thousand meters through open paddies that were filled with water, which made movement hard, and hard to move without making noise.

Lance Cpl. Kevin Kelly: We moved across open paddies to get to India and Kilo. When we reached India's position, we had a little trouble because India wanted to make sure we were Marines. There were a few enemy soldiers outside their lines who were throwing grenades and trying to get us to fire into India's position and India to fire into ours. We took a few casualties from grenades, and the 3rd Platoon commander was wounded.

Staff Sgt. Craig Sullivan: When we moved up on the hill, a sniper shot at us, but we were not allowed to fire back. We might be firing into the other companies' lines, and the men in the other companies were so keyed up that they probably would have fired back at us. We held our discipline, and not one of our men fired a round. They finally got things worked out, and we moved in.

Pfc. Bob Whitfield: Next thing I knew, the sun was coming up, and there was not a shot being fired, and I felt awful. I was scared shitless because I didn't know who had won, and I didn't know until a corpsman came over to get me ready to be medevaced.

THE MORNING SUN SHONE ON eighty-eight enemy bodies around the position. The 3rd Battalion, 5th Marines, lost 34 killed and 109 wounded. Lieutenant Murray described the scene that morning as "nightmarish." There were bodies and body parts of NVA and Marines everywhere outside the perimeter.

Lance Cpl. Kevin Kelly: The next day we had to come back to the place where the 3/5 CP group was, and all the Marine KIAs were still there for the second day. This put a hurtin' on the morale for the men. I don't think it should have been done. They should have somehow been taken out.

Chapter 18

The Second Battle at Vinh Huy

On the same day, September 6, two companies of the 1st Battalion, 5th Marines, ran into two battalions of the 1st VC Regiment near the notorious Vinh Huy village complex. The Marines moved through the first hamlet without incident, finding that only the very old, the women, and the very young occupied it. They moved through a second hamlet and it, too, was quiet, although it was honeycombed with bunkers and tunnels that yielded a good supply of NVA ammunition and medical supplies. Then they took a break for chow. By this time the 3rd Platoon had moved up to take over point for Bravo Company, and Bravo was the lead company for the battalion. After the break, they moved out again, and the point walked only a few meters before a sniper took a few pot shots at them. Then an automatic weapon fired a short burst, slightly wounding Private First Class Austin.

About forty-five minutes later, they started across another paddy, and the 3rd Platoon drew heavy fire on their right flank from yet another of the hamlets, which stopped the company. When the enemy hit Bravo Company, the attached company, Delta Company, 1st Battalion, 1st Marines, flanked the enemy and tried to take enough pressure off Bravo so that the two companies could join up and consolidate. The NVA did everything they could to prevent the consolidation process. It was a long and bloody business. The enemy force was once more two battalions of the 1st VC Regiment near Vinh Huy, the same place where Capt. Jim Graham's Foxtrot Company, 2nd Battalion, 5th Marines, ran into the buzz saw on June 2.

Lance Cpl. Lonnie Henshaw: As we crossed the open paddy, we could see some NVA on the other side. When we moved across and got hit, the NVA moved in and poured around us and pinned our rear down too. When the fire slacked up again, we moved out again, and a squad leader from the 3rd Platoon was killed and our acting gunny hit, but we couldn't get a corpsman out to him until after he died. We set up and returned a lot of fire and called in air strikes.

Pfc. Stanley Darius: The NVA let the 1st, 2nd, and part of 3rd Squads into the rice paddy before they opened up from the right flank with heavy machine gun fire and accurate sniper rounds.

Lance Cpl. Lonnie Henshaw: They were pinned down and couldn't move at all. We heard, "Corpsman up, corpsman up." I didn't know how bad it was going to be.

Cpl. Gregory Crandall: The 3rd Platoon was pinned down for about twenty minutes before they called our platoon up to give them fire support so they could pull out of the paddy. This did not work, because the enemy was putting out about ten rounds to our one. Before we knew what happened, we were pinned down too, behind small graves and a hedge row. The 3rd Platoon was still down in the paddy. Corporal William Erling was shot in both legs. Sergeant Rider picked up Erling and ran him back under fire to a safer position, but he died about five minutes after he was hit.

CAPTAIN REESE SENT HIS 2ND PLATOON around to the right to provide covering fire so that the 3rd Platoon could withdraw, but the 2nd Platoon, too, was stopped by enemy fire. Reese then sent Lt. Ben Drollinger's 1st Platoon farther to the right in an attempt to flank the enemy. The 1st Platoon found itself outflanked and was forced to withdraw.

Lt. Ben Drollinger: They came out of spider holes, and my squads had to fight their way back to the perimeter.

Cpl. Gregory Crandall: The skipper sent the 1st Platoon, still on the trail, over to the 3rd Platoon's right flank and told them to attack the ville where the heavy volume of fire was coming from. Before the 1st Platoon knew what happened, they were outflanked, outmaneuvered, and almost completely surrounded, and were taking casualties, including KIAs. They had to pull back almost immediately. They left a few KIAs behind but got all their wounded back. After an intense exchange of fire, 3rd Platoon also managed to back out of the paddy, regroup, and then set up a perimeter with the 1st Platoon. The 2nd Platoon laid down a base of fire to cover them.

The enemy attained fire superiority and then sent a ground attack right at the Marines.

Cpl. Gregory Crandall: The enemy closed in and came across the paddies, and we could see that some were falling, but more kept coming.

Pfc. Stanley Darius: Before you knew it, they were coming at us and toward the battalion CP from all directions. There were so many that we were fighting hand to hand. We tried to seal up the holes the enemy was knocking into our lines, and they kept coming across the paddy trying to overrun us. Then Bravo called in an air strike of 250-pound bombs and napalm, and that slowed them down.

Lance Cpl. Lonnie Henshaw: Then we looked up, and we saw more NVA in full uniform running at us across the paddy. I got a glance at them and then had to get down again because of the fire. I popped up and fired several shots and saw three go down. Nothing could stop them; they acted like they were doped up and didn't care. They were enveloping to our right to outflank us. We moved back around a bomb crater and set up a perimeter. The NVA were getting very close to us. We started to get air strikes that were very close because we were sure we were going to get overrun in a very few minutes. Several people from Delta 1/1, including their XO, came running in, and they were all wounded. I was firing and loading and firing and loading. I had to keep putting oil on the chamber of the rifle to keep it from jamming. If I fired a lot, it would stick, and then I would have to clear the jam, coat the chamber with oil, and fire again. I kept firing and firing. Sometimes the fire was so great that we couldn't move and fire back.

Pretty soon the NVA got so close that we had no choice, we had to pull back. The battalion and the rest of the company were putting in a perimeter somewhere to our rear, but we weren't sure exactly how far. Slowly, a few men at a time, we moved back to the perimeter. I was the last man in the trench to go, and I came by another position that was supporting me so I could move back. I had the radio on my back and two hundred or three hundred rounds of machine gun ammo. They told me to go, but I didn't know where, because there was nothing I could do except go out in the open, so I ducked my head and ran as fast as I could and dove into the hedge row. When I went through it, I lost my helmet and almost lost the radio. I picked the radio up and ran as fast as I could. Then I heard men yelling, "Over here, over here, over here." I ran to them and lay down.

THE FRONTAL ASSAULT AND ENVELOPMENT of the 2nd Platoon by the enemy nearly succeeded. The platoon commander, Lt. John Brackeen, saw the enemy's flanking attempt and ordered the platoon to fall back fifty meters and set up a perimeter in a trench line. The NVA closed quickly, and the enemy attack turned into a grenade duel. Twenty-five-year-old Sergeant Rodney Davis stood fast and pointed out targets to his men in an attempt to repel the enemy attack.

Cpl. Gregory Crandall: We pulled back from the small rice paddy about fifty meters on the other side of a hedge row, where there was a trench and a large bomb crater about twenty meters wide. After we got in this trench, we got a huge volume of fire from our front. There were air strikes all around us, and the platoon commander was trying to get a hold of these jets and have them drop their ordnance closer because there were so many of the NVA very close to our position, we were in fear that we would be overrun. The NVA were so close that they were throwing grenades into our positions.

Lance Corporal Robert Sadler, who had taken over Corporal Thompson's squad after he was hit, was trying to get everyone's head up out of the trail to show them where the NVA were coming across the paddy, down the trail, and through the hedge rows. Sadler got hit in the arm and fell down into the trench. After a moment of rest, he got up, wrapped a rag around his wound, and ran down to the other end of the trench to point out the enemy and was hit again by a burst of machine gun rounds that instantly killed him.

ANOTHER SQUAD LEADER, LANCE CPL. MANUEL CASTILLO, was in that large bomb crater and trying to figure out what was going on. He kept his head down, but, in order to direct the fire of his squad, he lifted his head three or four inches above the trench to see what was going on, and that was all an NVA gunner needed to shoot the round through his head that killed him. The alternate radioman ran over to help Castillo, but there was nothing he could do. A machine gun with the 2nd Platoon jammed early that day, and the gun crew was trying with everything they had to get the gun to fire again. The gunner was kicking and hitting the gun. Private

Sergeant Rodney Davis, Kilo Company, 3rd Battalion, 5th Marines, threw himself on an enemy hand grenade to save his comrades on Operation Swift, September 6, 1967. He was posthumously awarded the Medal of Honor. *USMC*

First Class Petrus, the assistant gunner, closed his eyes and said, "Oh, God, please make this gun fire." And before he even finished saying it, the gun put out a fast volume of fire.

Cpl. Gregory Crandall: The NVA threw three grenades at our position but with little accuracy. Then, all of a sudden, an M26 grenade sailed into the trench not too far from where I, Lieutenant Brackeen, Lance Corporal Henshaw, and Sgt. Rodney Davis were. Henshaw rolled free of the trench, trying to get away from its explosion. Sergeant Davis saw the danger that Lieutenant Brackeen and I were in, and dived forward onto the grenade on his stomach. The blast of the grenade lifted him about three feet out of the trench, where he did a complete flip and came down on his back. While his head was still over the trench from the blast, he was shot through the head. If it had been had not been for Sergeant Davis, I, Lieutenant Brackeen, and Lance Corporal Henshaw would be dead or seriously wounded. After this happened, Lieutenant Brackeen saw that there was no choice but to pull back farther and join the rest of the company. He had a man with a tear gas launcher cover what was left of the platoon, and we moved back to the battalion position with our casualties.

Doc Larry Casselman: That day, the sixth, we were trying to push the enemy south. My platoon was rear security, and we waited for the column to move. We had just got on our feet and saddled up when all hell broke loose. It was worse than Operation Union: they were closer, and there were a lot more small arms. I was with a group of ten or twelve, and everyone was hit, except for two of us, in the first few minutes. No one was mortally wounded, but they weren't able to fight. As soon as the column was hit, the company pulled quickly into a perimeter, and our platoon got cut off from everyone else, and before we realized it, we were a hundred yards outside the company perimeter with NVA all around. There was a lot of enemy grazing fire.

Casselman and the Marines crawled toward the sound of the M16s firing and tried to shut out the sound of AK-47s that were very close by. The ground was littered with weapons, M16s and AKs, so Casselman picked one up. He emptied a rifle at the NVA and was hit in the foot for his troubles. Now everybody was wounded. His little party kept moving toward the perimeter, crawling and pushing or dragging the worst-off casualties. They also tried to retrieve the abandoned weapons and ammunition that they found in their path.

Doc Larry Casselman: Once we found the perimeter, we had to figure out how to get into it without the Marines shooting us. One of our guys got their attention, and we hauled ass into the perimeter about dusk.

Lance Cpl. Lonnie Henshaw: Most of our rifles had jammed. As we were moving out, a man from 1st Platoon ran up to us. He was shot in the back, and the enemy thought he was dead. The NVA took his pack and his weapon and his gear. We took him back to our corpsman. Our skipper called up Sergeant Snook and his radioman, Corporal Cox, and they came running up to take us back to the CP. We still had eight or nine men who attached themselves to the 2nd Platoon. After my squad leader was shot, I used his weapons, a grenade launcher and a .45 that he got from a man whose M16 was working well. We put loaded magazines in our weapons and fixed bayonets. We had LAAWS, grenades, and a gas launcher. The enemy closed in using gas masks that were similar to ours.

When the gas man used his launcher and sprayed gas in the area, it slowed down the fire quite a bit. The lieutenant, I, Lance Corporal Selfbach, and Lance Cpl. John Call were the last ones to leave the area. Lance Corporal Call laid down a base of fire so everyone else could clear the area. Call crawled along this trench, and when he reached this rise, an M79 round hit him in the head, killing him instantly.

HENSHAW AND THE OTHERS DITCHED THEIR PACKS in a bomb crater and sank them in the four feet of water. They had to crawl another fifteen meters, the longest fifteen meters in their lives, before they reached their perimeter that was set in a trench around a small ville. Captain Reese was carrying a wounded man named "Frenchy" Borgett who was shot in the back, and his hand was hanging on only by flesh at the wrist. As Reese reached his destination, a hooch he thought would be better cover, a machine gun walked down the trail and hit him and Borgett at the same time.

Lance Cpl. Lonnie Henshaw: I immediately jumped out of the trench and ran over to the captain and saw that he had been shot in the lower abdomen, just above his thigh. I thought he was going into shock, and he kept screaming things I could not understand. All he was talking about was that he was not going to have his baby. He thought he was wounded right where it hurt him the most.

HENSHAW TOOK REESE'S PACK AND CARTRIDGE belt off, and he and another Marine, Private Berry, carried the skipper behind the hooch and called for a corpsman. The captain was almost out of his mind with pain and kept trying to sit up and look at his wound. Henshaw knew this wouldn't do him any good, but he would not stay down, so Henshaw reluctantly had to haul off and hit his captain. Then he pinned him down so the corpsman could take his trousers off and treat his wound.

After Reese was wounded, Maj. Charles Black, the battalion operations officer, showed up at the Bravo Company position to help organize their perimeter. The Marines were still getting a lot of fire, and Reese told the major that the lines were set in but they were a mish-mash of the various squads and fire teams, which were not with their original platoons because of the confusion of pulling back. With Major Black's help, they began sorting out the mess.

Henshaw's platoon commander, Lieutenant Brackeen, asked his Marines who the senior remaining man was in each squad. Lance Corporal Henshaw replied that he was for the 2nd Squad but that he could find only one other man from the squad, Private First Class Ledeen. He thought there might be two other survivors, but he did not know where they were. Brackeen told him not to look for them just then but to wait until morning.

Lance Cpl. Lonnie Henshaw: I was standing with Lieutenant Brackeen in an open space talking with him and a Marine named Krall and Krall's squad leader, Corporal Volkman. Three rounds came in on each side of Lieutenant Brackeen, and we hit the deck. One round went through the lieutenant's pocket and destroyed his notebook but didn't touch him. I asked, "Are you hit?" and he said he wasn't, and then he said, "Maybe I am." As he got up, he tripped and was trying to catch himself with his left hand. Another three-round burst went under his arm, and caught the middle finger of his left hand and almost took it off. The doc sewed it back on as best he could, and the lieutenant kept working.

AFTER THE CORPSMAN BANDAGED THE LIEUTENANT'S HAND, Brackeen and his squad leaders sat behind the hooch and tried to figure out who could still fight. They could only account for eight men in the entire platoon plus a few Marines from Delta Company, 1st Battalion, 5th Marines, and Delta Company, 1st Battalion, 1st Marines, who were mixed in with Bravo Company in the confusion of the fight.

Dusk was upon them, and the Marines expected a mortar attack, so those who had not yet dug holes did so. The corpsman had given Lieutenant Brackeen morphine, so Sergeant Posey took over the platoon. Sergeant Posey, Henshaw, and a couple of others decided that the hooch would provide them with little cover, and they dug in behind a large haystack about ten meters back. They were still digging when mortars and a great number of M79 rounds pounded them. The NVA continued the barrage for nearly an hour until the Marines got air on station and artillery on call and ringed their position with fire. The fire support was "danger close" because the NVA assailed the lines and were close enough to throw grenades.

Lance Cpl. Lonnie Henshaw: Suddenly, I got a call over the radio that there was a Huey overhead spraying gas and to tell everyone to put on their gas masks. This was useless, because we had gone through so many rivers that none of them were working very well any more. But we were pretty well shielded from the gas because the haystack filtered a lot of it out.

THE GAS DISSIPATED, AND THE NVA RESUMED their assault right through the twilight and into the night. They increased the volume of rocket and machine gun fire as cover for their soldiers who continuously crawled up to the Marine lines and hurled grenades, trying to cause enough confusion that other NVA could infiltrate the Marine lines. Major Black checked the

Bravo Company lines and encountered and personally killed several of these infiltrators and rallied the Marines to drive out the rest. In the dying light, Lance Cpl. Thomas Driscoll, the courageous young artillery forward observer who had proven so valuable in the fight on September 4, spotted two wounded Marines lying in the open about a hundred meters from his position. He moved forward and carried the men to safety one at a time. He dropped the second casualty within the perimeter and turned around. Right on his heels, a force of fifteen to twenty of the enemy attempted to penetrate the perimeter. Driscoll ran back at them in a one-man assault, a furious, grenade-hurling attack that broke up the enemy formation and sent them packing back to their own lines.

Doc Larry Casselman: That night I was in a hole with Chuck Jenkins, a sergeant who had been shot in the ass and was hurt pretty bad. Our hole was about five meters inside the perimeter and alongside a trail that came through the position. In the middle of the night, I looked up, and there were these two NVA walking down the trail and into our perimeter with their rifles slung on their shoulders. About the same time that they realized where they were, we realized who they were. Everyone opened up at point-blank range, and we shot them down. A Marine just inside the perimeter received a nonfatal but painful wound. One of the NVA was killed outright, and the other fell outside the perimeter and lay there moaning. We found him dead the next morning holding a grenade on his chest. During the night, we tried to get medevacs in, but every time a chopper approached, all hell broke loose, and we could not get a helicopter in until later.

Casselman was medevaced next day and did not get back to his unit until November.

Lance Cpl. Lonnie Henshaw: I got little sleep that night. First, there was the gas, and then the M79s and mortars. We were scared. When it was all over, I heard the screams of "Corpsman up." There were quite a few Marines hit, including some in the CP group. The eight men of my platoon that we could find that night surrounded the 81 mortars, and the mortars surrounded me. I sat in a trench right next to a sort of bridge that went over it. Lance Cpl. David McBeth, from 81s, manned a machine gun about sixty to seventy yards in front of us. For some reason, he got up and gave another man his rifle and took his pistol. As soon as he stood up, he got round in the chest that knocked him back down. We screamed, "Corpsman up," but no corpsman came. Within a few minutes he drowned in the blood that filled his lungs. Most of the night we heard rounds go off around the perimeter. Puff put out flares that night but not as many as before, and there were times when it was completely dark.

Pfc. Stanley Darius: Because so many of our machine gunners were killed or wounded, some guns had inexperienced assistant gunners on them who would open up at noises in the night, giving away their positions. The enemy 60mm mortars were so close that we were able to use M79 grenade launchers to counterbattery them. The enemy tried to get in the lines, and a few got in, but the Marines got hand-to-hand with them, using bayonets on the ends of rifles and KA-BARS. At one time the enemy overran the Bravo Company 60mm mortars and captured all three of them. We eventually got two of them back. There was only one officer left, and he took command and got everything under control that night. They got the wounded back to the perimeter, but we couldn't get a medevac to get them out that night, and some bled to death by morning.

The enemy continued circling the battalion and harassing the Marines with grenades until 0200, when they left, abandoning sixty-one bodies.

Lance Cpl. Lonnie Henshaw: We were on full alert all night. About 0400 we finally got some medevacs in. Almost all the machine guns worked and most of the rifles on the line, because two men would remain on watch, and two would clean weapons. It was a tight perimeter all night.

The Marines lost thirty-five killed and ninety-two wounded. At first light on the seventh, the Marines found a dead NVA with a map that showed numerous enemy positions and storage areas. Acting on this information, the 1st Battalion, 5th Marines, swung to the east, blasted through some enemy positions with supporting arms, and uncovered large ammunition and weapons caches.

Cpl. Gregory Crandall: By morning the enemy had completely withdrawn. We regrouped and found that we had fifteen men left in our platoon. The skipper was once more First Lieutenant McInturff, who sent us on a patrol to cover the area where we had left some dead and some gear the evening before. We collected all our gear, including an M60 whose bolt had been removed, about five feet from our trench, outside the perimeter. On the other side there was a large haystack and a lump where fresh hay had been thrown over something. One of the men took a long pole to the hay, and we saw two bodies, both in NVA uniforms. I grabbed the arm of one who pretended to be dead. After I stepped on him a bit, he opened his eyes and tried to give us the impression he was wounded, and he wouldn't get up and walk at all. He didn't have a scratch on him. They had an AK-47 and a rocket launcher. We left these men with Sergeant Smith and went out to the bomb crater where we had been the night before, before we had to pull back. The first body we came upon was that of Sergeant Davis, who had saved my life and others when he jumped on the grenade. He was unrecognizable. His body was almost completely dismembered. We carried all the bodies back—Lance Corporal Castillo, Lance Corporal Call, Lance Corporal Sadler. And we picked up all the gear. We found another PRC25 radio that belonged to Delta Company.

After we got all the bodies and gear to the LZ, I had to make up reports on the wounded and dead. In midmorning a platoon-size patrol went out. There were so few of us left than it took nearly all the men who were left in the company to make up a platoon patrol. I was left behind on radio watch when they moved out.

Lance Cpl. Lonnie Henshaw: Eight men from each platoon were sent on a search mission to a ville where I found my missing men. We went around to the west, in the direction from which the NVA had come the night before. We saw live NVA all over the place to our front, and it looked like they were trying to get us to come across the paddy. We weren't going. The patrol route said we were supposed to go there, but Sergeant Posey said he wasn't going, because he knew they were trying to pull us over there, and we'd all get wiped out. We came back, and they sent us out again on a different route. We found a man from 1st Platoon who looked like he had been captured alive and tortured to death. He looked so bad that I almost throw up when I think about it. We brought his body back on a poncho and put it down on the LZ. The 3rd Battalion, 5th Marines, moved in, and we expanded and strengthened our lines.

Cpl. Gregory Crandall: The patrol saw four enemy across a paddy. The enemy saw us too, and two of them ran away. The other two just stood there, open targets. The platoon opened fire and a lot of rounds ripped through them but they didn't fall. It turned out that they were dummies wearing rice paddy hats and black pajamas. Then a Marine in the patrol spotted twenty to twenty-five NVA trying to outflank us on the right. The dummies were to distract the Marines so the enemy could hit them in the flank. The platoon withdrew to the CP and called artillery in, but they wouldn't fire the mission, as it was too close to us. The patrol went out again by a different route to try to outflank the enemy but found no one.

What they did find was the body of Lance Cpl. Colin Hipkins, who was listed as MIA from the day before. He was lying in a bamboo stack, and he appeared to have been tortured. His legs were severed from his body, and he had been shot through both wrists and into his forehead. It looked like he had his hands in front of his face and trying to shield himself. They brought him in, and we stayed in the same perimeter for another very long night.

That afternoon as they were picking up the enemy bodies for burial, the stench was unbearable. The tropical sun had already rotted some of them to the point where an arm or leg would come off when the body was picked up.

Pfc. Stanley Darius: My squad went out that morning, and we found several of our Marines who had been tortured and cut up. One man had his tongue cut out. The NVA took food out of their packs and took their rifles and magazines. They also took the helmet liners and the camouflage covers.

We moved out to another ville, found some enemy holes, and set in for the night. My fire team had an LP that night outside Alpha Company's lines, and we'd been out there no more than forty-five minutes before we heard movement to the front: there was splashing in the water and movement in the trees. We only had two grenades and limited ammo. We threw one grenade that was a dud. The second one went off, and the movement stopped for a while and then started again, and we heard talking. Our M79 man shot two rounds at this noise and some talking.

The movement stopped, and we called in, and they told us to stay there and see if we could hear anything else. When the movement started again, they called us back into the perimeter. Lance Corporal Walters looked back and saw two of the enemy following us; he fired four quick shots and was positive of dropping the first man. The rest of the night was quiet, and the next morning we moved back to the battalion area.

Cpl. Gregory Crandall: The next morning we received word that our company was to be lifted out. Out of the forty-three men of our platoon, I, Lance Corporal Askin, and Private First Class Petrus were the only ones not either killed or wounded.

Lance Cpl. Lonnie Henshaw: I was the squad leader for the first time since I had come into the Marine Corps. I was not very sure about what my job was, although I had seen many good squad leaders before who had been over me. I had to go on instinct and hope that I would make the right decisions. That night nothing happened. We got word in the middle of the night that our company was supposed to move out in the morning, and Alpha Company 1/5 was going to take our place. We couldn't have been any happier. We had seen so much in a short time that nobody wanted to see it again. Before Operation Swift, I didn't mind going out and getting a few rounds shot at me. From that day on, I always hated going outside the perimeter for a patrol. I hope I never see another day when I watch my buddies die.

On September 7, farmers told the Marines that the NVA lost more than 300 killed in action where the 3rd Battalion, 5th Marines, were fighting the day before.

Chapter 19

The Hotel Fight

Three days later, the 3rd Battalion, 5th Marines, got into a fight, and Hotel Company, 2nd Battalion, 5th Marines, Capt. Gene Bowers, was chopped to their operational control. The battalion ordered Captain Bowers to double back from his current route and try to intercept an NVA unit that was supposed to be in the vicinity of Hill 43, the scene of one of the India/Kilo/Mike fight on September 6. The battalion suggested that they send squad-size patrols. Bowers decided, wisely, to send reinforced platoons. He chose his 1st Platoon, commanded by Lt. Allan Herman, for the mission. Sergeant Harold Wadley, an old Korean War hand, asked to go with Herman and take two machine guns and two 60mm mortars with them.

Lieutenant Herman and Wadley discussed the area that they passed through earlier and thought that they may have bypassed some caves and tunnels. Sergeant Wadley convinced Lieutenant Herman that a single man on point was not enough, and Herman agreed. Staff Sergeant William Stutes, Herman's platoon sergeant, was standing nearby and made a strong plea for being one of the men on point. Lieutenant Herman reluctantly agreed, and Stutes joined Lance Cpls. James Braswell and Michael Wolf on point. The platoon doubled back and headed for Hill 43.

The NVA were there and were well dug in along a dogleg position, and so well camouflaged that the Marines did not see them until they were a few feet away. The three-man point moved down one side of the dogleg and straight into the enemy trenches. The NVA were lying in wait with a lot of firepower, including at least four machine guns. The point—Stutes, Braswell, and Wolf—were right on top of them when the enemy opened up and were all

Corporal John "Juice" Jessmore crosses a stream in Antenna Valley, 1967. *Courtesy Harold Wadley*

Machine gunners Cpl. Melvin Johnson (rear) and Sgt. Harold Wadley, 1967. Wadley was awarded the Silver Star in Vietnam. *Courtesy Harold Wadley*

Sergeant Harold Wadley was one of the heroes of Operation Swift. He had been awarded the Bronze Star in Korea and left the Marine Corps before returning for the Vietnam War. Laos can be seen in the distance, with the Thu Bon River flowing past the napalm-scarred landscape. *Courtesy Harold Wadley*

killed. Sergeant Wadley and a corpsman named Dennis Noah went through the fire toward the point. An enemy round went through Wadley's gas mask pouch, set it on fire, and knocked him to one side and down on one knee. Another round got his helmet and tore it off his head. Wadley and Noah paused to check the point men and saw that they were beyond all help, and then Sergeant Wadley took off after a .50-caliber machine gun to their front. He heard a bolt click and knew that their gun jammed. This gave him the break he needed. Three enemy soldiers were sitting behind the gun trying to clear it when Wadley ran up and killed them, and they rolled off into a trench. Then he saw another NVA come out of a spider hole; he remembers it like it was a slow-motion movie. Wadley was on one knee and trying to react when the enemy soldier shot right into the point of his left shoulder and blew his shoulder blade and scapula out. Another Marine, Benny Burns, shot the

NVA and stayed up on one knee firing while Sergeant Wadley struggled to get his weapon reloaded with one hand. He thought his left arm was already gone, because when he looked down, he could see the top of his arm socket right under his chin.

Lieutenant Herman came out to get Wadley. First he threw his hand grenades at another machine gun and silenced it, then said to Wadley, "I'm getting you out of here," and picked him up just as several enemy soldiers came out of the next set of holes. One of them shot Herman through the head, killing him. Another enemy soldier crawled into a bomb crater about four feet from Doc Noah and Wadley, and Wadley knew the NVA was going to get one of them. Wadley said, "Shoot him, Doc!" Doc Noah, who had never shot anyone, before said, "I can't." Wadley lay there and was trying to get his rifle turned around toward the enemy when the doc finally shot the NVA in the head as he came up out of the hole.

The Marines were pinned down there for several hours. Corporal Steve Rader, a LAAW man, crawled out and got up on one knee to fire his weapon at a machine gun emplacement, and the LAAW misfired. The young corporal stayed on one knee and stayed calm. He wet his finger by sticking it in his mouth and then reached back with that hand and found the magneto connection on the LAAW, held the connection together, and then jerked the trigger. He got the enemy gun.

Lance Corporal Leo Aukland, a 60mm mortar man, was carrying the tube and a few mortar rounds and had gotten separated from the man carrying the base plate and bipod. He crawled out to a firing position, sat up, and jammed the tube in the ground. Then he wrapped his leg around it, pointed it toward the enemy, and began dropping rounds down the tube. He just eyeballed the enemy position and fired away. He had only the burner increment on the rounds, and they barely cleared the bamboo treetops before coming down on the enemy position. He got six rounds off before they killed him.

A helicopter support team (HST), attached to Hotel Company and led by Cpl. Kenneth Long, fought as infantrymen. When Long heard there were Marine casualties in the field, he and his three men ran toward the sound of the guns. They crested a hill and saw wounded Marines lying in the paddy. They reached the casualties but then, according to team member Billy Joe Stapleton, NVA fire pinned them in place.

The HSTs had not yet been issued M16s, and their M14s, operating on full automatic, poured a torrent of fire into the NVA position. Private First Class Kyle Furkins tried to raise the Hotel Company command group on his radio but had not the proper call signs, and the company CP thought it was the enemy on their frequency. The fire of the HST, added to that of the Marines of Hotel Company and Mike Company, 3rd Battalion, 5th Marines, eventually let them reach and evacuate the casualties.

A Mike Company Marine recalled that one of Hotel's platoon patrols "got hit pretty bad, but they didn't need any help at first. We got ready because we knew that they would ask us for help, and about a half hour later they called. We left one platoon behind and went out with two platoons."

Mike Company, still depleted from the September 4 battle for the knoll, fought their way to Hotel Company. Lieutenant Mike Hayden, who now had the 1st Platoon of Mike Company, gathered a small group of eight Marines and tried to maneuver into the no man's land between the Marine positions and the village where the NVA were. They got to a point about twenty meters from the casualties and ran into a .50-caliber machine gun that knocked down and wounded half of Hayden's small force. The lieutenant then adjusted fire for Mike Company's organic 60mm mortars and wiped out the fifty, killing about fifteen NVA. Mike Company got to the Hotel Company command post and explained the situation. Half of Lieutenant Herman's platoon was either in the paddy or on the other side. In any case, they were all pinned down. Hotel had not yet set up a perimeter, so they consolidated and set in. Then Lieutenant Murray talked with the Hotel skipper about how to get his Marines back. Lieutenant Murray yelled out to where Wadley and Doc Noah were, and wanted to know if anyone out there was still alive. He heard a voice shout back at him and came up with a plan to retrieve the stranded Marines and their equipment.

The Hotel Company commanding officer suggested getting his men together and assaulting the tree line without putting any artillery or air strikes in on the enemy position. For one thing, his FAC team was reluctant to call in air strikes, because the Marines were very close to the enemy. Murray refused to assault without prep fires and had the Mike Company FAC, Cpl. Chuck Goebel, do the job without causing any friendly casualties. After several bomb and napalm runs, the enemy broke and ran, and the Marines retrieved the wounded.

When the Marines brought the casualties back, a medevac chopper came in, they loaded the casualties, and the bird left under fire. Mike Company stayed with Hotel for the rest of the night. The next day, they pulled back about four or five hundred meters and called in air strikes before they went in to recover Hotel's dead. The recovery party found that six of the nine Marine KIAs in front of the enemy position had broken down their M16s in an attempt to remove cartridges stuck in their chambers. The enemy shot all of them at close range; all had bullet holes surrounded by powder burns in their heads.

Cpl. Larry Nunez: I took a patrol out on that morning and had just set up an ambush at the bottom of a hill when word came over radio to move out. They told us to move back uphill and set up an observation post. We went up this trail just as it began to get light, turned down a right-hand dogleg, and walked directly into a column of NVA regulars coming off that hill. For a split second I could see the column out of the right side of my vision. What saved my life that day was the lead NVA soldier was loaded with canteens, and he was going to a water source near there. Their procedure was similar to ours: they would send someone to a water source, fill canteens, and then pass them out to the column, which was moving. The regular behind him had an AK-47 and was as stunned as I was, and we fired at the same time. I don't remember him falling, nor did

A lance corporal remembered only as "Underdog" lights a cigarette for his wounded comrade, Lance Corporal Wasson, while awaiting medevac. *Courtesy Harold Wadley*

Corporal Larry Nunez's squad from Mike Company, 3rd Battalion, 5th Marines, sometime after Operation Swift. Front row, left to right: Lance Cpl. Keith Rounseville, Lance Cpl. Richard Giebe (killed in November on Operation Essex), Pfc. Victor Sosa-Acosta, and Cpl. Larry Nunez. Back row, left to right: Pfc. Carlton Clark, Pfc. John Noelle, Lance Cpl. William Talliferro (with machine gun), Pfc. David Pizana, Pfc. Tony "Short Round" Martinez, and Pfc. Bert Watkins. Corporal Nunez was awarded the Silver Star for gallantry in action during the knoll fight on September 4, 1967. *Courtesy Larry Nunez*

I get hit. When we engaged that group, they went into a ditch, and my guys couldn't see them, because they were shooting through a tree line. We put some heavy fire into them and they took off and abandoned a 60mm mortar. It was painted a dark red, and I think that it had been in storage, that they had a cache somewhere nearby.

Their column was between thirty and fifty men in single file. They were on the hill the same time we were during the night, and we didn't hear them, and they didn't hear us, and we couldn't have been a hundred yards apart. We moved out some distance, and on the night of the eleventh, I went out to an ambush site to find another water source. I set in near a two- or three-hooch village, knowing there would be a water source there. I moved my fourteen men, three fire teams, a machine gun team, and a radio operator as close to the well as we could. We set in inside a ditch in an ambush position

In the fall of 1967, Marines are cleaning weapons at a battalion area south of Da Nang. Ron Pizana faces a disassembled M60 machine gun, while Bert Watkins is at center. *Courtesy Steve Lovejoy*

near the well and two trails. During the night there was no enemy activity. Early that a.m., Puff fired on us, and one of my men was hit in the arm, Pfc. Talmadge Carnell was hit in the chest and killed, and I was hit in the wrist and tricep.

AT 0330 ON THE MORNING OF THE TWELFTH, AN INDIA Company squad outpost got into a firefight with a large enemy force. Supported by air, the Marines held on until just before dawn, when the enemy withdrew. The NVA force was thought to have bumped into the Marines by accident. It cost the enemy thirty-five confirmed dead.

Cpl. Ron Pizana: On September 13, we moved onto a hill, and that evening we moved down to an LZ to helilift us out to help the Vietnamese Rangers at Thang Binh. From our position we could see that they were in heavy contact, and we could see .30- and .50-calibers firing and our air support. After India Company and a platoon from Hotel lifted off, the LZ came under attack. The helicopters that were supposed to lift us were driven off by ground fire, and the mission was aborted.

Lieutenant J. D. Murray's 1st Platoon commander and his radio operator were seriously wounded.

That night, Lieutenant Murray's Marines marched over seven thousand meters before reaching the battalion command post at Hill 35 at about dawn. Murray is certain he fell asleep at least once while walking.

In J. D. Murray's estimate, reinforced by the testimony of nearly every Marine in the field that year, half of the Marines who died since the beginning of Operation Union in April were lost because of malfunctioning M16 rifles.

Cpl. Tim Hanley: After Union II, Captain Burke asked squad leaders and above to write up what they thought of the M16. I got called to the battalion CP to explain myself, and I was scared shitless. Oh, my God, I have got to go before colonel. He listened to what I had to say about the M16 and then said, "I agree totally with you."

I was relieved because I thought I was going to get my ass chewed for knocking the government's new weapon. After Operation Swift, I probably would have told General Walt himself where to shove the weapon.

Heading from a patrol to the Mike Company, 3rd Battalion, 5th Marines' base south of Da Nang in the fall of 1967, Ron Pizana is at the front with an M60 machine gun. *Courtesy Steve Lovejoy*

THE 2ND NVA DIVISION FLED THE QUE SON VALLEY in tatters. The Marines' newspaper in Vietnam, the *Sea Tiger*, reported 1,480 enemy were killed on Operation Swift by body count. The total, according to evidence uncovered after the war, was more than twice that. Operation Swift was the biggest battle in the bloodiest campaign of the Vietnam War. Two months later, in November, during Operation Essex, the Marines set out once more to pursue the 2nd NVA Division's units in a smaller basin to the west known as Antenna Valley.

Chapter 20

Golf and Hotel: Essex End Game

In October the badly battered 2nd NVA Division received new orders from Hanoi that told them little about the coming Tet Offensive. Their immediate task was to prepare to draw the Americans away from the major population centers. Hanoi also ordered them to preposition supplies to establish the logistics "nose" that they would need for a major offensive.[11] Although the enemy did a good job of not leaking their plans for Tet, U.S. intelligence sources accumulated evidence that the 2nd NVA Division was staging units and materiel near the western borders of the Que Son Valley for something big.

Thus far in 1967, the NVA had massed large units in the valley and sent them against the Marines in daylight. It was now obvious to the allies that the NVA prized control of the valley enough to fight for it, even the face of enormous manpower and equipment losses.

Everywhere they looked in Vietnam that season, American intelligence analysts saw the specter of invasion. Whole enemy divisions massed west of the Central Highlands and in Cambodia, not far from Saigon. The siege of Con Thien had ended, but other divisions sat on the north side of the DMZ. They worried that the 2nd NVA Division, possibly with the help of other unnamed units, would make a major thrust through the Que Son Valley. If unopposed, toughened NVA units could move from the western foothills to the South China Sea in a vigorous overnight march and cut off most of I Corps, including Da Nang, the second largest city in South Vietnam, from the rest of the country. Alarmed by this possibility and the many indicators of preparation for a major enemy campaign, Gen. William C. Westmoreland of the U.S. Army, commander of all U.S. forces in Vietnam, ordered a U.S. Army offensive in the Que Son Valley. Operation Wheeler/Wallowa began under the command of the U.S. Army's Americal Division and squeezed the North Vietnamese forces out of the valley. Some retreated to the far western hills. Others only went as far as Antenna Valley, a small basin just to the west and connected to the Que Son Valley proper by a dirt and gravel track that winds through mountainous terrain.

The Marines were directed to move into Antenna Valley, interrupt the enemy withdrawal, and drive them eastward, into the arms of the Americal Division. In all of the operations so far this year, the Marines had pushed the enemy out of the valley toward their sanctuaries in the west. This time they hoped to cut off their avenue of escape, push them up against the army units in the Que Son Valley, and then trap and crush them.

On October 30, the 5th Marines sent their 2nd Battalion, commanded by Lt. Col. George McNaughton, a warning order to be prepared to launch a new operation, codenamed Essex. Two of the battalion's organic companies, Echo and Foxtrot, were engaged in other operations, so the 5th Marines chopped Delta Company (1st Battalion, 5th Marines) and Mike Company (3rd Battalion, 5th Marines) to McNaughton's operational control. He still had his other two organic companies, Golf and Hotel.

There is always a lot of scuttlebutt before a big operation. One of the stories this time was that there were five thousand enemy soldiers in Antenna Valley, and they were making coffins, for themselves. The valley had fewer than six hundred civilians, and they were not supposed to be there. The allies cleared them out earlier in the war to prevent the enemy from feeding itself on their rice. With the civilians absent, the NVA fortified most of the villages. The Marines expected to them to vigorously defend the great number of supply and equipment caches they had stored in preparation for their major offensive, and they prepared for the worst.

On D-day, November 5, Mike Company made a long trek from the An Hoa Combat Base into the objective area, a long hike over a very narrow track. Private First Class Tony "Short Round" Martinez was fairly new to Vietnam and was intimidated when his column had to pass a Vietnamese farmer leading a water buffalo on the trail. Other Marines told him tales of water buffaloes. According to pop knowledge, they were offended by the smell of Americans, whom they sometimes attacked and severely wounded. He got by the beast without incident.

All of the civilians were evacuated from Antenna Valley in early 1967. About six hundred remained during the brutal fights of Operation Essex, November 1967. Because most civilians had been evacuated, the Marines were able to employ supporting arms more freely. *USMC*

Likewise, Capt. Edward "Buck" Dyers's Golf Company moved on foot from the Que Son Valley. Private First Class Joe Snead, rifleman, Golf Company, 2nd Battalion, 5th Marines, an FNG, spent his nineteenth birthday walking to Antenna Valley from Nong Son. It was not the happiest one he ever had.

Cpl. Jeff Lyon (squad leader, Golf Company): That same day the lieutenant gave me four new men. I had a full squad plus a gun team and a corpsman. The new guys had been in the platoon for a while and were experienced, but I had to move the squad around. All four of the new guys got it on the operation.

I loaded my squad up with extra everything—grenades, ammo bandoliers. I carried twenty-four loaded magazines all the time, plus bandoliers. Most of us had NVA packs, if we could get them, since the Marine packs were too small and nearly useless. Our platoon's mission was to set up security around the battalion command post.

CH-34 helicopters set down as they insert Hotel Company, 2nd Battalion, 5th Marines, into Antenna Valley for Operation Essex, November 1967. *USMC*

LIEUTENANT COLONEL MCNAUGHTON set his command post on Hill 171, which he reckoned was the center of where he expected enemy contact.

Cpl. Jeff Lyon: As soon as we got set up, we saw Hotel getting lifted in over us. They came in H-34s with no gunships. They weren't on the ground very long before they got hit as they started across a paddy. The gooks were on the other side and were entrenched with good bunkers and barbed wire. They caught a platoon of Hotel in the middle of the paddy and drilled them all.

Lieutenant Eugene "Gene" Meiners's 3rd Platoon of Hotel Company landed in the second wave. He was pushed out of the chopper from about ten feet and landed flat on his face. As he got up, he saw that the first wave was setting fire to the uninhabited ville next to the landing zone.

Captain Gene Bowers's Hotel Company did not have to look very hard to find the enemy. At about 1130 Captain Bowers told Lieutenant Meiners to take his platoon off to the first objective, which was the hamlet of Ap Bon (2). The official report of the fight says that the hamlet was hit with air and artillery. According to Lieutenant Meiners and Corporal Lyon, there was no prep fire. Meiners's platoon went through a little stream and then across a rice paddy and to an embankment, and that was ten yards short of a barbed wire fence.

Lt. Gene Meiners: There was a trail that ran through the creek and the little-bitty rice paddy, up onto a four- or five-foot embankment. There were some big-assed trees on the embankment—two or three or four big ones and a lot of grass. The grass was all shot away by the next morning; there wasn't any left. We came through there and came through the creek and through the little rice paddy up onto the embankment, and my point started to cross, and they killed him. There was a spider hole, and the guy in it had a machine gun and took him out.

Then my machine gun team jumped up on that embankment. I cannot remember these guys' names, but they were black Marines, and they were just gorgeous. One of them was so black that if he stood in front of an ace of spades, you couldn't see him. In the sun and the heat we were sweating, and he was glistening, just gorgeous—he looked like an apparition. And his buddy was not as big, not as meaty, and not as black, but they were both great big, huge guys. They took on the NVA machine gun, but they were both standing up in the rice paddy firing at the NVA, and both of them got knocked down.

Corporal Jimmy Floren saw that the gun team was down. He pulled one casualty to safety, and then he got up on the dike and picked up the machine gun. The members of the gun team were all hit, but the gun was okay. Floren took on this enemy machine gun at ten yards: two guys having a machine gun fight. The NVA was in a hole; Floren was out in the open. The gooner shot Floren and wounded him and destroyed the machine gun. So Floren went back and got an M79 and went back at it. He was so close to the gooner that the M79 rounds wouldn't detonate. He was just firing beanbags. And then the gooner killed Jimmy.

Duane Sherin, Hotel Company, 2nd Battalion, 5th Marines. The first photo was taken on the first day of Operation Essex before the Marines boarded the helicopters. The second was taken a day later after a big firefight. When seen individually, there is nothing particularly unusual about the photos. But seen side by side, these two photos demonstrate like few ever taken the effect of combat on a Marine. Lieutenant Sherin was awarded the Silver Star for valor during that fight. *Courtesy Eugene Meiners*

Even though his lead platoon was badly hurt, Captain Bowers thought that the enemy force was one he could handle.

Lt. Gene Meiners: Then I put my people on line on top of that little embankment, and we fired at the ville. The ville fired back at us with at least three machine guns. People who later went into the ville told me that they were firing from concrete emplacements. One guy said there were fifties firing from the flank. There were three machine guns firing at me out of that goddamn ville, and all the riflemen in the world. About that time, Lt. Bob Miller came up on my left flank. And then Lt. Duane Sherin went around farther to the left and tried to see what he could do about getting into the ville, and he lost a couple of people trying to do that, and he came back.

Captain Bowers recollects that he pulled Sherin's platoon back and ordered an intensive air and artillery strike on the village.

Lt. Gene Meiners: Then Bowers called me on the radio, and this is a quote, "Gene, I'm sorry, but I've got to get into that ville." End of request.

I never could locate where those guns were shooting from. I was a former enlisted machine gunner, and I knew about the trick of putting some wet sandbags in front of the guns to not give away the muzzle flash, and I don't know if they did that or not. We could see tracers but not the guns.

Then Bowers called me up again and said, "What is taking so long?" At the time, I was lying behind Corporal Wilson's squad, and he had about ten yards to go to the wire, through the wire, and then he had another twenty-five or thirty yards to go to get to the ville. The other squad had about thirty-five to forty yards to go to the fence, and once they cleared the fence, they would have been in the ville. I decided to go with the guys that had the longest way to go. I said "Ready, go," and I rolled over and I got behind that second squad and got up on that dike and out into the rice paddy in a matter of seconds. I looked, and Wilson's squad was dead, and the part of the other squad was dead. I think four of them made it to the fence and no farther. I looked and got my dumb ass down in a slight depression in the ground along with my radio operator. I can remember looking at him, and he was looking at me, and we were almost nose-to-nose, and his eyes were as big as saucers. I asked him later what was going, on and he said that they were shooting a quarter of an inch above my head. He could see it, but I had my back to it.

I started that morning with thirty-one Marines and ended up with six, including me. We had nine dead and sixteen serious medevacs. Now my platoon was a squad. And that was not enough for Captain Bowers, and he tried to take the village with Bob Miller. The thing is that Bob Miller had about twice as far to go as I did. We had been cut to shit, literally, by this time. I looked up and here came Bob Miller, attacking across to my left flank. This was the same area I had gone through, but his distance of transit was twice as long as mine. That damned rice paddy was alive with tracers. It was like a mad moment. Bob Miller began his attack across there, and I could see his people going down. I was watching Bob, and he stopped and sort of stood there for a while bent over, and then he went down. He was hit again. It looked like he had pulled himself up and was resting his head on his helmet. And that is how he died. The radio operator came up and bent over him, and he went down too.

At 1600, Capt. Edward "Buck" Dyer's Golf Company arrived on the scene and began an assault on the village on Captain Bowers's right flank. As Bowers remembers it, Golf Company did not even pause to coordinate their assault with him but moved right into the attack. Golf ran into the same obstacles as had Hotel Company and was repulsed after making a slight penetration of the enemy perimeter. Corporal Lyon remembers it differently.

Cpl. Jeff Lyon: We got a call for help and left the battalion command group to go across the valley. It took us an hour. There were so many NVA that they sort of opened up a horseshoe and let us into where Hotel was. Hotel told us that they had a platoon down and out in front, and they wanted us to go down a stream bed around the flank. And once we got down there in the bed parallel to the paddy where the men were down, we were going to get on line and assault across and into the hedge row across the paddies. All the paddies were dried out or a bit muddy.

Lance Cpl. Ronnie Powers (member of Lyon's squad): They dropped tear gas, and we had a hard time with gas masks because they kept fogging up.

The Marines were trained on how to use gas masks but not how to fight or even run in them.

Lance Cpl. Ronnie Powers: We went down stream knowing that there was a machine gun in front of us. We crossed a paddy dike to get on line and were going to try to assault the gun.

Powers crossed the dike and went into a trench; he had a sixth sense that something was wrong and stopped. The gunfire quieted down for a moment.

Cpl. Jeff Lyon: One of the enemy machine guns had a bolt come loose on the gas cylinder, and you could hear it slow down as it worked its way loose. One of my guys yelled, "Kill him, he can't shoot," but it wasn't a minute or two later before it was back into action.

The Marine behind Lance Corporal Powers crossed the trench, came up out of it, and took three bullets in the face. The fight started again, and the company was cut in three; some were in the trench, some in the paddy, and some in the stream.

Cpl. Jeff Lyon: When we started down the stream bed, one of the other platoons went first. We had a good view of the rice paddies and could see what we were facing. My platoon went about seventy-five yards when machine gun fire opened up down the stream bed, forcing us to the side. One Marine was killed, and a corpsman assaulted the gun with a .45 when the gun jammed and he killed both men. Lieutenant Arndt told me, "Lyon take your squad up out of the stream bed, and try to hook up with Hotel Company's platoon that is down in the paddy."

I told my men what we were going to go, and we got ready. The problem was the stream bed was about seven to eight feet deep, with a steep, muddy bank. "Everybody out of the stream bed." We had to pull ourselves up on whatever branches we could find, and guys were boosting each other. My M79 man, Lance Corporal Bressner, was right behind me, one of the Marines I had just gotten in my squad. The paddy was right in front, and the village wasn't visible because of growth, but we could see an old concrete building.

I saw two NVA standing on top of a little knoll. And I let a magazine go, and they went down. Bressner started across, and the rest of the squad was coming up. Lieutenant Arndt told me the rest of the platoon would be right behind me. I put in another magazine and was still running when Bressner stepped on a "Bouncing Betty" [antipersonnel mine] and was blown up.

I got some slight wounds but was dazed by the explosion and blown forward, and I thought I was going to pass out. I kept firing until everyone else was across. We put our backs down against the paddy dikes because we were taking machine gun fire and grenades. I was waiting for the rest of the platoon, and they never came. Because of the swift action of Corpsman Moore, Bressner lived. Moore picked him up and took him back to be medevaced by the only choppers that got in that day.

I called Arndt, and he told me to send a fire team out into the paddy to my front and see if they could hook up with the dead and wounded of Hotel Company. We were out in the paddy, and the rest of Golf Company pulled back and went back to where Hotel was.

Golf Company never did assault; only Lyon's squad did so. He feels that the officers failed that day, and the sergeants took over and did the right thing.

Cpl. Jeff Lyon: I sent the fire team forward, and then I was going to try to move up. I was at the stream bed, and the rest of the platoon never showed up. We had arty and air, and I couldn't fire in front of me, because I didn't know where my men were because of the foliage. We were yelling out to them, and they didn't answer, and I assumed they were dead. I told Arndt that I was missing three guys, there was no answer, and I thought they were all KIA. He told me to pull back. I told him no, "I am not pulling back. I have guys down in front of me, and I don't know if they are dead or wounded or just can't answer. I am not leaving here." He gave me a direct order, and I refused the order and said, "I am not pulling back." I stayed out there.

I called guns up to lay down a base of fire so we could go out and see what happened to this fire team and get them back. The gun came up, and the gunner told me, "I don't have any barrels, both of my barrels are burnt out." I went totally ape shit. I said, "What?" He said he could only shoot one round at a time. I was screaming at him. "Yesterday we were told there were five thousand gooks in the valley, and you come out with two burnt-out barrels." He was giving me this whole load of shit. I found out later that it wasn't the barrels but that the gas piston had been put in backwards when the gunner cleaned it. If the barrel was burned out, it just meant you wouldn't have accurate fire.

Now I had no M79 and no machine gun. I had five LAAWs. I fired one into a grass hooch, two into the concrete building, and two into the bunkers. The dead and wounded from Hotel were to our front, so we fired to our right front so we wouldn't hit any of them. The gooks had a trench line along the edge of the paddy, and they were running down into the trench and throwing grenades and firing AK-47s and then running back. I was up front, and I had my guys pass grenades up to me. I threw all of them myself because I was worried about hitting the dead and wounded to my front, and I didn't want anyone else to hit them. I rose up one time, and they threw a grenade at me that lay on the side of the trench looking like a soup can. I ducked and it went off.

Now we were out of LAAWs and grenades. I also used up all the ammo in my twenty-four magazines and told all my men to fire just one round at a time to save ammo. I was reloading my magazines and talking to Arndt on the radio and trying to figure out how to get our dead and wounded back. They were only ten feet in front of us, but the gooks were only about fifteen feet to our right front. We couldn't do anything except stay up against the paddy dike. We had arty and air coming in. I was reloading magazines, and the lieutenant kept telling us to pull back, and I told him no. Our guys were right between us and the Hotel guys who were maybe thirty feet in front of us.

I told my other guy, Pfc. Ardenia Freeman, to go back and get whatever he could—LAAWs, ammo, M79 rounds—and tell the lieutenant we need help up here. He went back and got an M79 and all the ammo he could carry. I sent one of the machine gun team back to get a barrel, and he came back empty-handed. Freeman fired about ninety M79 rounds at the gooks, but it didn't faze them. There were so many of them, and they were so dug in.

Eighteen-year-old Freeman was killed that day.

Cpl. Jeff Lyon: I was reloading magazines, and my radio operator was behind my back. I had Lance Corporal Rearick and Private First Class Cobbs next to me, and my radioman was Lance Cpl. James Lucky Jenkins, his real name. We used to call him "Dean" because he looked like James Dean. He was on the radio and telling me that Arndt was telling me to pull back again. I told him that we were not pulling back. Jenkins just lost it and started to run. The next things happened in about twenty seconds. Jenkins got up and started running around me. I tried to kick him with my legs to knock him down and yelled, "Get down! Get down!" As he was running around me, a grenade went off and blew up Rearick and Cobbs, and Rearick came flying back on top of me. I got up to run after Jenkins, who made a turn and jumped into the trench. As soon as he got in the trench, they opened up with a machine gun and must have put twenty rounds in him, through the throat. This was the trench the gooks were in, and the guys in the trench were Lance Cpl. Ron Powers, Cpl. Clarence Scott, and Private First Class Shumbarger—the fire team I was missing. Scott and Shumbarger were dead, and Powers was having his own grenade duel with the gooks.

I had been letting the grenade spoon flip and holding it a bit before I threw it. Powers was doing the same thing. He was trying to get an airburst. When the machine gun concentrated on Jenkins, Powers came flying out of the trench, the top of his helmet was smoking on fire, and the look on his face was the look of death. I grabbed him and said, "Are you all right, are you all right?" He had been in the trench for about two hours and went through hell with those two guys. He went back with this other new guy, Lance Cpl. John Tooke, who was later killed that night. When they blasted Jenkins with the machine gun fire, his blood was splattered all over everybody. My gunner had big chunks of flesh and lots of blood over his back, and I thought he was hit. He was screaming and yelling and in shock.

I went back to see how Rearick and Cobbs were. Rearick was on his back yelling, "Corpsman up, I need a corpsman, I'm shot in the head." The sun was up, and he had his hand up to shade his face, and blood was dripping on his face. I told him to get the hell up and fight: "You are only shot in the hand, not in the head." I sent him back. Then Arndt sent one guy up. He was a coward and was scared shitless. He wasn't in my squad, and I didn't care.

The next thing that happened is that Cobbs was blown up by a Bouncing Betty that went off, and part of it hit one of my canteens, and I thought I had been shot. Cobbs was okay, just a little shocked. His pack was on fire, and he had to rip it off. A bullet hit a flare in the pack, and it didn't go off but was smoking. All my guys could have gotten Purple Hearts that day, but most of the guys in Golf Company thought that Hearts were bad luck.

Now I had no radio, which was good, since I didn't have to listen to the lieutenant. I had no M79 rounds left and no grenades and no LAAWs. I had plenty of machine gun ammo but no machine gun. We knew where Jenkins got hit, and we wanted to get him out of there. I had a rope in my pack with a hook on the end. Private First Class Freeman volunteered to go into the trench with a .45 to try to get Jenkins out. A jet was coming in, and I told Freeman to wait. The jet was coming really low. We got down and got our backs to the paddy dikes, and I looked up, and two silver cylinders were tumbling at us. I screamed, "Get down!" I thought they were napalm. They were headed for us, and they blew up in the air. The guys started yelling, "Gas!" but most of them had thrown the gas masks away and filled the pouches with C-rations. The gooks got down until the gas subsided.

Freeman said he was going in now to get Jenkins and the radio, which was on Jenkins. First he hooked the rope on the radio, and we couldn't get him out. Sergeant Parke and Corporal Lofton came out with the 2nd Squad after we had been out there for about four hours. They helped us trying to get the bodies out, but they were stuck, and we couldn't get them. Freeman went in there several times and was taking fire, and we still couldn't get the bodies out.

After three attempts to get them out, Parke ordered me back, and I wanted to cry. It was the saddest time of my life. It was such a bad taste because no matter our tradition, I had to leave three guys out there. Hotel had about thirty guys, and they left them out there too.

THE TEAR GAS DROP HAD BUT A TEMPORARY effect on the enemy, and they were soon back in the fight. The Marines were low on ammunition of all types; their 60mm high explosive rounds were all gone, but they fired what they had left—illumination rounds that they disarmed in hopes that the sound of the rounds leaving the guns would help keep the enemy's heads down. The two companies collected what casualties they could reach and moved back to set up in what Bowers described as a "comma" shaped defensive position for the night. The wounded were surrounded by their comrades in the tight curl at one end of the comma, where the corpsmen feverishly worked on them. Captain Bowers had over a dozen emergency medevacs, men who might die if he did not get them out immediately. Two choppers came in over the battlefield and asked for him to pop a smoke to mark the landing zone. Bowers told the pilots that he was under heavy fire and could not secure a landing zone. The two H-34s, one piloted by a squadron commander, flew through the fire anyway, kicked off ammunition, and lifted out fourteen emergency medevacs. As the choppers sat on the ground, the red rays of the setting sun shone through the dozens of bullet holes in them.

Cpl. Jeff Lyon: When we pulled back with Hotel, it was getting dark. I had four guys dead and four wounded. At twilight, we found gooks in our position in spider holes. They started jumping out and running out of our position. Ronnie Powers was at the end of our position, in a hole at the end of the dike that was in the open. One of the NVA that was running out ran by and opened up with an AK as Powers was trying to pull Tooke down. Tooke was hit. Then the NVA ran over the top of them and took off, and a corpsman carried Tooke back. He might have been saved with another medevac, but we got no more that night. He lived about an hour.

Just at dark, Captain Bowers was on the edge of his perimeter when an NVA popped up and tossed a grenade in his direction. It rang his ears but caused no other damage. He quickly reacted and threw a grenade of his own, killing the enemy soldier. The NVA harassed the two companies with small-arms fire until late that night despite the best efforts of their FO and FAC teams. The Marines were greatly relieved when their old friend Puff came on station and worked the village over for several hours.

Cpl. Jeff Lyon: When it got really dark, we got Puff, who came over and dropped flares and hosed down the area. Part of the paddy had dead Marines covered with ponchos, and the flares would swing, and the shadows on ponchos glittered black with blood. Tooke was there, and we were talking to him when he died. He had gone to the States to get married on his R&R to Hawaii. His last words were, "Tell my wife I love her." I said, "Don't worry, I'll tell her." Lieutenant Arndt said not to worry, that he would write a letter and take care of it. To this day it bugs me that maybe no one told her.

The rest of the night it was all flares and Puff. Every now and then, when the flares went out, the gooks ran around the position like crazy. One gook

Corporal Mansil Hurlbutt III, a rifleman, eats a can of peaches after an assault on NVA bunkers, 1967. *Courtesy Harold Wadley*

came up out of the creek bed, and the Marine shot him right in the head with an M79 round that didn't detonate. The next day it was like his head was split in half. We went out before dawn, at 0500.

They said we are going after the gooks, and we went up the stream bed, but the gooks had disappeared. We collected our dead and went to get Jenkins and Shumbarger and Scott out of the trench. The gooks had taken all their stuff but didn't mutilate them. We lost a radio and a .45 and some M16s.

THE MARINES ASSAULTED THROUGH THE VILLAGE that morning without resistance. They discovered that behind the barbed wire the enemy had a communications trench, dotted with firing platforms and with deep tunnels dug into the sides, where the enemy could take shelter during artillery and air attacks. The village was located near the mountain foothills, where the enemy easily melted into the rugged terrain beyond.

An NVA officer cadet captured a few days later stated that he was at Ap Bon (2) during this action. He told the Marines that an enemy headquarters battalion occupied the hamlet and that a direct bomb hit from a Marine aircraft on the command bunker killed the battalion commander.

He also said that more than 60 NVA were killed at Ap Bon (2). The day had cost the Marines 23 killed and 56 wounded.

Cpl. Jeff Lyon: It was only a matter of about eighteen hours since our guys died, and the stench, body waste, and red ants were horrible. It was muddy and slippery, and we needed three to four guys to carry each guy out. We struggled to get them out. One of them was bloated, and the ants were coming out his nose and eyes and ears. As we were moving out, I looked over in the paddy where Hotel's dead, about thirty guys, were still lying out there. All these guys were bent, and legs were twisted around their heads; some were on their knees and bent backwards and arms wrapped around their backs. I was ashamed that we didn't do more to get these guys. There should have been some officers up there calling air strikes or whatever. The problem wasn't getting out to where we had been, it was getting back.

We got some artillery rounds, and Corporal Krieger was with his squad across the paddy. The arty went into where he was, and he called for corpsmen. Two corpsmen ran over to help. I ran out, and then I heard more rounds come in. One of the corpsmen had to be medevaced. And Krieger. He died later in the hospital. The arty round cut his stomach wide open.

Hotel and Golf Companies, 2nd Battalion, 5th Marines, lost radio contact with their parent battalion the evening of November 6, and Lieutenant Colonel McNaughton called for an air observer as soon as it was light enough to see. The duty officer awakened air observer Lt. Robert "Rob" Whitlow an hour early on November 7 because of the emergency in Antenna Valley. Well before dawn, he squeezed into the back seat of an O-1G Bird Dog spotter plane behind the pilot, Capt. Dave Marshall. The Bird Dog's mission was to find the missing companies.

Captain Marshall had been an A-4 Skyhawk attack pilot until he was shot down in the North Vietnamese coastal city of Vinh. The story was that Marshall had completed his bomb run and then put down his flaps, speed brake, tail hook, and landing gear and made a touch-and-go landing on the town's main street. Whatever the truth, Captain Marshall was widely known as a highly skilled and completely fearless aviator.

Antenna Valley was completely covered by a deep fog layer that curled around the valley and reminded Whitlow of a thick, white, fuzzy caterpillar. Marshall said, "Hold on, Rob, this is going to get interesting," and put the aircraft into a dive through the opaque fog. Lieutenant Whitlow could see no visual reference point, and only the rapidly unwinding altimeter told them how high they were. At the last second, Marshall leveled off under the fog and flew along the Thu Bon River just a few feet above its muddy surface.

Lt. Rob Whitlow: I was glad that we had drawn one of the newer models of the Bird Dog. Our newer planes were, of course, proving much more reliable. Skimming along the river's surface, even a slight hiccup from the engine would make for a long, messy day. The light conditions and the heavy fog bathed the river in a ghostly gray cast. A light mist hugged the water, and I could barely make out the dark riverbanks flashing past my open rear windows. The expression "flying by the seat of your pants" took on a whole new meaning that morning.

WITH WHITLOW NAVIGATING, Marshall made his way to the site of the battle where Golf and Hotel Companies were engaged the previous day. As they flew over them, Captain Marshall said, "Holy shit, did you see that?" Whitlow and Marshall agreed that it was the single worst sight either of them had seen in Vietnam. Lieutenant Whitlow added that it could have been a scene from Dante. The terrain was completely devastated, the survivors grouped together in a tight perimeter atop a small hill, and there were bodies everywhere, Marines and NVA. Whitlow called in air strikes on the surrounding terrain to discourage any NVA remaining in the area.

That morning, Hotel Company reorganized as best they could. They formed the six survivors of Lieutenant Gene Meiner's platoon and the seven survivors of the fallen Bob Miller's platoon into one thirteen-man platoon.

Chapter 21

Mike Company Fights Again

During the day of November 7, Mike Company of the 3rd Battalion, 5th Marines, moved toward Golf and Hotel Companies of the 2nd Battalion, 5th Marines. Private First Class Brad Reynolds was a rocket man with Mike.

Pfc. Brad Reynolds: Around noon we pulled off the trail for a break. Corporal Donald Kretsinger was hollering at everybody. "Watch out for booby traps; this doesn't feel right. Don't go between trees." We looked up as he went between two trees, and, "Boom!" He was completely disintegrated, and three or four other guys were hit. We had to find the pieces.

Pfc. Tony Martinez: A corpsman carried what was left of Kretsinger to the rear in a plastic bag.

Lance Cpl. John Lobur: Kretsinger seemed to love it out there; he was always upbeat, and everyone liked him. He had been carrying a couple of bandoliers of M79 ammo, and a couple of dozen of them went off.

Private First Class Brad Reynolds had a close encounter with a tiger pit, a camouflaged hole full of punji stakes, sharpened bamboo spikes that were often covered with human excrement to aid infection. Reynolds did not see it and might have become its victim had an NVA not shot at him at just the right moment. He dove for cover on the side the trail, his foot kicking away some of the brush covering the pit. "I don't know what gook it was, but I have always thanked him for shooting at me just as I was about to step on the camouflaged pit.

Pfc. Brad Reynolds: We went on to the next objective and set-in a perimeter and got probed that night. We looked the next morning to try to find trails where they had gone and didn't find any, but they began mortaring us.

ANTENNA VALLEY WAS INFESTED WITH NVA and fortified villages. The next afternoon, less than a kilometer from where Golf and Hotel companies were stopped on the edge of Ap Bon (2), Mike Company found a similarly protected village, Ap Hai (1). As they approached, the NVA raked their ranks with mortar, machine-gun, and small-arms fire, wounding three Marines and pinning down several more. This marked the beginning of a very long night.

Lieutenant Dale Loudin quickly moved his platoon into the attack and was just a step or two in front of his radio operator, Cpl. Peter Schrader. The enemy quickly knocked down and killed Loudin. Corporal Schrader took charge of the platoon and stood, ignoring the fire, maneuvering the Marines out of the rice paddy and back into friendly positions. With their attack stalled, the Mike Company Marines poured round after round of artillery into the village, turning it into a smoldering ruin. Then they went at it again.

Pfc. Brad Reynolds: We got strung out there in the paddy. Schrader and the 1st Fire Team, 1st Platoon, went into the paddy. They got hit and were hollering for guns and rockets up, and we went running up there and came through the tree line, and there was a big rice paddy with a dike that was about five feet tall. Schrader and the rest of them were probably seventy-five yards out in this rice paddy. The NVA killed everybody except him. Every time the NVA tried to get over the dike, they would get hit, and every time we tried to go for them, we would get hit.

Several of us were running behind the dike, trying to find out where the gooks were. The machine guns were firing, and we were trying to call in air strikes. They had snipers up in the trees. One of the platoons that was strung out behind us was getting fire from the rear. The NVA were trying to surround the ten of us behind that big dike. The rest of the platoon was in the tree line or strung out along the trail, and they were being hit sporadically. Within about forty-five minutes, they were firing at us from both flanks and dropping in mortar rounds.

The Marines called up air support as quickly as they could and hammered the enemy to good effect, greatly reducing the enemy fire.

Pfc. Brad Reynolds: After things quieted down because of the air strikes, we were ordered to spread it out and get to the other side of this massive rice paddy. Somehow we got bunched up again, and mortars hit us again, and we got fire from a machine gun that was fairly close to our rear. The gun was firing from heavy brush, and we could not see it, but some of our guys were firing to our rear, where they thought the NVA were. The next day we found that the NVA had tunnels through the brush, but we couldn't see them at the time. We got stuck in the mud on a little trail, and the machine guns raked us. We lost a lot of guys right there, and we shouted to the rear and told them to stay put and not to try to reach us.

I was the ammo humper for the 3.5-inch rounds, and the gunner told me to stick close by. He quickly fired all the rounds we had, as our machine guns fired over the top of us. The 2nd Platoon fell back to the tree line, but when the 1st Platoon fell back, they could only find little pockets of bamboo. Some of the guys were killed just trying to scramble up out of the stream bed to reach them.

By 1900 the enemy found the range of the company and rained violence on them from all directions with small arms, automatic weapons, and mortars. Mike Company was spread out, front to rear, several hundred meters. The new company commander had lost control of the command-and-control functions amidst the carnage and confusion. The NVA raked the trail on which the company command group was advancing, killing eleven of the fifteen Marines on the trail, including the artillery and mortar forward observers and the forward air controller. Luckily, the heroic young corporal Steve Cottrell, who kept his head, manned the battalion radio. When the battalion commander began getting incoherent reports from the company commander, he asked to speak to the radio operator, and Cottrell gave them a report of the situation and did all he could to keep the company together. Private First Class Michael Callahan, the company radio operator, crawled up alongside Cottrell to assist him and was shot to pieces by a swarm of machine gun bullets. Corporal Cottrell took over both radio nets and, working constantly under fire, got location reports from the scattered elements of Mike Company and gradually helped bring most of them together to form a perimeter. In the meantime, the fight continued among the scattered Marine force.

Corporal Peter Schrader, the radio operator who had performed so heroically earlier in the day, moved with his platoon across a rice paddy. Mortar and machine gun fire killed the acting platoon commander and, once more, Schrader took charge. Though wounded, he directed the men to cover while he fired at the enemy and stayed on the radio, letting the rest of the company know what his situation was. He moved his position in an attempt to get better radio reception and was killed.

Not far away from where Corporal Schrader was desperately engaged, Cpl. Richard Duncan, a machine gun squad leader, maneuvered his gun team across an open area to a position behind a dike, where they laid down heavy fire against the enemy. The curtain of steel permitted the withdrawal of the Marines that were trapped in the open. When it became time for him to move back, he was seriously wounded. Then his platoon was redeployed, and Duncan's gun team was designated to provide security for the left flank. The nineteen-year-old corporal surveyed the line and placed his guns in the best defensive positions. As darkness fell, the NVA launched an assault, but they were driven back by Duncan's machine gun. All along the line, enemy soldiers crawled up to a few meters outside Marine lines and heaved grenades into their position. When Corporal Duncan saw that one of his Marines was exposed and wounded, he ignored his own wound and crawled out to help him. Another grenade came flying at him, and he shielded his man with his body and was wounded again. Enemy pressure forced him to pull back his squad, and he lay in the open to cover their withdrawal. His men safe, he attempted to join them and was shot and killed.

Later that evening, on another part of the scattered battlefield, Staff Sgt. Adam Banks became separated from his platoon commander during the firefight. Seeing that many Marines had moved across a river to a more advantageous position, Banks joined them and began organizing a perimeter defense for an NVA attack he felt was sure to come. As he predicted, the enemy lay down a base of fire and then launched a ground attack. Banks was all over the place, moving wounded Marines to safety and redistributing ammunition. The Marines drove them off. Banks stayed awake all night, checking on his Marines and waiting for a second attack that never came.

Sometime during the night, enemy fire slackened and then stopped as they departed the battlefield and made for the hills. Corporal Cottrell did what he could to impede their flight by calling in artillery missions to interdict their probable escape routes. Just after midnight, Hotel Company, which had been on the move for several hours, established contact with Mike Company.

Pfc. Brad Reynolds: Sometime in the early morning the next day, someone from 2/5 came to our rescue. They approached from our right flank. I saw movement, and they looked like Marine uniforms, but we had the radio operator call them and told them to get down, and they got down until the sun popped and we could see them.

I volunteered to go back out with a few guys, and that is when I found Jack Swann. He had gotten stuck that night with a new guy in a bamboo grove and had NVA walking over them. Neither Marine was hit.

There was a corpsman that that stayed with a Marine who was hit in the legs outside the lines, and the NVA found them that night. An NVA officer spoke English and said he had gone to college in the U.S. He prevented his men from killing them and told the corpsman, "You guys are fierce fighters," and they took his medical bag for their own casualties and left the two of them untouched on the field. The NVA officer told them not to move or he would kill them. We could hear the wounded men screaming in the night, and it took us a long time to get to them.

The next morning I couldn't see anyone I recognized from 1st Platoon. There was a machine gun just sitting there, so I sat down behind it. A helo came in, and a lot of officers got off, and this colonel was asking questions. He asked me where the rest of my outfit was, and I told him, "I don't know, I think I am the only one." He said, "No, there is a guy named Jack Swann over around the bend, if you want to get to him." I told him, "No, I better stay with the gun." He said, "What if I relieve you off that gun?" And I said okay. He said, "You are relieved," and he knelt down by the gun, and when I looked back, he was covering the gun. Then I got around the bend and wasn't sure what happened.

Tony Martinez remembered that Lance Cpl. James Navarro was a fanatic about cleaning his weapon. Any time there was a pause, he would meticulously clean it. They found Navarro's body that morning with a jammed rifle in one hand and a knife in the other.

Pfc. Brad Reynolds: They were loading bodies, and—this was the only time I saw this in Vietnam—they were loading bodies in cargo nets under the CH-46s. We were all upset about this.

The Marines went across to where the enemy had been and saw many bodies and trees still smoking, and I saw tunnels that had ladders and went down ten feet before they went off horizontally. I checked out several, and in the last one there was a live gook about halfway down the ladder that had been badly burned, probably by napalm. All the hair had been burned off his head. I got him back up. He had a lot of stuff all over his uniform and was probably an officer. He had big blisters. I gave him to a fire team that came up: "Here, you can be heroes and say you captured him."

ON THE MORNING OF NOVEMBER 10, Delta Company, 1st Battalion, 5th Marines, detained a Vietnamese civilian who told them that 180 NVA, with Chinese advisors, had fled from the area of the Mike Company contact on November 8. They had another 60 dead and wounded with them. In the 2nd Battalion, 5th Marines' command post, the Marines monitored an enemy radio frequency over which the NVA were transmitting and heard both Vietnamese and Cantonese.

In the face of allied firepower and aware that the U.S. Army was waiting for them to the east, the NVA abandoned their supply caches in Antenna Valley and took to the western mountains again.

All told, Operation Essex cost the Marines 40 killed and 127 wounded. The enemy lost 112 confirmed killed and another 125 probably killed.

Chapter 22

Victory

The action on November 8 was the last significant fight of Operation Essex, and Essex was the last major operation for most of the 1st Marine Division elements in the Que Son and Antenna Valleys. The New Year was to bring with it the Tet Offensive and a major shift of Marine units northward.

As a result of the long and bloody seven-month campaign, the 2nd NVA Division was so exhausted, demoralized, and reduced in numbers that it could not complete its assigned mission when the Tet Offensive of 1968 began on January 30. Their higher headquarters assigned the 2nd NVA Division, in concert with some main-force and local-force guerilla units, the mission of attacking Da Nang during Tet. The division's regular troops were to neutralize allied, mainly U.S., units stationed in or near the city of Da Nang. Once the allies were fixed in place, the guerrillas, who knew the names and addresses of all the government officials and sympathizers, were to seek them out and eliminate as many as possible. At the same time, they were to organize the popular uprising against the Saigon regime that they expected would follow.

In December, allied intelligence sources watched as the 2nd NVA Division headquarters came out of the far reaches of the valley and set up housekeeping on Go Noi Island, a large, swampy, and overgrown piece of terrain formed by two rivers near the coast south of Da Nang. Further, all three battalions of the 31st NVA Regiment (Red River Regiment), 2nd NVA Division, were closing Da Nang. According to retired NVA Col. Tran Nhu Tiep, who was then the commander of the

1st Battalion, 31st Regiment, his battalion did not receive their final orders for Tet until January 15. His unit had to move nearly forty kilometers, in secrecy, to get in place and only had two weeks to do it. The division's other two regiments, the 1st VC and the 3rd NVA, moved to join their division headquarters on Go Noi Island. From there, they expected to be able to close Da Nang on short notice and in the confusion of the offensive.

Prisoner interrogations and documents captured after Tet indicated that the entire 2nd NVA Division was in poor shape. It suffered from having to fill out its ranks with inadequately trained, unseasoned soldiers. The new troops were absorbed too rapidly to train them in the skills they needed before being sent into combat. Moreover, the enormous losses the division sustained in the Que Son Valley the previous year still weighed heavily on the minds of the troops, weakening their morale. NVA prisoners taken during the Tet Offensive confirmed that the division's objective was the city of Da Nang.

When the offensive began, Colonel Tiep's battalion was not able to accomplish much. Their only success came when they ambushed a platoon from Golf Company, 2nd Battalion, 5th Marines, killing ten Marines. Even that was costly. Allied supporting arms savaged them mercilessly. Only one platoon from this enemy regiment made it into the city of Da Nang, and they were ineffective.

The Marines expected the other two regiments, the 1st VC and the 3rd NVA, to attack on the evening of January 30. Large formations from these units were spotted by Marine Recon Team Rummage, which smashed them with supporting arms and took the equivalent of an entire battalion of the enemy out of the fight. The 1st VC and the 3rd NVA Regiments did not reach their points of departure for the attack until the night of February 5–6, six days behind schedule. By that time, the allies had overcome their shock at the offensive and had regained the initiative. The NVA came against the Da Nang defenses in a weakened and halfhearted attack that was easily turned back.

In the face of failure, the division ordered Colonel Tiep's 1st Battalion, 31st NVA Regiment, to retreat some eight kilometers west, where they holed up, hiding there for twenty-four days until it was safe to move on. Then the battalion moved some sixty kilometers west and hid in the western jungles.[12] The 2nd NVA Division, battered by the fights in the Que Son Valley, lost an estimated 1,200 to 1,400 killed in their abortive attempt to invest Da Nang.

The North Vietnamese Army's own official history, usually full of exaggerations about their victories, has this to say:

> At Da Nang City the Military Region's main force 2nd Division, sapper battalions, the Quang Du province local force battalion, and mass forces participating in the political struggle had been preparing since October 1967. However, because we did not have a firm grasp on the situation, our preparations had been cursory, the movement of our forces forward to seize attack positions had not been well organized, and because enemy forces were too numerous and responded fiercely when we attacked, the forces that attacked the city on the night of 29–30 January 1968 were unable to seize their assigned objectives.[13]

This is the only instance in their official history that the North Vietnamese admitted being beaten during Tet. It is as complete an admission of defeat as will ever be found in their public records.

Their defeat was due to the outstanding courage and skill of the Marines and corpsmen, fighting with defective rifles and at great cost to themselves, who wore the NVA forces down and destroyed their effectiveness in the long and bloody Que Son campaign of 1967. They may have saved Da Nang from the same fate as Hue, which the enemy held for nearly a month, murdering thousands of innocent civilians.

Mortal ground combat is the province of the young. The average age of the Marines and corpsman who served at the company level or below during the Que Son campaign was twenty years. Two-thirds of those who fought so valiantly, suffered grievous wounds, or were killed were not old enough to buy a beer in their hometowns. Moreover, they fought a war that became increasingly unpopular at home, and they were held accountable for the failed policies of U.S. politicians. Their service was not even acknowledged until two decades after they returned from the war, and then only grudgingly, and only rarely were they given a feeble "welcome home."

Yet these men endured as much hardship and horror and fought as valiantly as their forebears did at Belleau Wood, Iwo Jima, or the Chosin Reservoir. America owes them a debt that can never be repaid.

Chapter 23

Parting Shots

Sgt. Harold Wadley: Que Son Basin is full of memories and ghosts: some so terrifying, sleep still comes in troubled waves, and some so hilarious, like the night the ARVN pinned us down in a village's crapper area. We nearly puked! Our web gear stunk so bad we had to survey most of it.

The smell of the foul, muddy, red creek water we dumped colored Kool-Aid into to make it taste appetizing still flavors my soft drinks.

A beautiful, red, flaring sunset can bring a smile as I recall the night the dumbest Viet Cong on the planet decided to throw a parting .50-cal shot as Puff the Magic Dragon passed by, and for his effort got lit up quick by Puff's red, arching tongue! We nearly felt sorry for him; but not quite.

The ghosts of Hotel Company, 2nd Battalion, 5th Marines, frequently come silently in my dreams to renew our many patrols, assaults, and ambushes. They are forever the hard-charging, light-of-step, bright-eyed, boyish mavericks of 1967. Being out of the Corps for fourteen years, I had wondered if these young Marines would have the same old fire in their bellies we had in Korea. I soon found that regardless of how exhausted they were, they responded as one and went straight to the enemy at the crack of the first round.

Some will forever remain eighteen, nineteen, or twenty in my memory. They never grow old. Out of one blood-soaked, shattered tree line and paddy, where unselfish, devoted Marines once answered to the roll call of Aukland, Baptist, Braswell, Horvath, Herman, Irving, Rosales, Stutes, Wilson, and Wolf, would come a beautiful blessing called Catherine Stutes. She was barely six months old and had never seen her father, Sgt. William

Stutes, when he died hanging onto my boots, trying to get up when another North Vietnamese round hit him. Twenty-five years later my phone rang. A female voice said, "I'm Catherine Stutes, my Dad was a Marine killed in Vietnam, do you remember him?" The sounds and smells of that last day in Vietnam as I watched the light of life slowly fade from Stutes's eyes flooded over me. "Remember him?" I replied, "How on earth could I ever forget him?" She flew to Idaho to meet me and learn more about her Dad. My son, Neal, just happened to be home on leave from the Marine Corps. As they say, "And the rest is history." They married and later had a little boy called William and two daughters, Kacie and Lacie. We all too soon lost Catherine to cancer. The ghosts are many from Que Son Basin, but as Cpl. "Russian" Rasmussen and Cpl. Hunton Witt once said, "This is the best time of my life!" I am so thankful I could be counted among them.

Lance Cpl. Gerry Reidenbach: Rudy Galiana died in the Que Son Valley. I know, as I was with him and wounded when he died. We were in the midst of a horrific and chaotic struggle with our enemy for a piece of land no bigger than a football field. The fact that a lot of Marines behind us were dependent on us holding that position was not known to us. Our motive at that point was survival. We were going to keep each other alive. Rudy didn't try to be, but he was, a hero. He was also a quiet guy with a giant smile on his face that never seemed to go away. In fact, to this day I would swear that he had that smile when he died, and he and I lay on that piece of ground so many years ago, both of us broken. My body mended over time from some of the wounds; unfortunately, Rudy didn't. There were a lot of heroes during that campaign, most likely on both sides, some decorated, some not. However, when I think of Que Son, my thoughts turn to a quiet guy with a big smile that asked nothing from life but gave it all. Rudy *is* the story of Que Son in my mind: fearless and unselfish dedication to a brotherhood. That's what I remember about Que Son and will tell my grandkids. I'll tell them about a quiet guy with a big smile that gave it all. I'll tell them Rudy's story.

Lance Cpl. Greg Miller: I tell my former colleagues whom I worked with at George Washington University, "While you guys were dodging the draft and protesting the Vietnam War, I and my Marine colleagues were writing another glorious chapter in the magnificent history book of the United States Marine Corps in the Que Son Valley in 1967."

Cpl. Gary Peterson: After forty years, I still think of that day and all the suffering we went through. Every day I wish there was something else I could have done to keep our men alive so they could have come home like I did.

Lance Cpl. Paul Malboeuf: For all those Marines and corpsmen that walked that ground and paid dearly, "We Remember" all those lost and those that survived that Hell. Semper Fi.

Lance Cpl. Steve Lovejoy: Several times during that summer and fall, my platoon was so decimated that those of us who survived were placed with other platoons until replacements came on board. We grunts had to contend with a lot of political posturing that kept us from fully doing our job. The ridiculous rules of engagement were the cause of a lot of frustrations, but, more importantly, a great number of our casualties. Of course, we constantly had to deal with misfiring M16s.

Lance Cpl. John Lobur: Back then, no one had heard the term *political correctness.* For example, the little yellow bastards who were engaged full time in trying to make each moment the *big moment* were known as *gooks.* They were trying to kill us; it wasn't a game. If they scored first, they didn't kick the ball to you: the game was over. We did not call them gooks as a sign of hatred or respect or compassion. We knew them as brave, professional soldiers. They were often fearless, possessed of tremendous endurance. They were underequipped, physically weak, and barely trained. They had no air support and no modern transport near the battlefield. But they just kept coming.

Cpl. Bill Clark: I have never been able to adequately describe my feelings about that period in my life. I saw men perform acts of profound and unselfish bravery for which they expected and received no honors or awards. They did this for each other and because of that bond that ties us together as Marines. These things never leave me, and not a day of my life has passed without my remembering them and the things they did. I do know that I cringe every time my local news describes all members of the military as "hometown heroes." We all know that not everyone in uniform is a hero, and I believe that using heroes in this manner dilutes the word and diminishes the real heroes.

Lance Cpl. Jim Mullen: When we landed in the Que Son Valley on April 21, 1967, we had no idea what we were getting into. After hitting the ground, we fought as hard as any Marines ever have under similar circumstances. For all these years our story has gone unreported because of the media's antipathy toward the Vietnam War and, by extension, those who fought in it. If our efforts had happened during World War II, they would have made a movie about us. In closing the chapter on the Que Son Valley campaign, we don't want a movie. We just want the truth. It speaks for itself.

Capt. Joe Tenney: Those who served in Vietnam had the unique situation of facing opposition not only abroad but at home. What is not generally acknowledged is that the fighting in Vietnam did help to slow the spread of world Communism, which at the time was the main threat to the free world. By blocking and opposing the Soviet Union's effort to spread Communism, the American military bought time, first in Korea and then in Vietnam.

Lance Cpl. Harvey Newton: We fought as we had been taught and seldom questioned our cause. Regardless of what one thought, coming into the Corps and going to Vietnam, most young grunts quickly realized the fallacy of the "domino theory" and recognized the angst of the local Vietnamese citizen, caught in a no-win situation. We fought for our lives and for the Marines next to us. For those of us who survived the battles here, our scars run deep and are permanent. I hope what we did and the price we all paid served a purpose. From the standpoint of a nineteen-year-old lance corporal earning a base pay of about $120 per month, this was one helluva way to spend your summer.

Lt. Rick Phillips: The Que Son Valley Campaign started with a small Marine unit contact with a small enemy unit that soon grew into an NVA Division and a no-holds-barred, all-out battle. The Marines who fought this horrific battle were truly magnificent, and they won a major victory against an enemy that prior to that time had been largely illusive. We Marines in the air were proud to do all we could to support them.

The enemy was attacking the Marine position with such large numbers that the Marine artillery pieces had been drawn into a circle in a graveyard, and Marine infantry had taken up positions between the guns. It was night, and the 155mm towed and 105mm artillery barrels had been lowered to chest level for firing canister, as I pushed the H-53 helicopter into a steep-spiral diving approach from five thousand feet. I landed hard on top of gravestones with a large internal resupply of 155mm canister shot and powder bags. The big guns were blasting with huge flashes, and the ferocity of the battle was everywhere. After a very quick offload, I put the big bird's collective in my armpit and spiraled back up to five thousand feet. The next morning, the enemy dead were in large piles, and the Marines still held the position. It was that kind of a battle, and God, those Marines were magnificent!

Lance Cpl. Dennis Delaney: We went in young boys and exited hardened men. It gave true meaning to the phrase, "You haven't lived until you have almost died." My time there will never escape my memory.

Lance Cpl. Bob Kreuder: It was not until many years later that I found out that Union I, Union II, and Swift all took place in the same valley. I still remember the beauty of the valley in my dreams and the carnage in my nightmares. The faces of the dead are still there, etched in the dark recesses of my mind, the feelings of fear and confusion felt during the heat of battle sometimes escaping to my consciousness, surfacing as a great sadness for those who were lost. I live with a deeply hidden guilt that I survived and had what those Marines who did not, could not have. Today I find solace during those infrequent gatherings of comrades who had watched my back as I had watched theirs, who had fought in the same valley and had shared the same hardships. I will never forget them or the faces of those who did not return.

Cpl. Lynwood Scott: While fighting in bitter battles against the NVA and VC for control of the Que Son Basin, I witnessed Marines and corpsmen risking their lives one for another. John 15:16 says, "Greater love has no one than this, that he lay down his life for his friends." There is hardly a day that goes by that I don't think about those men and the sacrifice they made for fellow Marines, country, and freedom.

Afterword

Debunking Myths about Vietnam

Richard Nixon was right when he said that Vietnam was the least understood war in our history. Many myths that were created by the antiwar movement and the media during the war persist to this day. A poisonous legacy of misunderstanding has corrupted our political process, distorted our foreign policy, obscured the valorous service of a generation of veterans, and led us to the brink of disaster in Iraq. The public knows little about the Vietnam War or the Vietnam veteran; many of the things that they think they know are not true at all. Most of these issues are beyond the scope of this book. The lot of the Vietnam veteran is not.

No one who has read the foregoing pages can fail to be impressed by valorous and selfless service of the men who fought this unpopular war. Yet during the Vietnam War the antiwar faction blamed the men and women who fought that war along with the politicians who created it and the military leaders that squandered their chances of success. Vietnam veterans were spat upon, called "baby killers," denied employment opportunities, and harassed when they attended college. Most damaging of all, the pronouncements on the floor of both houses of Congress that the war was a failure had a corrosive impact on the morale of U.S. servicemen and women, all of whom know better.

There is a whole collection of misunderstandings about the character and service of the Vietnam veteran that has become part of the tapestry of urban myth. All of these were caused by the untrue and emotional accusations by the antiwar movement and the indifference of our citizenry. The list includes the following:

DRAFTEES

Tom Brokaw's Greatest Generation was indeed great. It endured the Depression, fought World War II with courage, and returned home to build the greatest economy on earth. However, the images of countless thousands of volunteers flooding recruiting offices are misleading. Only 33 percent of those who served in World War II were volunteers: the other two-thirds were drafted. In Vietnam, by contrast, 78 percent of those who served were volunteers. Which is the greater generation?

MINORITY GROUPS

Minority groups served in Vietnam with courage and skill, and I have included many instances of minorities performing above and beyond. African-Americans accounted for 12.5 percent of combat deaths in Vietnam, Hispanics about 5 percent. Census figures show these numbers to be slightly *below* their percentages in the draft-age population of the United States at that time. Thus, these groups were slightly *underrepresented* in terms of casualties. Adding credence to this myth that minorities were carrying an inordinate burden of the war was Martin Luther King Jr.'s uninformed declaration that blacks in Vietnam "fight and die in extraordinarily high proportions relative to the rest of the population."[14]

ATROCITIES

Atrocities have been an ugly side of warfare since the dawn of time. The My Lai Massacre undoubtedly occurred as reported, and there were others of a lesser scale or that went unreported. Atrocities are associated with the Vietnam War because of motion pictures like *Platoon* and *Apocalypse Now*. Although the antiwar movement portrayed these incidents as common, independent studies prove that, on a per capita basis, atrocities in Vietnam were far fewer than in any other of America's wars.

DESERTION AND DRAFT DODGING

Much was made of those who refused to serve. Once again, independent studies have confirmed that the percentage of deserters and draft dodgers were fewer in the Vietnam War than in World War II. Everyone remembers the safe haven Canada offered during the war. Ten thousand Americans took advantage of that and went north. A little known fact is that over thirty thousand Canadians came to the U.S. and enlisted in our armed forces. About ten thousand of them served in Vietnam.

DRUG ADDICTION, HOMELESSNESS, AND JOBLESSNESS

Several studies by the Veterans Administration and by outside agencies demonstrate that the incidence of drug addiction was lower among Vietnam veterans than among those of the same age group who are not veterans. Other carefully researched studies demonstrate that the Vietnam veteran is better educated, is more affluent, and lives a fuller life than the non-vet of the same era. Freeloaders looking for a handout, the Vietnam veteran wannabes, have distorted public perceptions about the real Vietnam veteran.

Some years ago, Dan Rather produced *CBS Reports: The Wall Within*, a special about the Vietnam Veterans Memorial. Rather's team interviewed eighty-seven of them, choosing six of the "saddest cases." Most of those selected looked like the longhaired, unshaven, drug-addicted bums that were frequently seen around shopping centers with their "Vietnam Veteran, please help" signs begging for money. Rather's program was hailed as "extraordinarily powerful." After *The Wall Within* was aired, an independent researcher, using the Freedom of Information Act, investigated the background of the "veterans" that appeared in the special.[15] He found that only one was an actual combat veteran of Vietnam. The others were bogus. One was an equipment repairman who spent most of his army service in the stockade. Another was a sailor who served on a ship that never left the California coast but who claimed to have post-traumatic stress disorder (PTSD) because of an incident that he said he witnessed but in truth, he only heard about. Another never saw combat and spent most of his time in the brig for going AWOL, and so on. *The Wall Within* may have been the most egregious example of the media view of the Vietnam veteran, but it was far from uncommon. CBS still stands by it.

The truth about the Vietnam veteran is this: Vietnam veterans served with as much honor, courage, and commitment as any of America's warriors who went before them or who followed. They fought with hand-me-down equipment from World War II and Korea. The Marines fought the desperate campaign in the Que Son Valley for most of a year with a defective rifle, the "experimental" model of the M16. Equipment was in such short supply that sometimes they had to recover the flak jackets, and even the boots, from the dead for reuse by the living. Yet they fought on. The survivors returned to an America they did not recognize and which scorned them. Corporal Vito

Lavacca recalls, "The change was just shocking. It was totally devastating. Clothes had changed. People's attitudes had changed. Close friends that you had that had been clean-cut athletic types when you last saw them now had hair down to their shoulders. They were wearin' big medallions around their necks. And . . . beards. Christ . . . earrings. And bell-bottom pants and high-heel boots. And . . . givin' peace signs."

These men did not expect parades when they returned, but they wanted acknowledgment of their service. And in spite of a cold homecoming and decades of contempt and scorn for their efforts, they put together better and more useful lives than the nonveteran of the same era.

One might ask why they served with such courage and determination. This is a question that has vexed nonveterans for centuries. Why did twenty-five-year-old Sgt. Rodney Davis throw himself on a grenade, knowing that to do so would kill him? Why did eighteen-year-old Pfc. Gary Martini give his life away to save a comrade? Why did Father Vincent Capodanno trade his life for the sake of assisting an obviously dying Marine on his own journey from this world to the next?

The outstanding historian of the American Civil War, Bruce Catton, addressed this very problem without really answering it. "It may be that life is not man's most precious possession, after all. Certainly men can be induced to give it away very freely at times, and the terms hardly make sense unless there is something about which we don't understand." Warriors understand. Those who are not, never will.

Acknowledgments

My sincere thanks to the Marine Corps Heritage Foundation for their generosity in giving me a grant to complete this work. Thanks, also, to my friend and retired Marine Bill Benner for his encouragement while I was revising the text. Thanks, most of all, to the aging warriors, Marines, Corpsmen, Viet Cong and North Vietnamese Army soldiers who trusted me with their stories. I hope I have provided a good account of their courage and determination. And to my friend, fellow Marine and agent, Stu Miller, for his help in getting this published—Semper Fidelis.

If you are able, save for them a place inside of you and save one backward glance when you are leaving for the places they can no longer go.

Be not ashamed to say you loved them, though you may or may not have always. Take what they have taught you with their dying and keep it with your own.

And in that time when men decide and feel safe to call the war insane, take one moment to embrace those gentle heroes you left behind.

—Maj. Michael Davis O'Donnell, Vietnam
Listed as KIA February 7, 1978

Appendix

Awards for the Que Son Valley Campaign

In mid-1968, President Lyndon Johnson attached a streamer signifying the award of the Presidential Unit Citation to the battle colors of the 5th Marines. This award is the unit equivalent of the Silver Star Medal that is given to individuals.

The following list of individual awards is incomplete. There is no single repository for the records of all the valorous acts in the Vietnam War. It is relatively easy to find the Medal of Honor and Navy Cross citations. But from there downward, it is increasingly difficult. The Bronze Star and Navy Commendation Medals I included were found by chance. A complete list of these awards would run in the hundreds. I included as many as I could and apologize to those whom I left out. There were thousands of Purple Hearts awarded, probably an average of more than one for every Marine and corpsman who participated in the Que Son Valley Campaign. Many were wounded multiple times. The reader should understand something I learned many years ago: there are always more heroes in any battle than there are medals. There are many whose efforts will never be commemorated, except by those with whom they served. For most Marines, that is enough.

MEDAL OF HONOR

Capodanno, Vincent, Lt., U.S. Navy, Chaplain Corps, 3/5

Citation: For conspicuous gallantry and intrepidity at the risk of his life above and beyond the call of duty as Chaplain of the 3d Battalion, in connection with operations against enemy forces. In response to reports that the

President Lyndon Johnson affixes the streamer of the Presidential Unit Citation to the regimental battle colors of the 5th Marines for Operations Union I and II, October 18, 1968. The second Marine to Johnson's left is Brig. Gen. Kenneth Houghton who, as a colonel, commanded the regiment during these operations. *USMC*

2d Platoon of M Company was in danger of being overrun by a massed enemy assaulting force, Lieutenant Capodanno left the relative safety of the company command post and ran through an open area raked with fire, directly to the beleaguered platoon. Disregarding the intense enemy small-arms, automatic-weapons, and mortar fire, he moved about the battlefield administering last rites to the dying and giving medical aid to the wounded. When an exploding mortar round inflicted painful multiple wounds to his arms and legs, and severed a portion of his right hand, he steadfastly refused all medical aid. Instead, he directed the corpsmen to help their wounded comrades and, with calm vigor, continued to move about the battlefield as he provided encouragement by voice and example to the valiant marines. Upon encountering a wounded corpsman in the direct line of fire of an enemy machine gunner positioned approximately 15 yards away, Lieutenant Capodanno rushed a daring attempt to aid and assist the mortally wounded corpsman. At that instant, only inches from his goal, he was struck down by a burst of machinegun fire. By his heroic conduct on the battlefield, and his inspiring example, Lieutenant Capodanno upheld the finest traditions of the U.S. Naval Service. He gallantly gave his life in the cause of freedom.

Davis, Rodney, Sgt., B/1/5

Citation: For conspicuous gallantry and intrepidity at the risk of his life above and beyond the call of duty while serving as the right guide of the 2d Platoon, Company B, in action against enemy forces. Elements of the 2d Platoon were pinned down by a numerically superior force of attacking North Vietnamese Army Regulars. Remnants of the platoon were located in a trench line where Sgt. Davis was directing the fire of his men in an attempt to repel the enemy attack. Disregarding the enemy hand grenades and high volume of small arms and mortar fire, Sgt. Davis moved from man to man shouting words of encouragement to each of them while firing and throwing grenades at the onrushing enemy. When an enemy grenade landed in the trench in the midst of his men, Sgt. Davis, realizing the gravity of the situation, and in a final valiant act of complete self-sacrifice, instantly threw himself upon the grenade, absorbing with his body the full and terrific force of the explosion. Through his extraordinary initiative and inspiring valor in the face of almost certain death, Sgt. Davis saved his comrades from injury and possible loss of life, enabled his platoon to hold its vital position, and upheld the highest traditions of the Marine Corps and the U.S. Naval Service. He gallantly gave his life for his country.

Graham, James, Capt., F/2/5

Citation: For conspicuous gallantry and intrepidity at the risk of his life above and beyond the call of duty. During Operation Union II, the 1st Battalion, 5th Marines, consisting of Companies A and D, with Captain Graham's company attached launched an attack against an enemy occupied position with 2 companies assaulting and 1 in reserve. Company F, a leading company, was proceeding across a clear paddy area 1,000 meters wide, attacking toward the assigned objective, when it came under fire from mortars and small arms which immediately inflicted a large number of casualties. Hardest hit by the enemy fire was the 2d platoon of Company F, which was pinned down in the open paddy area by intense fire from 2 concealed machineguns. Forming an assault unit from members of his small company headquarters, Captain Graham boldly led a fierce assault through the second platoon's position, forcing the enemy to abandon the first machinegun position, thereby relieving some of the pressure on his second platoon, and enabling evacuation of the wounded to a more secure area. Resolute to silence the second machinegun, which continued its devastating fire, Captain Graham's small force stood steadfast in its hard won enclave. Subsequently, during the afternoon's fierce fighting, he suffered 2 minor wounds while personally accounting for an estimated 15 enemy killed. With the enemy position remaining invincible upon each attempt to withdraw to friendly lines, and although knowing that he had no chance of survival, he chose to remain with 1 man who could not be moved due to the seriousness of his wounds. The last radio transmission from Captain Graham reported that he was being assaulted by a force of 25 enemy soldiers; he died while protecting himself and the wounded man he chose not to abandon. Captain Graham's actions throughout the day were a series of heroic achievements. His outstanding courage, superb leadership and indomitable fighting spirit undoubtedly saved the second platoon from annihilation and reflected great credit upon himself, the Marine Corps, and the U.S. Naval Service. He gallantly gave his life for his country.

Martini, Gary, Pfc., M/3/1

Citation: For conspicuous gallantry and intrepidity at the risk of his life above and beyond the call of duty. On 21 April 1967, during Operation UNION elements of Company F, conducting offensive operations at Binh Son, encountered a firmly entrenched enemy force and immediately deployed to engage them. The marines in PFC Martini's platoon assaulted across an open rice paddy to within 20 meters of the enemy trench line where they were suddenly struck by hand grenades, intense small arms, automatic weapons, and mortar fire. The enemy onslaught killed 14 and wounded 18 marines, pinning the remainder of the platoon down behind a low paddy dike. In the face of imminent danger, PFC Martini immediately crawled over the dike to a forward open area within 15 meters of the enemy position where, continuously exposed to the hostile fire, he hurled hand grenades, killing several of the enemy. Crawling back through the intense fire, he rejoined his platoon which had moved to the relative safety of a trench line. From this position he observed several of his wounded comrades lying helpless in the fire-swept paddy. Although he knew that 1 man had been killed attempting to assist the wounded, PFC Martini raced through the open area and dragged a comrade back to a friendly position. In spite of a serious wound received during this first daring rescue, he again braved the unrelenting fury of the enemy fire to aid another companion lying wounded only 20 meters in front of the enemy trench line. As he reached the fallen marine, he received a mortal wound, but disregarding his own condition, he began to drag the marine toward his platoon's position. Observing men from his unit attempting to leave the security of their position to aid him, concerned only for their safety, he called to them to remain under cover, and through a final supreme effort, moved his injured comrade to where he could be pulled to safety, before he fell, succumbing to his wounds. Stouthearted and indomitable, PFC Martini unhesitatingly yielded his life to save 2 of his comrades and insure the safety of the remainder of his platoon. His outstanding courage, valiant fighting spirit and selfless devotion to duty reflected the highest credit upon himself, the Marine Corps, and the U.S. Naval Service. He gallantly gave his life for his country.

Newlin, Melvin, Pfc., 2/5

Citation: For conspicuous gallantry and intrepidity at the risk of his life above and beyond the call of duty while serving as a machine gunner attached to the 1st Platoon, Company F, 2d Battalion, on 3 and 4 July 1967. PFC Newlin, with 4 other marines, was manning a key position on the perimeter of the Nong Son outpost when the enemy launched a savage and well coordinated mortar and infantry assault, seriously wounding him and killing his 4 comrades. Propping himself against his machinegun, he poured a deadly accurate stream of fire into the charging ranks of the Viet Cong. Though repeatedly hit by small-arms fire, he twice repelled enemy attempts to overrun his position. During the third attempt, a grenade explosion wounded him again and knocked him to the ground unconscious. The Viet Cong guerrillas, believing him dead, bypassed him and continued their assault on the main force. Meanwhile, PFC Newlin regained consciousness, crawled back to his weapon, and brought it to bear on the rear of the enemy, causing havoc and confusion among them. Spotting the enemy attempting to bring a captured 106 recoilless weapon to bear on other marine positions, he shifted his fire, inflicting heavy casualties on the enemy and preventing them from firing the captured weapon. He then shifted his fire back to the primary enemy force, causing the enemy to stop their assault on the marine bunkers and to once again attack his machinegun position. Valiantly fighting off 2 more enemy assaults, he firmly held his ground until mortally wounded. PFC Newlin had single-handedly broken up and disorganized the entire enemy assault force, causing them to lose momentum and delaying them long enough for his fellow marines to organize a defense and beat off their secondary attack. His indomitable courage, fortitude, and unwavering devotion to duty in the face of almost certain death reflect great credit upon himself and the Marine Corps and upheld the highest traditions of the U.S. Naval Service.

Peters, Lawrence, Sgt., M/3/5

Citation: For conspicuous gallantry and intrepidity at the risk of his life above and beyond the call of duty while serving as a squad leader with Company M. During Operation SWIFT, the marines of the 2d Platoon of Company M were struck by intense mortar, machinegun, and small arms fire from an entrenched enemy force. As the company rallied its forces, Sergeant Peters maneuvered his squad in an assault on an enemy defended knoll. Disregarding his safety, as enemy rounds hit all about him, he stood in the open, pointing out enemy positions until he was painfully wounded in the leg. Disregarding his wound, he moved forward and continued to lead his men. As the enemy fire increased in accuracy and volume, his squad lost its momentum and was temporarily pinned down. Exposing himself to devastating enemy fire, he consolidated his position to render more effective fire. While directing the base of fire, he was wounded a second time in the face and neck from an exploding mortar round. As the enemy attempted to infiltrate the position of an adjacent platoon, Sergeant Peters stood erect in the full view of the enemy firing burst after burst forcing them to disclose their camouflaged positions. Sergeant Peters steadfastly continued to direct his squad in spite of 2 additional wounds, [and] persisted in his efforts to encourage and supervise his men until he lost consciousness and succumbed. Inspired by his selfless actions, the squad regained fire superiority and once again carried the assault to the enemy. By his outstanding valor, indomitable fighting spirit and tenacious determination in the face of overwhelming odds, Sergeant Peters upheld the highest traditions of the Marine Corps and the U.S. Naval Service. He gallantly gave his life for his country.

NAVY CROSS

Burnham, Thomas, Cpl., F/2/5
Caine, Lawrence, Cpl., I/3/5
Driscoll, Thomas, Cpl., D/1/5
Duncan, Richard, Cpl., 3/5
Fisher, Thomas, Lance Cpl., M/3/5
Floren, Jimmy, Cpl., H/2/5
Green, John, Gunnery Sgt., F/2/5
Houghton, Kenneth, Col., 5th Marines
Leal, Armando, HN, M/3/5
Long, Melvin, Sgt., F/2/5
Mosher, Christopher, Lance Cpl., K/3/5
Murray, John, Lt., M/3/5
Myers, William, Pfc., D/1/5
Panian, Thomas, Sgt., I/3/5
Peterson, Dennie, Lt., FO/2/11
Reid, John, Cpl., C/1/3
Ross, David, Maj., VMO-2
Rusth, John, Cpl., C/1/5
Sanders, Thomas, Cpl., C/1/3
Strode, Gerald, HM3, B/1/5
Woods, Lloyd, Cpl., F/2/5

SILVER STAR

Allen, Melvin, Cpl., C/1/3
Banks, Adam, Staff Sgt., M/3/5
Blackburn, Glenn, Pvt., D/1/3
Brandon, Wayne, Lt., K/3/5
Brown, Marc, Lance Cpl., M/3/1
Brown, Richard, Sgt., K/3/5
Burke, Francis, Capt., I/3/5
Byrne, Gerald, Pfc., H/2/5
Call, John, Lance Cpl., B/1/5
Caswell, Russell, Capt., C/1/5
Davis, Stanley, Col., 5th Marines
DeAtley, Hillmer, Lt. Col., 3/1
Dennis, Dan, Cpl., M/3/5
Esslinger, Dean, Lt. Col., 3/5
Farlow, Gary, Lance Cpl., C/1/5
Flood, Dennis, Pfc., M/3/5
Floren, Jimmy, Cpl., H/2/5
Fulford, Carlton, Lt., D/1/5
Galiana, Rudolph, Pfc., I/3/1
Giordano, Andrew, Lance Cpl., 3/5
Hatzfield, William, Cpl., 1/5
Hayes, J. Michael, Lt., FO/1/11
Hilgartner, Peter, Lt., Col., 1/5
Hill, Byron, Lt., FO/1/11
Horton, Charles, Gunnery Sgt., I/3/1
Houghton, Kenneth, Col., 5th Marines
Inscore, Roger, Cpl., 3/5
Irvin, Stephen, Lance Cpl., H/2/5
Jenkins, Charles, Staff Sgt., D/1/5
Johnson, Robert, Sgt., K/3/5
Leshow, William, Cpl., C/1/5
Madden, Ernest, Cpl. C/1/5
Manfra, Howard, Sgt., M/3/5
Marcombe, Stephan, Lance Cpl. M/3/5
McElroy, James, Capt., M/3/5
McInturff, David, Lt., H&S/1/5
McKeon, Joseph, Lt., B/1/3

McNally, Paul, Lance Cpl., C/1/5
Miller, Russell, Pfc., D/1/3
Mitchell, Curtis, Pfc., B/1/5
Mixon, Michael, Sgt., B/1/5
Moore, Kenneth, Lt., I/3/5 (two awards)
Moser, Keith, Pfc., F/2/5
Moy, William, Cpl., M/3/5
Murphy, Edmond, Maj., HMM-363
Murphy, Edward, Cpl., B/1/5
Nunez, Larry, Cpl., M/3/5
Orlett, Paul, Staff Sgt., K/3/5
Ortiz, Melicio, Cpl., I/3/5
Parmelee, Bruce, Pfc., I/3/1
Pettengill, Harold, Capt., L/3/5
Rawson, William, Lt., I/3/5
Richardson, Benjamin, Cpl., L/3/5
Richardson, Jerry, Sgt., I/3/5
Riley, James, Pfc., B/1/3
Rousseau, Joel, Sgt., I/3/5
Rozanski, Edward, Lance Cpl., C/1/5
Schmidt, Joseph, Cpl., H&S/1/5
Schon, John, HM, L/3/5
Schrader, Peter, Cpl., M/3/5
Sherin, Duane, Lt., H/2/5
Smith, Ralph, Cpl., C/1/5
Soderling, Jerry, Staff Sgt., A/1/5
Tenney, Joseph, Capt., K/3/5
Tilley, Robert, Lt., K/3/5
Vanzandt, Ray, Cpl., D/1/5
Wadley, Harold, Sgt., H/2/5
White, Harry, Cpl., 3/5
Winston, William, Cpl., C/1/5
Woods, Sterling, Cpl., B/1/3
York, Hillous, Sgt., C/1/5
Zell, Rick, Lt., A/1/5

BRONZE STAR

Delaney, Dennis, Cpl., I/3/5
Dinota, Dennis, Gunnery Sgt., M/3/1
Grappe, Buford, Cpl., M/3/5
Kelly, Kevin, Cpl., M/3/5
Mollenkamp, David, Cpl., engineer attached to I/3/5
Moore, Kenneth, Lt., I/3/5
Richardson, Jerry, Sgt., I/3/5
Sanchez, Juan, Sgt., C/1/5 (two awards)
Seablom, Gordon, Cpl., M/3/5
Sullivan, Craig, Staff Sgt., M/3/5
Teague, Frank, Lt., M/3/1
Warner, Jack, Lt., HMM-363

NAVY COMMENDATION MEDAL

Cottrell, Steve, Cpl., M/3/5
Goebel, Chuck, Cpl., M/3/5

Notes

1. Later, Major General Deegan.
2. Marine units are designated among themselves and will be so designated in this book in this fashion: the letter is the designator of a rifle company or artillery battery, the first number is the battalion, and the second number the regiment to which it belongs.
3. Later, Brigadier General Hayes.
4. Despite the irreverent nickname, Lieutenant Colonel Bell was a storied warrior and the holder of two Navy Crosses.
5. Later, Major General Kenneth Houghton.
6. Smith told the author a hilarious story about a captured enemy who made a statement about U.S. Marines issuing sex toys to their men. Upon further questioning, they came to believe this because the Marines called an air mattress a "rubber lady."
7. Phillips later became a major general.
8. Later, Brigadier General McKay.
9. Later, Four-Star General Carlton Fulford.
10. The 1st VC Regiment captured two 105mm howitzers from the ARVN in the fight for Ba Gia in 1965. They may have been the source of the occasional mysterious artillery rounds received by allied forces. A member of the 1st VC Regiment told the author in 2004 that the VC later buried these weapons, but the ARVN discovered and recaptured them toward the end of the war.
11. Statement of retired NVA Col. Tran Nhu Tiep, November 2008.
12. Ibid.
13. Merle L. Pribbenow, trans., *Victory in Vietnam: The Official History of the People's Army of Vietnam, 1954–1975* (Lawrence: University Press of Kansas, 2002). It was originally published under the title *Lich su Quan doi Nhan dan*

Viet Nam in 1996 for the Military History Institute of Vietnam, Ministry of Defense by the People's Army Publishing House.

14. Martin Luther King Jr., "Declaration of Independence from the War in Vietnam," *Ramparts,* May 11, 1967, 33.

15. B. G. Burkett and Glenna Whitley, *Stolen Valor: How the Vietnam Generation Was Robbed of its Heroes and its History* (Dallas: Verity Press, 1998), 87–108.

Glossary

3.5-inch rocket launcher: Designed as a tank buster, this was used in Vietnam against bunkers and crew-served weapons.

105: A 105mm howitzer.

106: A 106mm recoilless rifle

155: A 155mm howitzer.

782 gear: Web gear—packs, cartridge belts, suspenders, canteens, ammunition pouches, and the like. Also called *deuce gear* for the 2 in 782.

A-4 Skyhawk: An attack aircraft used for close air support.

a-gunner: Assistant gunner. In a machine gun team, he was responsible for feeding the gun and changing barrels when necessary. In a rocket team, the a-gunner loaded the rocket tube and tapped the gunner on the head to let him know that he was cleared to fire.

air: Air support.

AK or **AK-47:** An assault rifle designed in the Soviet Union and copied by the Chinese. After about 1967, it was the most prevalent weapon used by the NVA.

ALO: Air liaison officer, a pilot temporarily assigned to ground duty to provide close air support for infantry units. He was in charge of the tactical air control party (TACP) and the forward air controllers (FACs).

AO: An air observer, generally flying in a small Cessna aircraft. The AO was trained to call in artillery and air support for ground units.

AOR: Area of responsibility.

arty: Slang for artillery.

B40: A shoulder-fired rocket, also known as an RPG or rocket-propelled grenade.

Bald Eagle: A reaction force of company size or larger, sent out to help a unit that is in trouble.

BAR: Browning automatic rifle. Used by the U.S. forces in World War II and Korea. Most BARs in Vietnam were in the NVA and VC service; they had either captured the weapons from the ARVN or received them from the Chinese Communists, who had captured them in the Korean War.

Basic School: The school where all Marine lieutenants are trained to be infantry company commanders.

Bird Dog: A nickname for the light Cessna aircraft flown by air observers.

BLT: Battalion landing team, the forces that made up a special landing force. In addition to an infantry battalion, the BLT usually had a battery of artillery, a recon platoon, helicopters, and other odds and ends attached.

Bouncing Betty: An antipersonnel mine with two charges. The first charge blew it into the air, and the second charge blew deadly fragments in every direction. Because it detonated in an airburst, its killing radius was increased.

CH-34 or **H-34:** The older of the two medium helicopters used by the Marines in Vietnam.

CH-46 or **H-46:** The newer and largest of the two medium helicopters used by the Marines in Vietnam.

CH-53 or **H-53:** The Marines' heavy-lift helicopter.

Charlie: Viet Cong, for Victor Charlie, the pronunciation of the phonetic alphabet for VC.

Charlie Med: Charlie Company, 1st Medical Battalion, where a great number of 1st Marine Division casualties were treated.

Chicom: Chinese Communist; applied as a nickname for the grenades most often used by the NVA and VC. They were manufactured in China—hence the name—and were not particularly reliable.

chieu hoi: A soldier from the communist forces who rallied to the allied side.

chop: Usually chop opcon, or assign operational control of a unit to a headquarters that was not normally their parent unit.

click: A kilometer.

CO: Commanding officer.

COC: Combat operations center. At the battalion level, this was the center for running an operation and coordinating the various supporting arms.

Cosmoline: A greasy preservative for metal, usually found on new weapons.

CP or **CP group** or **command group:** For the purposes of this book, it is the commanding officer and his immediate staff, usually when deployed to the field. CP can also simply mean command post.

Crusader: *See* F-8 Crusader.

danger close: Friendly fire that is so close to the Marines as to be nearly as hazardous for them as for the enemy.

entrenching tool or **E-tool:** A small but very durable folding shovel each Marine carried on the outside of his pack.

F-4 Phantom: Designed as a fighter and attack aircraft, this was one of the workhorses for close air support.

F-8 Crusader: A fighter aircraft that was sometimes used for close air support, a role for which it was unsuited.

FAC: Forward air controller. The man on the ground who controlled close air support and helicopters.

fifty: A U.S. .50-caliber machine gun. The communists used a 12.7mm gun that was essentially the same caliber. The term *fifty* was used to indicate both machine guns.

fire team: The smallest Marine Corps tactical unit, consisting of a fire team leader, an automatic rifleman, and two riflemen. After the M16 was issued to the Marines in 1967, the lines between the automatic riflemen and the riflemen were blurred since all had automatic weapons.

final protective fires: *See* mad moment.

FNG: Fucking New Guy.

FO: Forward observer for mortars or artillery. Artillery FOs were generally artillerymen from an artillery regiment, temporarily assigned to infantry Marine units to call in and adjust artillery fire.

frag order: A fragmentation order: a brief combat order, usually issued in a hurry and called a fragmentary order because it leaves out part of the standard five-paragraph order.

grease gun: A .45-caliber submachine gun that throws a large volume of bullets. Inaccurate in ranges farther than a few yards, it looks like a grease gun used by mechanics.

gunnery sergeant or **gunny:** A pay grade, E-7, and also a title for the operations NCO in a rifle company.

H&I: Harassment and interdiction (fire).

H&S: Headquarters and service.

hamlet: One of several subunits that make up a village. Most of the settlements that the Marines refered to as *villes* were in fact hamlets.

HE: High explosive.

HMH: Marine heavy helicopter squadron. These units flew the CH-53.

HMM: Marine medium helicopter squadron. These units flew the CH-34 or the CH-46.

Ho Chi Minhs: Rubber sandals made from old tires.

hooch: A peasant hut, or a makeshift shelter rigged by a Marine in the field.

howtar: A 4.2-inch mortar mounted on a howitzer frame, hence the name.

Huey: The nickname for a light helicopter that served as troop transport and gunship. It got its nickname from the designation of the original model, which was HU-1E.

I Corps: (Eye Corps) The northernmost five provinces of South Vietnam. The Marines fought nearly their entire war in this region.

KA-BAR: The fighting and utility knife used by the Marines.

Kit Carson scouts: Former enemy soldiers who defected to the allied side and acted as scouts.

LAAW: Light antitank assault weapon. Used as a bunker buster in Vietnam.

LP: Listening post. A small group, usually two to four Marines, placed well outside the lines at night to warn of approaching enemy.

LZ: Landing zone.

M14: The U.S. service rifle that was used prior to the adoption of the M16. It fired a 7.62mm cartridge and was highly reliable and accurate.

M16: The rifle issued to the Marines in the spring of 1967. The army got the M16A, which was fairly reliable. The Marines got the M16E (E for experimental). It was defective and a great number of them jammed in combat, unnecessarily causing friendly combat casualties. It fired a small projectile, about the size of a .22 Magnum.

M26: The high-explosive, fragmentation grenade used by the Marines.

M60: The workhorse 7.62mm machine gun used in Vietnam. Highly reliable.

M79 grenade launcher: A 40mm weapon that could fire a grenade up to 250 meters with a fair degree of accuracy. It fired high-explosive, buckshot, flechette, white phosphorus, or tear gas rounds.

mad moment: A unit firing their final protective fires, or FPF, usually in desperation and using every weapon available. It is generally fired in a prearranged pattern.

mechanical mule: A small vehicle that looked like a large door lying flat, with four wheels and a small driver's seat. They were used for everything from moving supplies to mounting weapons.

medevac: Medical evacuation.

mustang: A former enlisted man who has become an officer.

NSA: Naval Support Activity in Da Nang, where many Marine casualties were treated.

NVA: North Vietnamese Army. This was used interchangeably to refer to the army as a whole, a group of their soldiers, or even to an individual soldier.

opcon: Operational control.

PF: Popular Forces. Local village troops, generally poorly led, poorly equipped, and not very reliable.

Phantom: The F-4 Phantom.

pogue: A term of derision, usually applied to clerks and the like who served in the rear. Candy and sweets have been called "pogie bait" by generations of Marines.

PRC25: A tactical radio used by the Marine artillery and infantry.

PRC41: The ground-to-air radio used by the Marine forward air controllers.

Presidential Unit Citation (PUC): An award given in the name of the president of the United States to a unit that has performed courageously. It is the unit equivalent of a Silver Star.

Puff: Puff the Magic Dragon, also known as Spooky. An older-model C-47 aircraft equipped with a type of Gatling gun that could put a round in every square inch of a football field every minute. It could also put out a great many flares and illuminate the battlefield at night.

punji stakes: Sharpened bamboo stakes often laid alongside a trail or in a pit and camouflaged to catch the unwary. They were often tipped with human feces to promote infection.

R&R: Rest and recuperation, the only break, lasting but five days, that the infantryman received during his thirteen-month Vietnam tour.

RPG: Rocket-propelled grenade, also known as a B40 rocket.

S3: The operations officer of a unit.

SKS: Rifle used by the NVA and VC.

Skyhawk: *See* A-4 Skyhawk.

SLF: Abbreviation for special landing force. The theater reserve, it served aboard ship and was committed to ground action whenever needed but only with the permission of commander in chief, Pacific Fleet, in Hawaii.

snake and nape: Snakeye bombs and napalm, a terrifying combination that was commonly used to support ground Marines.

Snakeye bombs: Bombs with fins that popped out upon release from the aircraft, thereby slowing their descent and allowing the aircraft to get out of range before they detonated.

Sparrow Hawk: A platoon-size reaction force.

Special landing force (SLF): Made up of a battalion landing team (BLT) that consisted of an infantry battalion, an artillery battery, a helicopter squadron, engineers, and other attachments.

spider traps or **spider holes:** Deep, one-man fighting holes, usually well camouflaged, named after the spider that lives in a similar dwelling.

squad: For the Marines, this was made up of three, four-man fire teams and a squad leader.

TAOR or **AOR:** Tactical area of responsibility.

Thompson submachine gun: Also called a Tommy gun. A .45-caliber weapon that put out a lot of fire but which was inaccurate beyond a few yards.

village: A series of several hamlets that are tied together by family or tradition. Many of the hamlets in a village have the same name, but with a numerical designator, e.g., Chau Lam (1), Chau Lam (2), and so on. The average village was made up of about 2,500 souls.

ville: Village or hamlet.

VMO: Marine observation squadron.

XO: Executive officer, the second in command of a unit.

Index